Beginning SQL
Joes 2 Pros

The SQL Hands-On Guide for Beginners

(SQL Exam Prep Series 70-433 Volume 1 of 5)

By
Rick A. Morelan
MCDBA, MCTS, MCITP, MCAD, MOE, MCSE, MCSE+I

ISBN: 1-4392-5317-X
EAN: 978-1-4392-5317-5

Rick A. Morelan
Rick@Joes2Pros.com

Table of Contents

Chapter 6. Data Manipulation Language (DML) Scripting 122

Chapter 7. Maintaining Tables 159

About the Author

In 1994, you could find Rick Morelan braving the frigid waters of the Bering Sea as an Alaskan commercial fisherman. His computer skills were non-existent at the time, so you might figure such beginnings seemed unlikely to lead him down the path to SQL expertise at Microsoft. However, every computer expert in the world today woke up at some point in their life knowing nothing about computers.

Making the change from fisherman seemed scary and took daily schooling at Catapult Software Training Institute. Rick got his lucky break in August of 1995, working his first database job at Microsoft. Since that time, Rick has worked more than 10 years at Microsoft and has attained over 30 Microsoft technical certifications in applications, networking, databases and .NET development.

Acknowledgements

As a book with a supporting web site, illustrations, media content and software scripts, it takes more than the usual author, illustrator and editor to put everything together into a great learning experience. Since my publisher has the more traditional contributor list available, I'd like to recognize the core team members:

Editor: Peter D. Kendall, Jessica Brown, Doug Fritz
Technical Editor: Peter Bako (MCTS), Jong Jin Lee (MCTS)
Cover Illustration: Jungim Jang
Technical Review: Hugo Rossini, Ed Hartmann
Software Design Testing: Michael Baker (MCTS), Eugene Kim (MCTS)
Content Review: Rhonda Chesley (MCTS), Allan Fridson
User Acceptance Testing: Cyrus Despres, Anthony L. Walker
Book Title: Nathaniel J. Purdy
Index: Sean Harrison
Website & Digital Marketing: Gaurav Singhal

Thank you to all the teachers at Catapult Software Training Institute in the mid-1990s. What a great start to open my eyes. It landed me my first job at Microsoft by August of that year. A giant second wind came from Koenig-Solutions, which gives twice the training and attention for half the price of most other schools. Mr. Rohit Aggarwal is the visionary founder of this company based in New Delhi, India. Rohit's business model sits students down one-on-one with experts. Each expert dedicates weeks to help each new IT student succeed. The numerous twelve-hour flights I took to India to attend those classes were pivotal to my success. Whenever a new generation of software was released, I got years ahead of the learning curve by spending one or two months at Koenig.

Dr. James D. McCaffrey at Volt Technical Resources in Bellevue, Wash., taught me how to improve my own learning by teaching others. You'll frequently see me in his classroom because he makes learning fun. McCaffrey's unique style boosts the self-confidence of his students, and his tutelage has been essential to my own professional development. His philosophy inspires the *Joes 2 Pros* curriculum.

Hades Meza, one of my most technically advanced students, tells aspiring SQL professionals that you need two things to clinch a job: "First, you need to know the SQL language and have SQL Server development skills. Then, you need to be able to pass a SQL Server job interview." Meza has given and has been subjected to dozens of SQL technical interviews. His hiring question insights are woven into the Points to Ponder labs and quizzes in this book.

Numerous colleagues such as Peter Bako, Jessica Brown, Anne Hunt and Peter D. Kendall contributed their skills and experience to make this book possible. Peter Bako is a hands-on master of computer hardware, software and programming languages. Whenever a challenge arises he either has the answers, he knows how to quickly get the answers, or invents a working solution on-the-fly. Jessica Brown and Anne Hunt have very sharp eyes for details and contributed greatly to the smooth progress of the book. Peter D. Kendall, a professional journalist whose expertise earned my admiration right away, combined the conciseness and punch of AP style with his own SQL knowledge to bring cohesion to this project. What better technical editor could there be than a former newspaper editor who is now a certified SQL server MCTS.

The first student to read the entire book and provide review suggestions was Ernie Li. Ernie used his daily bus commute to read the entire book when it was a mere jumble of papers in a 3-ring binder. If you like the big readable figures, then give him some credit. He suggested the figures be vivid, easy to read, and that they zoom in to draw your attention to specific points. Ernie gives the illustrations a big "thumbs-up" as we go to print, and I'll always be grateful for Ernie's diligence, thoroughness, and his eagerness to learn and apply new skills.

Finally, a special thank you goes to Ed Hartmann who has taught so many students at Bellevue College over the years. Ed's experienced and careful eye caught a few 11th hour items which really raised the quality standard of this book.

Preface

How do you build a raging fire of learning from a single spark of curiosity? If you take that little spark and add some paper, a few twigs and a stick, eventually even the largest log can be tossed on to the raging fire. You, too, can evolve from flame to firestorm, from Joe to Pro, when you take the steps outlined in this book. Regardless of your skill level, this is the ideal way to learn.

Viewing a large and unruly database that someone else wrote is like throwing a huge log directly onto a match. What if that large database, which included complex relations, started off as a smaller database with just three tables and 12 employees? You will learn how to build that large database one chapter at a time over the course of studying these Joes 2 Pros books. When you are a part of building something, you comprehend each new level of complexity that is added. Afterward, you're able to stand back and say, "I built that!" Your *Joes 2 Pros* journey will soon make databases appear fun and familiar.

Introduction

Does the following story sound familiar to you? The first SQL book I bought left me confused and demoralized at chapter one. Enrolling in my first class totally overwhelmed me and left me nearly hopeless – and with only a partial tuition refund. Progress was expensive and slow. Countless times I was tempted to give up.

After years of trial and error, I finally got into my groove. While grinding away at my own work with SQL, those key "ah-ha" moments and insights eventually came. What took me over five years of intense study is now a high tide that lifts my students to the same level in just a few months.

Each lesson and chapter builds sequentially. The labs have been created and delivered by me over several years of teaching SQL. If a lab offered one of my classrooms an exciting "ah-ha" experience with students leaning forward on every word and demo, it's a keeper. However, when a lab caused more of a trance or tilted squint, it was discarded or revised with a better approach. The labs in this book are the end result, and each one consistently elicits "ah-ha" moments in my classes.

This book follows what students told me worked for them and launched their careers. This curriculum has helped many people achieve their career goals. If you would like to gain the confidence that comes with really knowing how to get things done, this book is your ticket. This book offers the following ways to help:

Most learning for the money: What if you could get more from this book than the average $1,800 class? Perhaps there is even more material here – proven teaching tools presented by someone whose goal is for you to succeed and achieve a high level of SQL knowledge and proficiency. More importantly, you can learn SQL with demos and practice. When you finish this book, you will be reading and writing in SQL with ease. This book can easily give you more than a typical 18-hour class costing $1,800.

Truly getting it: Is there a better way to learn SQL than a giant book of concepts with only a few examples? You bet there is, and you're reading it. Just wait until you finish the Points to Ponder section of each chapter. It exists in written and video format to bring life and action to concepts. Points-to-Ponder is a wrap-up of each chapter, like getting 10 pages of lengthy reading into one. To see these come to life, read them while watching the downloadable videos. This is a concise way to finalize the new points you have just used.

Downloadable files bring text to life: Answer keys, quiz games and setup scripts will prepare your SQL Server for the practices that will hone your skills. The files can be found at www.Joes2Pros.com.

Bug Catcher game reviews: After you have run the right code several times, you are ready to write code and help others do the same by spotting errors in code samples. Each chapter's interactive Bug Catcher section highlights common mistakes people make and improves your code literacy. In the classroom setting, this segment is a fun chapter wrap-up game with a wireless buzzer system. Try this game at home for yourself.

This book is an essential tool. When used correctly, you can determine how far and fast you can go. It has been polished and tuned for your use and benefit. In fact, this is the book I really wished was in my possession years ago when I was learning about SQL. What took me years of struggle to learn can now be yours in only months in the form of efficient, enjoyable and rewarding study.

Skills Needed for this Book

SQL stands for Structured Query Language. Since SQL uses English words like select, set and where, SQL statements can be created using basic English. Beyond that you only need to be able to turn on your computer, click a mouse, type a little, and navigate to files and folders.

You should be able to install SQL Server on your computer. Your options are to search the internet for a free download or buy a licensed copy. The official download site gets updated to a new location constantly. To get the most current installation steps go to the www.Joes2Pros.com site.

For the free download you can search for "SQL Server Express 2008 download" and follow the instructions. It's a junior or light version. However, the preferred option is to get "SQL Server 2008 Developer" for under $50. The Joes2Pros site has a link to make this purchase. Microsoft offers a real bargain for SQL students. For only $50 you can install and use the fully-enabled Developer edition as long as you agree to use it only for your own learning and to create your own code. This is an outstanding deal considering that businesses generally spend $10,000 to obtain and implement SQL Server Enterprise. More on these options and installation instructions can be found in the InstallingSQL2008Developer.wmv and InstallingSQL2008Express.wmv download files on the Joes2Pros.com site.

About this Book

Beginning SQL Joes 2 Pros project started in the summer of 2006. At that point it was just a few easy-to-view labs to transform the old, dry, text reading into easier and fun lessons for the classroom. The labs grew into stories. The stories grew into chapters. In 2008, many people whose lives and careers had been improved through my classes convinced me to write a book to reach out to more people.

After covering this entire book, something interesting happened with one of my most ambitious students. She purchased a brick-heavy SQL book with a similar title to expand her learning. After completing half the book she said, "I understand it all but didn't learn anything new compared to your materials, Rick." Reassured in her skills yet curious at the ease with which she learned them, she asked me how this irony was possible. Upon conducting a little research, I learned that page count is a selling point for publishers. People think they are getting a bargain when a book swells to 700 pages. It's easy to boost the page count without adding content. Wide margins that go in an inch or more from every edge and giant indexes can bloat the size of a 300 page book to 500 pages or more. Other than having a page at the beginning and ending of each chapter to take notes, you will find each page chock full of the visuals and a minimalist narrative geared toward your rapid learning.

Maybe the publishers are right about hooking the consumer with page count and padding. People buy on page count and read on content, but how rarely it is that bad, bloated books are returned? Perhaps readers are now ready to get the most from their investment. Trim off the fat and get what you deserve for less. When the world is ready, it will reflect in this book's success.

There are other ways to deliver good teaching without overdosing you on wordy ink. How many words would it take to describe your favorite shirt? Would you rather write them all out or show someone with pictures and videos? Every point made in *Joes 2 Pros* is demonstrated with life-like examples using real databases, thus the downloadable files are essential tools in your SQL learning. The instructional videos will further enhance your learning experience.

There was a time when the term "boot camp" meant something admirable. Too many programs today prey on students' dreams while delivering little in return. These incentives rule stronger than ever in the IT training business model. A worst-case example was a school where I briefly taught. It charged students the highest tuition rate I've ever encountered while paying instructors the least amount, yet spent far more on advertising in the form of radio spots to lure unsuspecting students seeking to gain IT skills. That school also has the lowest rate of students successfully completing the program than any I have encountered. *Beginning SQL Joes 2 Pros* was written to change this trend.

Most of the exercises in this book are designed around proper database practices in the workplace. The workplace also offers common challenges and process changes over time. For example, it is good practice to use numeric data for IDs. If you have ever seen a Canadian postal code (zip code), you see the need for character data in relational information. You will occasionally see an off-the-beaten-path strategy demonstrated so you know how to approach a topic in a job interview or workplace assignment.

To put it simply, there is a recipe for success. You can choose your own ingredients. Just learn the lesson, do the lab, view Points to Ponder, and play the review game at the end of each chapter.

How to use this Book and Videos

Some students like the Read-View-Do approach so they know the concepts of what they are about to see. Others like to View-Read-Do approach so they can visualize the concepts as they read.

In the Read-View-Do approach you read the chapter, view the videos, and do the challenges in the videos. For example, let's say you are on chapter 2. You will read the pages for Chapter 2, view the "Setup" video, and do the Skill Checks at the end of Lab2.1. In the View-Read-Do approach for Chapter 2 you will watch the Lab2.1_SingleTableQueriesSampler.wmv video, skip the Skill Check until later, read the book, and do the video Lab 2.1 Skill Checks.

Some readers already have SQL installed and want to know how to set up the labs. Other readers need to install SQL server then set up the labs. You can do this before you even start the book or you can start reading the book until you get to the first lab in chapter 2.

If you already have SQL installed then just view the BookSetupLabSteps.wmv file from the www.joes2pros.com web site. It commonly takes between 1 and 2 hours to complete all the steps of installing SQL server.

Sometimes you will notice many videos for one subject matter. For example lab 2.1 there is a Lab2.1_SingleTableQueries.wmv and a Lab2.1PointsToPonder.wmv files. To make knowing what to do next easy, all video files should be viewed in alphabetical order.

Taking the practice quizzes is another great use of this book. Some multiple choice questions may only have one answer, while others will require multiple answers. There is a standard that most tests have adopted, that is good for you to know as you study and prepare. Here is an example of a question with a single answer:

Q1.) What is 2 + 3?

O a.   2
O b.   3
O c.   5

The answer to Q1 above is C. Notice each choice has a round bubble next to the selection. This means that there is only a single answer for this question.

Sometimes there will be more than one correct answer, and you will see square boxes before the selection. For an example of this, see Q2 below.

Q2.) Which number is greater than 2?

☐ a. 0
☐ b. 2
☐ **c. 3**
☐ **d. 4**

I'm often asked about the Points to Ponder feature, which is popular with both beginners and experienced developers. Some have asked why I don't simply call it a "Summary Page." While it's true that the Points to Ponder page generally captures key points from each section, I frequently include options or technical insights not contained in the section. Often these are points which I or my students have found helpful and which I believe will enhance your understanding of SQL Server.

How to Use the Downloadable Companion Files

Clear content and high-resolution multimedia videos coupled with code samples will make learning easy and fun. To give you all this and save printing costs, all supporting files are available with a free download from www.Joes2Pros.com. The breakdown of the offerings from these supporting files is listed below:

Training videos: To get you started, the first three chapters are in video format for free downloading. Videos show labs, demonstrate concepts, and review Points to Ponder along with tips from the appendix. Ranging from 3-15 minutes in length, they use special effects to highlight key points. You can go at your own pace and pause or replay within lessons as needed. To make knowing where to start even easier, the videos were named alphabetically. You don't even need to refer to the book to know what order they can be viewed. There is even a "Setup" video that shows you how to download and use all other files. The second is called Chapter1AboutDatabases.wmv and the third is Chapter1DatabaseGeekSpeak.wmv.

Answer keys: The downloadable files also include an answer key. All exercise lab coding answers are available for peeking if you get really stuck.

Resource files: If you are asked to import a file into SQL, you will need that resource file. Located in the resources sub-folder from the download site are your practice lab resource files. These files hold the few non-SQL script files needed for some labs.

Lab setup files: SQL Server is a database engine and we need to practice on a database. The Joes 2 Pros Practice Company database is a fictitious travel booking company that has been shortened to the database name of JProCo. The scripts to set up the JProCo database can be found here.

Chapter review files: Ready to take your new skills out for a test drive? We have the ever popular Bug Catcher game located here.

What this Book is Not

This book will start you off on the cornerstones of the language behind SQL. It will cover the most commonly used keywords. In short, this book won't attempt to 'boil the ocean' by teaching you every single keyword and command in the SQL language. However, the ones you do learn here, you will become expert at using and will qualify you to begin working in positions requiring SQL Server knowledge, depending on your background. In your continued study of SQL Server through more advanced books, you will acquire more of these keywords and continually add to your fluency of the SQL language on your way to becoming a SQL expert.

This is not a memorization book. Rather, this is a skills book to make part of preparing for the MCTS 70-433 certification test a familiarization process. This book prepares you to apply what you have learned to answer SQL questions in the job setting. The highest hopes are that your progress and level of SQL knowledge will soon have business managers seeking your expertise to provide the reporting and information vital to their decision making. It's a good feeling to achieve and to help others at the same time. Many students commented that the training method used in *Joes 2 Pros* was what finally helped them achieve their goal of certification.

When you go through the *Joes 2 Pros* book series and really know this material, you deserve a fair shot at SQL certification. Use only authentic testing engines drawing on your skill. Show you know it for real. At the time of this writing, MeasureUp® at http://www.measureup.com provides a good test preparation simulator. The company's test pass guarantee makes it a very appealing option.

Chapter 1. Introduction to Databases

Structured Query Language (SQL) is the most used database language across the world. SQL contains words you will recognize as common English words. Often students ask me, "What's the difference between SQL and SQL Server?" My reply is simple: "If you were going to live and work in Germany, you'd be better off if you could speak German. If you're going to SQL Server-land, you'd better learn to speak the Structured Query Language or SQL." In other words, SQL Server is the name of the environment. SQL is the programming language that is spoken or used in that environment. Before all that, let's examine the hullabaloo about databases.

READER NOTE: *If you find the downloadable sample videos from Joes2Pros to be a helpful complement to this text then keep an eye on the Joes2Pros.com site for an announcement on the availability of a SQL video training DVD release that is designed as a video training companion to the material covered in this book.*

About Databases

If someone came up to you claiming to have a database and hands you a shoebox full of receipts, you should agree with them. A database is a collection of related information. A checkbook is a database. An address book is a database. A telephone book is a database. A family tree is a database. A report card is a database. A diary is a database.

Data vs. Information

A shoebox full of receipts will not provide much vocational advancement. So, what's the buzz about SQL? The things SQL can do that the shoebox can't do are critical. SQL organizes your stored data in a meaningful way and allows you to pull out just the information you need. These capabilities allow businesses to make decisions with that information.

OK, let's say you are just as fast at pulling the receipts from the box as SQL is at pulling data from a database. So, what else does SQL have to offer? Well, the shoebox of receipts may be in US dollars. Try to ask that box for the equivalent value in Canadian dollars at today's exchange rate. You are asking for information not even stored in the box. SQL can take your existing data, apply directions or calculations to your data, and the final result is not even information you have stored, but derived.

This gets us to the definitions of data and information. Data is just what you stored in a database, such as raw numbers. Information is what you look at and often build into business reports. In other words, information is data that is processed or structured in such a way as to have true value. It's useful for businesses to have the right information quickly. SQL is a true master at turning data into information.

A Simple Database

By looking at the shopping list on this page (Figure 1.1) you can tell how many items you want to have in your bag when you leave the store.

What is the cheapest item? What is the most expensive one? What does the third item cost?

The SQL language uses the pattern recognition, filtering, grouping and calculations you used to answer these questions. The difference is that humans can only query short lists. SQL lets you query trillions of records in related lists. SQL Server returns answers as result sets in mere nanoseconds. If you can answer questions, you can answer SQL queries.

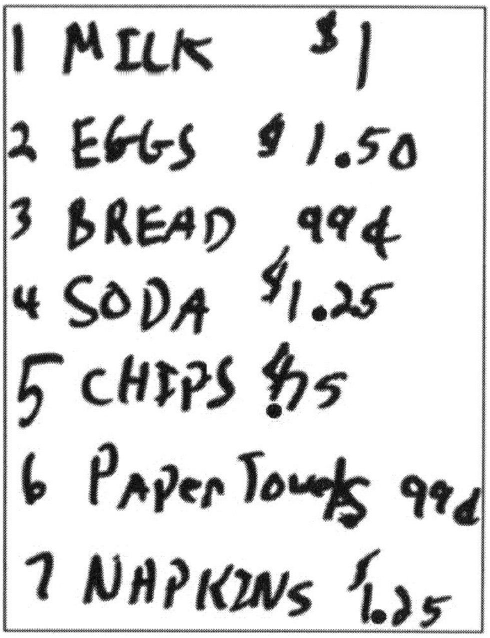

Figure 1.1 A flat database example.

There are seven items on this shopping list. The most expensive item is "eggs". The cheapest item is "chips". Item 3 costs 99 cents. It's listed as bread. The item on the list that costs one dollar is named milk.

Computer languages are literal and numerical. Imagine that you have an appetite and you ask a computer, "What's a good snack?" The computer might answer, '5'. People would interpret the language and simply say, Chips. From the short list in Figure 1.1, we have seven rows of information. There are three columns. The columns in this figure are not named but the first column lists the item number and could be named ItemNumber. The item Description column follows. Finally, we have a column we would logically name Price.

Part of what you must know is how to translate SQL "Geek Speak" into plain English. You must learn to translate business storing and reporting goals into SQL statements.

Database Geek Speak

Simple databases, such as shopping lists, use plain English. SQL Server can lay them out just as simply in a form that looks like a grid or spreadsheet.

To review in plain English, our Figure 1.1 and 1.2 shopping lists have seven rows and three columns. The first column is the ItemNumber. The second column is named Description. The name of the third column is Price. The first row has an ItemNumber of 1, a Description of Milk, and a Price that equals one dollar.

	ItemNumber	Description	Price
1	1	Milk	1.00
2	2	Eggs	1.50
3	3	Bread	0.99
4	4	Soda	1.25
5	5	Chips	0.75
6	6	PaperTowels	0.99
7	7	Napkins	1.25

Figure 1.2 A table in a database.

In Geek a collection of rows and columns of data is called a table. Figure 1.2 is a screen capture of a table from SQL Server.

"ShoppingList," the name of our table, is easier to read than the list written by hand on a napkin in Figure 1.1. This table has only seven rows. Calling them rows is just fine in Geek, but a few hardcore SQL folks might call them records. If you have seven rows you also have seven records.

The correct word for a column in Geek gives you two choices. You can actually choose between column and field. Here, you see three columns or three fields.

Each record in our table has an ItemNumber, a Description and a Price. Each record has three fields. In Geek we say, "This table is populated with seven records." Since we do not know the values that might be contained in the next record or eighth record, this is an unknown. Each of the three cells in this potential record contains what are called NULL values. NULL does not mean zero. NULL means we do not know the value. Maybe it's going to be "sugar" at $1.75 or "gum" at $1.10. For now, just think of NULL as unknown or not specified, but anything is possible later. NULLS will be covered more deeply later in this book.

After you have records in a table, you can delete some or all of them. If you deleted one record in the shopping list table, we would have six records remaining. If you deleted all of your records, you have an "unpopulated" table.

Once again, the ShoppingList table has three fields. The first field name in this table is ItemNumber. The second field name is Description. The third field name is Price. Oftentimes the first field is numeric and helps us prevent duplicates. For example, we don't want to have two items named number "4." A business might have two employees named David, but each would have a different employee number.

The fields offer you more than just a name label atop your data. You can see we have integer data for the ID, alphabetical data for the description, and decimals for the price field (Figure 1.2). It seems clear what type of data is acceptable for each field of any given record. In SQL Server, database fields are constrained so that they accept only a specified data type. The way this table is set up, if you accidently typed in "sugar" in the price field for the new records, SQL will not accept the entry. Fields are protected or *constrained* using data types. You can enter different numbers for Price like $1.95 or $22.50 so long as they match the data type accepted by that field.

If you look at where a field and record meet, you get a single *value*. A value sits inside what looks like a spreadsheet cell and acts similarly. In a table with seven rows and three fields, you get 21 values.

When you turn your data into viewable information it is often a grid just like you see in Figure 1.2. We don't call the resulting information a grid, but a "record set" or "result set."

Database Management Systems

What is a Database Management System? Well, it's not a shoebox full of receipts. Databases just store data. If your data is valuable and your decisions are driven by information, you may want your system to provide quick reporting. The value of your data may dictate a system which backs up daily or even hourly. A database management system like SQL Server can protect your data. Most importantly, you get to see exactly what you want as you turn data into information. Information is data laid out in a way that it can be viewed for business decisions.

Most databases have many tables, and those tables often relate to each other. Since SQL Server is a management system with related tables, it is called a Relational Database Management System or RDBMS. A shopping list is just a database. SQL Server is an RDBMS.

The true power in the RDBMS is when you want to tabulate the weekend gross of the latest weekend action movie across the nation. Do you want to ship all the ticket stubs from the box offices across the country to a central accounting desk and count by piles? The movie industry uses an RDBMS so that by Monday morning it instantly knows the weekend gross. That is the true power of turning data into information.

SQL at Your Service

In addition to being the most popular RDBMS, SQL Server is an extremely powerful program. It is like a software application, but falls under a different category we need to understand.

We are all familiar with applications. You run them, use them, and see them on the task bar when changing programs. Your computer runs application like processes to check for network connections and dozens of other processes to make things flow. These supporting applications and processes probably don't need to take up room on the taskbar. We need to keep your work area free for just user applications.

Applications or processes that run invisibly are in fact called Windows services. Think of a service as an application that can run without a user interface. A service has one other handy distinction from an application. A little background information on applications will clarify this distinction. Just share a machine with someone and notice your user theme compared to theirs. The co-worker who likes everything pink opens a popular spreadsheet to a pink theme. You log into a normal looking spreadsheet. Applications are customizable for different users. Nevertheless, regardless of who is logged onto the machine, the networking service had better run just fine. Services are like applications that are running on the machine regardless of who is logged on. SQL Server is a service. Actually, SQL Server is a collection of services that run together. SQL services run invisibly.

Since SQL Server runs invisibly, you might wonder how to manage it. The creator of a service often provides you with a special way to interact with the service. You must use a window to talk to the service. In the case of Microsoft SQL Server 2005 and 2008, we use "Management Studio." That is easier to say than the full name of "Microsoft SQL Server Management Studio." You will often hear people tell you to open SQL Server. Actually, you are opening Management Studio to a SQL service that has already been running.

On your SQL Server machine it is likely that the SQL Server service is one of many Windows services. Although this book only briefly mentions services, we thought you might want to see now how to view the invisible services that are running. If you right-click the "My Computer" icon and select "Manage" you will see the computer management console. Select "Services" on the left and view the list in the right pane (Figure 1.3).

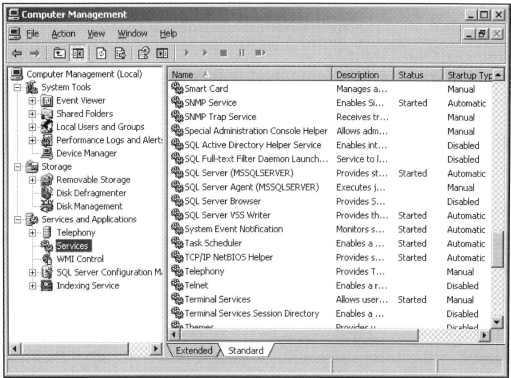

Figure 1.3 Your services can be viewed from your Computer Management console.

You can start or restart the SQL Server service without rebooting your computer. Simply choose the service and get a context menu as seen in Figure 1.4. Your service is up and running by selecting "Start" or "Restart." You can only use SQL Server and all of its tools if the SQL Server service is running.

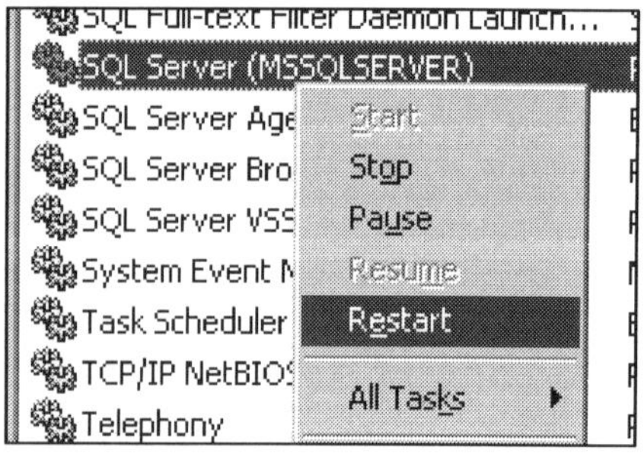

Figure 1.4 Restarting the SQL Server service is as simple as clicking a mouse.

22

Chapter Glossary

Column: A field in a database table.

Database: A collection of objects to store and retrieve data.

Database Management System: A set of software components and programs that creates, maintains, controls access to a database.

Datatype: An attribute of a field that tells SQL Server what kind of data it may accept. Examples include integers, dates and characters.

Field: A column in a database table.

Information: The data and calculation you choose to view from a database, usually for business purposes.

Management Studio: The user interface to talk with SQL Server services.

NULL: Unknown or unspecified values.

Populated: A term used to describe a table that contains data.

Query: A question you ask to get information from data in a database.

RDBMS: Relational Database Management System is a tool that allows for safe storage of data and quick retrieval of important business information.

Record: A row of data in a table.

Record Set: The set of data returned as an answer to a query.

Result Set: Another term for record set.

Service: A process, much like an application, that runs in the background of your system.

SQL: Structured Query Language.

T-SQL: Transact Structured Query Language is the computer programming language based on the SQL standard and used by Microsoft SQL Server to create databases, populate tables and retrieve data.

Chapter 2. Basic Queries

As you now know, data is what you store. By using the SELECT command you are choosing which stored data to retrieve and view as information. In case you are an intermediate level student and simply skimmed the first chapter, here is a one sentence recap: "*Data* is what you have stored and *information* is what you choose to show." It's information that you want to present. For example, your manager asks you to send her a report of books sold last week. If you viewed the raw data in the company's massive sales database, you would see an enormous amount of detail (such as title, author, price, ISBN, language, weight, quantity remaining in inventory, etc.) for every book sold. However, what your manager wants to see is key information regarding last week's sale, such as the total amount of sales expressed in US dollars, the total number of books, a comparison of last week's total sales versus the prior week, and the top 10 titles sold.

The way you retrieve data to get what your manager wants is to write a query starting with the word SELECT. This chapter will show you the core of the most commonly used keywords to retrieve data from your RDBMS known as SQL Server.

READER NOTE: *Is assumed at this point you have SQL installed on your computer. Please run the script Chapter2.0SetupAll.sql in order to follow along with the examples in the first section of this chapter. The setup scripts for this book are posted at Joes2Pros.com. If you need help running the script please download and view the video BookSetupLabSteps.wmv video from the Joes2Pros web site.*

Database Context

If you were to ask your best friend for their age you might get a different result than if you asked your child the same question. "How many employees work at your company?" could be a query. If you were working on a database for a pet store and looked for a list of employees, your results would differ greatly from the same query on the database of a giant global corporation. If you create the perfect query in the wrong database, it may run without error messages. When you query the right database, you get the information you need. Set your database context before you run your query.

In my career, every single server I've encountered has had many databases. You will find the same to be true and perhaps already have.

The Object Explorer inside Management Studio talks with the SQL Server service and finds all your databases. Databases appear as yellow cylinders inside the Object Explorer window. In Figure 2.1 we see three databases named dbBasics, dbTester and JProCo.

Figure 2.1 Databases appear as yellow cylinders inside Object Explorer.

The data inside these three databases are different. When you look for information you usually write a query on only one database at a time. Database context refers to which database you are running the current query against. Always set your database context before you run your query.

Notice the left side of Figure 2.2 shows the Object Explorer. The right side of the figure is your query window. The query window can have only one database context at a time. If you look in the toolbar above both windows, you see it is set to JProCo. You can change this connection by clicking the dropdown control and selecting the desired database from the list.

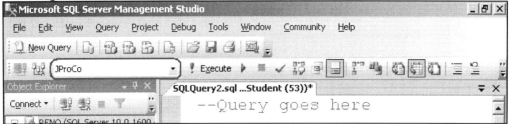

Figure 2.2 Full view of Management Studio with the database context set to the JProCo database.

There is always a risk that you will run code using the wrong database context. To avoid that situation, we simply change the database context to the correct database (Figure 2.2). You can also do this with a SQL statement. If we were in the JProCo database and wanted to change to the dbBasics database, we would type the USE command below:

```
USE dbBasics
GO
```

Running this SQL statement is the preferred way to modify database context. Alternatively, you can use the dropdown list which works just as well. However, the code method is best when writing code you plan to reuse, particularly when working on a team that shares SQL scripts.

When sharing your code, you want others to be in the correct database when it runs. Putting the USE statement in the top window changes the database context. Hit the F5 key or click the Execute button above the query pane to run this code (Figure 2.3).

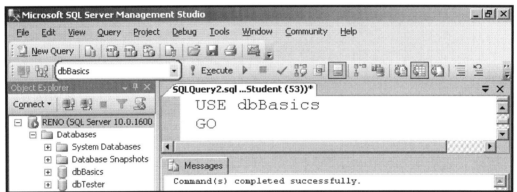

Figure 2.3 Changing context to dbBasics with the USE statement and then executing the code.

The SQL code tells the service to use the dbBasics database. The word GO means the statement above it must finish before going any further. So, GO really means stop, finish and then go. This is a safety feature since the next statement is dependent on the content already being set to dbBasics. If you're not in dbBasics, you can't query dbBasics. The GO makes sure the statement above it is completed in a batch before going further. Modern systems are capable of running many lines at the same time. GO means the statement above it must completely finish before proceeding to the next line.

Single Table Queries

When you want information from your database, you write a query. A query is a request for data from a database. In English you might say, "Show me the information!" In SQL you say, "SELECT." It's easy to spot a query statement since it always starts with the word SELECT.

Assuming you are in the right database, you can now write your query. In this example we will use the dbBasics database context. We are going to look at all fields and records from the ShoppingList table.

The word SELECT means you want to see all information displayed. The asterisk (*) is handy if you don't know the names of the fields, but want all of them to be displayed. The keyword FROM chooses the table you're querying. Run your query by hitting the F5 key or the Execute button (Figure 2.4).

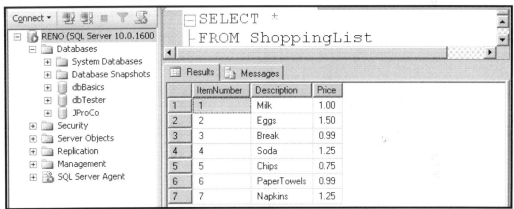

Figure 2.4 A query for all records and all fields from the ShoppingList table.

Basic Query Syntax

A simple guide to what the words in a basic SQL query mean was neatly summarized below by book editor Peter D. Kendall. My weekend class just loved it and insisted it be added to the book. For your viewing pleasure the code is seen below:

```
USE dbBasics        --choose DATABASE Context
GO                  --complete USE statement

SELECT *            --choose your Field(s)
FROM ShoppingList   --choose your Table(s)
```

Now is a good time to point out you can put words on your query screen that have nothing to do with SQL. You could write non-SQL words and notes like "I wrote this query today" above your select statement. If you do, you must tell SQL to ignore this text since it's not intended to be code. In fact, it should be non-executing code known as comments. To make comments, you need to begin the line with two hyphens. Change your context back to JProCo and use this example:

```
--This is my latest query
SELECT * FROM Location
```

The code above runs fine in JProCo. The first line is ignored by SQL because of the double hyphens. It's there only for your benefit. This is a useful way to make notes that later provide you or your team with key hints or details explaining what the code is attempting to accomplish.

Table names can optionally have square brackets around them. This does not change your result set. The two queries below operate identically. Changing back to dbBasics we see the two shopping list tables. One uses square brackets while the other does not:

```
SELECT * FROM ShoppingList
SELECT * FROM [ShoppingList]
```

When coding, you rarely use square brackets because it means extra typing. The only time it is helpful is when you can't tell when a table name starts or stops. For this demo, the dbBasics database has two identical tables named "ShoppingList" and "Shopping List." The latter contains a space in its name, which is generally a bad naming practice for any database object. You must use a delimiter, such as square brackets, in this situation. Without these delimiters, SQL will think the table is named "Shopping" and you have a command named "List" that it does not recognize (Figure 2.5).

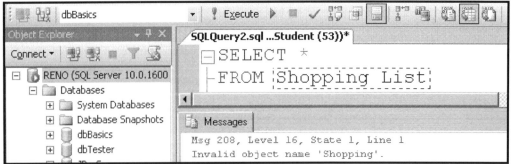

Figure 2.5 A table with a space in the name will not run without delimiters.

You can put square brackets around any table. In fact, automatically generated code always creates these delimiters. The only time you need to do this is when table names are not obvious to SQL Server.

Once you delimit the name of the Shopping List table with square brackets, the query runs without error (Figure 2.6). We get seven records in our result set.

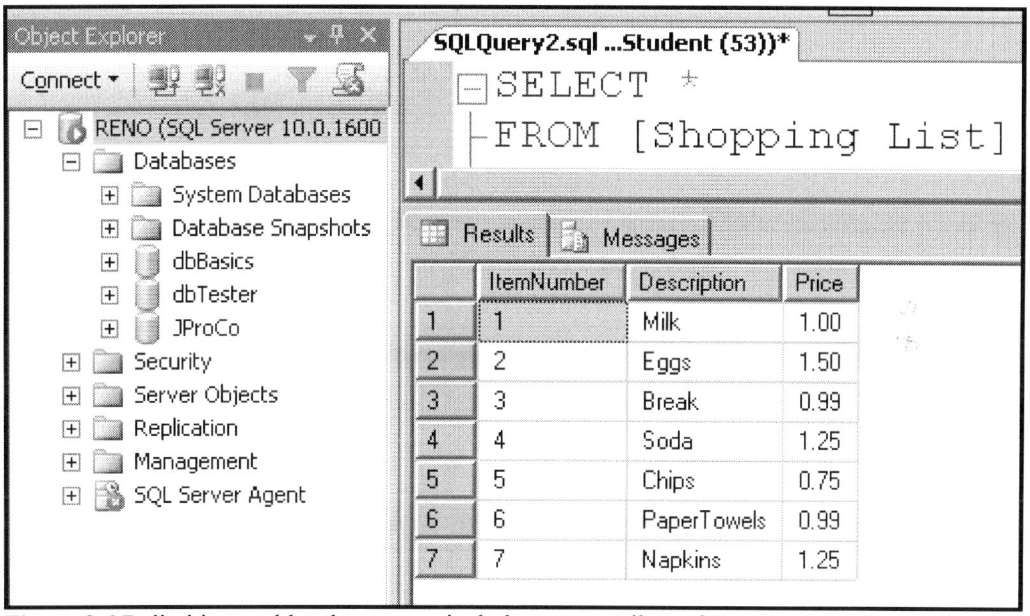

Figure 2.6 Delimiting a table whose name includes a space allows the query to run.

Delimiting table names helps us in another way, too. It would be a bad idea to name your tables after known keywords. For example, a table named "From" would look like this:

```
SELECT * FROM From
```

The vocabulary of SQL has grown over the years, and new keywords are continually added. Take an example where a company database that keeps track of charity grants is named "Grant." The company upgrades to a newer version of SQL Server where Grant is a keyword used to administer permissions. The following code would create problems:

```
SELECT * FROM Grant
```

It tries to use Grant as a keyword. You can solve table name and keyword conflicts by using delimiters. By putting square brackets around the table name of Grant, you tell SQL Server it's a table name and not the GRANT keyword.

```
SELECT * FROM [Grant]
```

	GrantID	GrantName	EmpID	Amount
1	001	92 Purr_Scents %% team	7	4750.00
2	002	K_Land fund trust	2	15750.00
3	003	Robert@BigStarBank.com	7	18100.00
4	004	Norman's Outreach	NULL	21000.00
5	005	BIG 6's Foundation%	4	21000.00
6	006	TALTA_Kishan Internati...	3	18100.00
7	007	Ben@MoreTechnology....	10	41000.00
8	008	@Last-U-Can-Help	7	25000.00
9	009	Thank you @.com	11	21500.00
10	010	Call Mom @Com	5	7500.00

Figure 2.7 Delimiters tell SQL Server Grant is a table name, not the keyword GRANT.

Square brackets will work on all table identifiers. You can put square brackets around the [Employee] table if you want. In reality, you only really need them occasionally.

This also works for fields. For example, the Location table has a field named state. STATE is also a keyword (beginning in SQL Server's 2008 version). There's more on selecting fields later in this chapter.

Exact Matching

There is a big difference between selecting everything and being selective. If you question the business importance of databases systems, ask yourself what a highly profitable search engine company does. The world has billions of web sites and you want your search narrowed down to just a few sites of interest to you. Without providing any new sites themselves, the search engine companies make the internet more selective than you need, and you are presented with a plethora of links, so you visit them. This drives the search engine's advertising business.

Trying to obtain information by looking at all records in a table is about as useful as trying to look at all web sites on the internet to find what you want. Instead, the preferred way is to add criteria to your query. With criteria you can deliver the information that gives people what they want. All queries must have the SELECT and FROM keyword clauses to be valid. We do have other choices available at our fingertips, such as the WHERE clause, which is the most common optional keyword.

When we query the entire [ShoppingList] table we have two items which cost $1.25. It's easy to spot two records out of seven. Two records from a million would be like looking for a needle in a haystack. So, let's tunnel through that haystack with the WHERE clause. We want to limit our result set based on the Price field being exactly $1.25. We add this specific criteria immediately after the WHERE clause (Figure 2.8).

```
SELECT *
 FROM ShoppingList
WHERE Price = 1.25
```

	ItemNumber	Description	Price
1	4	Soda	1.25
2	7	Napkins	1.25

Figure 2.8 The WHERE clause limits the number of records in your result set.

The WHERE clause is perfect for filtering your information. The amount of data in the [ShoppingList] table is still seven records. The number of records in our result set is now just two.

The WHERE clause can filter any type of data. If we wanted to see all employees named David in the JProCo database we can use the WHERE clause. When using character data we must use a single quotation mark.

The query seen in Figure 2.9 uses a WHERE clause to filter on the Firstname field to look for all employees with the first name of David. We still have twelve records of data stored in the Employee table. The WHERE clause shows us just the records in our result set that we asked to view. WHERE expects a logical

31

statement to evaluate each record. The logical statement "Firstname = David" is called a *predicate*. By predicating on Firstname, you filter your result set.

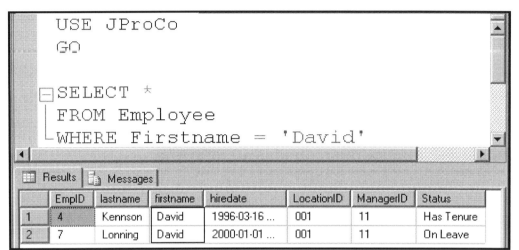

Figure 2.9 Using the WHERE clause shows employees with the first name of David.

Of the twelve employees, we have 10 who are not named David. To see all the records that don't have David as a Firstname, we use this query:

```
SELECT *
FROM Employee
WHERE Firstname != 'David'
```

When you put an exclamation point before the equal sign it means "Not Equals." Exact matches are filtered out of the result set. If you have used previous versions of SQL, you may be used to the < > operator as meaning "Not Equals." That is still true today with the code you see below:

```
SELECT *
FROM Employee
WHERE Firstname <> 'David'
```

The risk in using < > is it looks too much like an HTML or XML tag. When SQL needs to talk to other languages it's better to use ! = for "Not Equals" as seen in the query seen below:

```
SELECT *
FROM Employee
WHERE Firstname != 'David'
```

32

Using the equal sign gives you an exact match. What if you wanted to look for all the first names of Lisa or David? One option is to use the code below:

```
SELECT *
FROM Employee
WHERE Firstname = 'Lisa'
OR Firstname = 'David'
```

You can only specify one exact match after the equal operator. If you like using the equal sign then two exact matches require two equal signs. To enumerate a set of exact matches in your query with one criterion you can use the *IN* operator. The code below is another way to find the same result set:

```
SELECT *
FROM Employee
WHERE Firstname IN ('Lisa', 'David')
```

Lab 2.1: Single Table Queries

Lab Prep: Each lab has one or more Skill Checks. Start with Skill Check 1 and proceed until you reach the Points to Ponder section. Before you can begin the lab you must have SQL Server installed and run the Chapter2.1SetupAll.sql script. Since this is your first lab please make sure you have viewed the video on how to set up a typical lab called BookSetupLabSteps.wmv. This video shows you the steps involved in setting up all the labs in this book. View the lab video instructions for this specific lab named Lab2.1_SingleTableQueries.wmv.

Skill Check 1: Write a query that displays a result set of all records from the CurrentProducts table inside the JProCo database. Show all fields. When you are done your screen should resemble Figure 2.10.

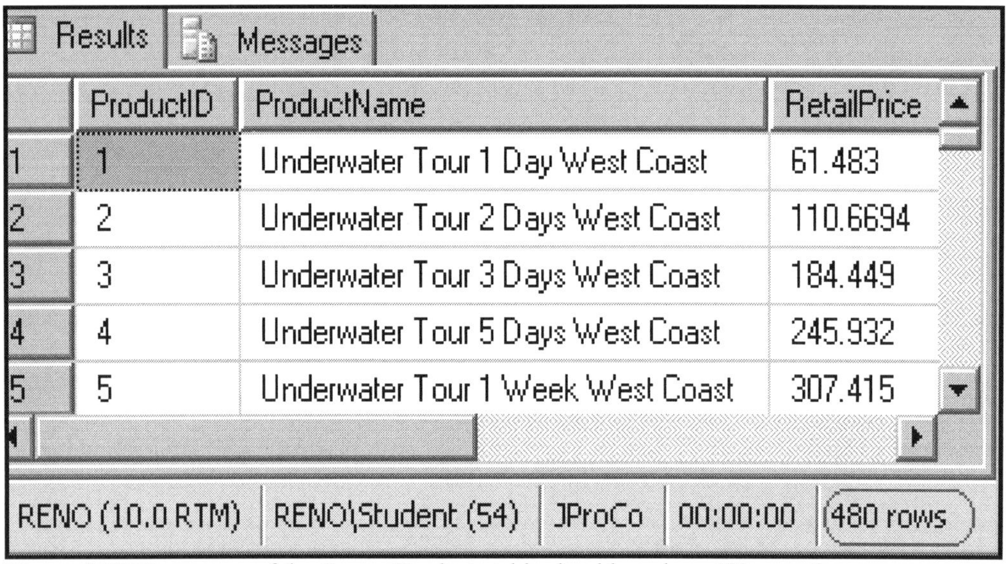

	ProductID	ProductName	RetailPrice
1	1	Underwater Tour 1 Day West Coast	61.483
2	2	Underwater Tour 2 Days West Coast	110.6694
3	3	Underwater Tour 3 Days West Coast	184.449
4	4	Underwater Tour 5 Days West Coast	245.932
5	5	Underwater Tour 1 Week West Coast	307.415

RENO (10.0 RTM) | RENO\Student (54) | JProCo | 00:00:00 | 480 rows

Figure 2.10 Your query of the CurrentProducts table should produce 480 records.

Skill Check 2: In the JProCo database, write a query that shows all records and all fields from the [Grant] table. Your result set should show 10 records.

Skill Check 3: In the JProCo database, write a query that shows all records from the [Grant] table that have an amount of $21,000. Your result set should show two records.

Skill Check 4: Write a query that displays a result set of all records from the Location table that are in the state of WA. When you are done your screen should resemble Figure 2.11.

	LocationID	street	city	state
1	1	111 First ST	Seattle	WA
2	4	444 Ruby ST	Spokane	WA

Figure 2.11 Your query should produce two Washington (WA) records.

Answer Code: The SQL code to this lab can be found from the downloadable files named Lab2.1_SingleTableQueries.sql.

Single Table Queries - Points to Ponder

1. A query is written in the SQL language and is a request for information from data in a database.

2. Microsoft SQL Server uses the Transact Structured Query Language (T-SQL).

3. Database context refers to which database you are running the current query against.

4. The FROM clause tells SQL which table or tables you are interested in viewing.

5. If you miss a letter, forget a punctuation mark, or make a spelling error in SQL, SQL Server will return an error message.

READER NOTE: At this point you can read pages 38-50 to help prepare you for Lab 2.2. on using criteria. Alternately the Lab2.2_UsingCriteria.wmv video will also cover the lab as well as summarize the information contained from pages 38-50. If you want to do the Read-View-Do approach then start reading the next page until you get to the skill checks. If you want to use the View-Read-Do approach then start watching the Lab2.2_UsingCriteria.wmv until you get to the skill checks.

Pattern Matching

What do the names Brian and Bo have in common? They both start with the letter B. Yes, there are other similarities, but let's go with the most obvious. If you use the = operator with the letter B, it wouldn't find either name. It would look for the name "B," which is only one letter long. This would give you an empty result set. We need to combine a more approximate operator with something called a *wildcard*.

The operator that allows you to do approximate predicates is *LIKE*. The LIKE operator allows you to do special relative searches to filter your result set.

To find everyone whose first name starts with the letter B, you need "B" to be the first letter. After the letter B you can have any number of characters. Using B% in single quotes after the LIKE operator gets all names starting with the letter B (Figure 2.12).

This is a good time to point out that SQL does not care if your name is Barry or barry. SQL is not case sensitive unless you go out of your way to change its default setting.

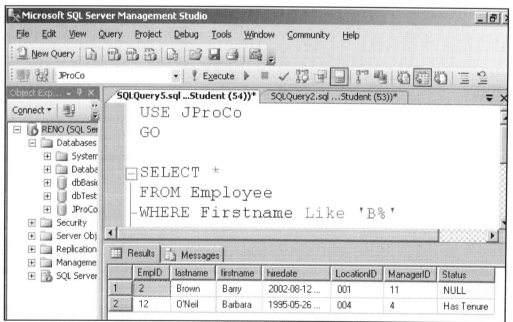

Figure 2.12 Using LIKE allows for a wildcard in your predicate.

The % wildcard symbol represents any number of characters of any length. Let's find all first names that end in the letter A. By using the percentage "%" symbol with the letter A, you achieve this goal using the code sample below:

```
SELECT *
FROM Employee
WHERE Firstname LIKE '%A'
```

Lisa and Barbara both end in the letter A. In this example, a capital A was used and it found all Firstnames ending in A, even if they were lower case.

Lisa has three characters before the ending letter A while Barbara has six. The % wildcard can mean three characters. It can also mean one, nine or even zero characters. If your Firstname was just "A" then you would also appear in this result set.

The next goal is to find Firstname records that have the letter A as the second letter. We want exactly one character of any type followed by an A, then any number of letters afterwards. A wildcard of exactly one character is represented by the underscore "_" symbol.

By asking for one character before the letter A and any amount afterward, we find David, James and others (Figure 2.13). The % symbol wildcard can represent many characters while the _ symbol wildcard always represents only one.

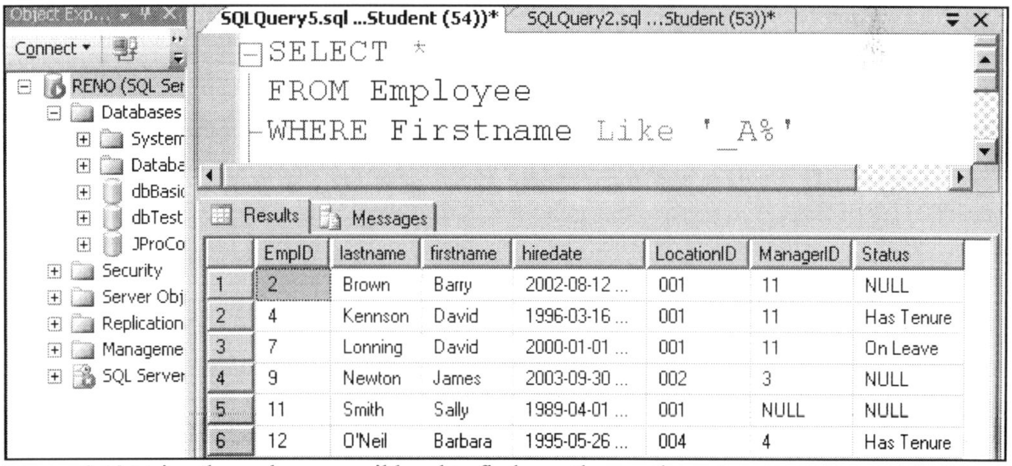

Figure 2.13 Using the underscore wildcard to find exactly one character.

Querying Ranges

If you want to find all Firstname values starting with the letters A or B you can use two predicates in your WHERE clause. You need to separate them with the *OR* operator. In Figure 2.14 you find records where Firstname starts with A or B.

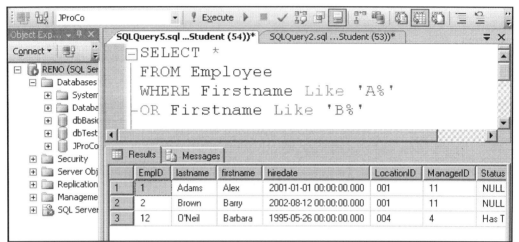

Figure 2.14 Using the OR operator to find Firstname values starting with letters A or B.

Finding names beginning with A or B is easy. This works well until you want a range of A-K as in the example below:

```
SELECT *
FROM Employee
WHERE Firstname Like 'A%'
OR Firstname Like 'B%'
OR Firstname Like 'C%'
OR Firstname Like 'D%'
OR Firstname Like 'E%'
OR Firstname Like 'F%'
OR Firstname Like 'G%'
OR Firstname Like 'H%'
OR Firstname Like 'I%'
OR Firstname Like 'J%'
OR Firstname Like 'K%'
```

The previous query does find Firstname values starting from A-K. However, if you need a range of letters, the LIKE operator has an even better option. Since

The previous query does find Firstname values starting from A-K. However, if you need a range of letters, the LIKE operator has many better options. We only really care about the first letter of the last name and there a several first letters that fit with what we're looking for. The first letter of the last name can be A, B, C, D, E, F, G, H, I, J or K. Simply list all the choices you want for the first letter inside a set of square brackets as in the example below:

```
SELECT *
FROM Employee
WHERE FirstName Like '[ABCDEFGHIJK]%'
```

We're looking for the first letter to be within a range, we specify that range in square brackets. The wildcard after the brackets allows any number of characters after the range. Note this range will not work if your LIKE was changed to an equal (=) sign. The following code will not return any records to your result set:

```
--Bad query (it won't error but returns no records)
SELECT *
FROM Employee
WHERE Firstname = '[a-k]%'
```

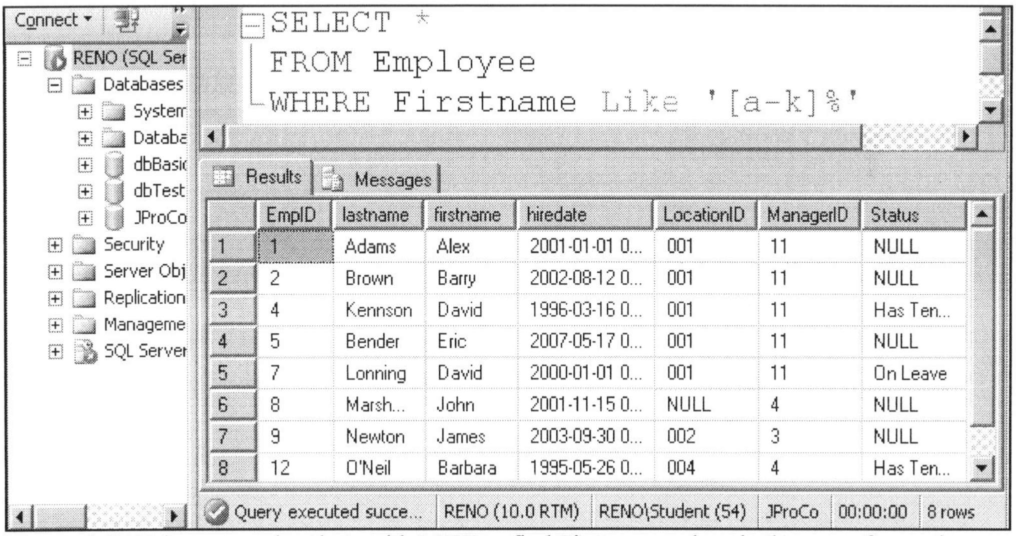

Figure 2.15 Using square brackets with LIKE to find Firstname values in the range from a-k.

A range of characters can be found using LIKE and the appropriate characters inside square brackets. The wildcard is considered a string pattern and must be enclosed in single quotes. Simply put, it's the starting letter followed by a hyphen and then the ending letter of your range (Figure 2.15). Notice you get Alex in

39

your result set. This is because A is considered to be in the [a-k] range. The same logic applies to John. There is a similar trick you can play with number ranges. If you look at the Grant table, you will notice we get amounts as low as $4,750 and as high as $41,000 for the Amount field (Figure 2.16).

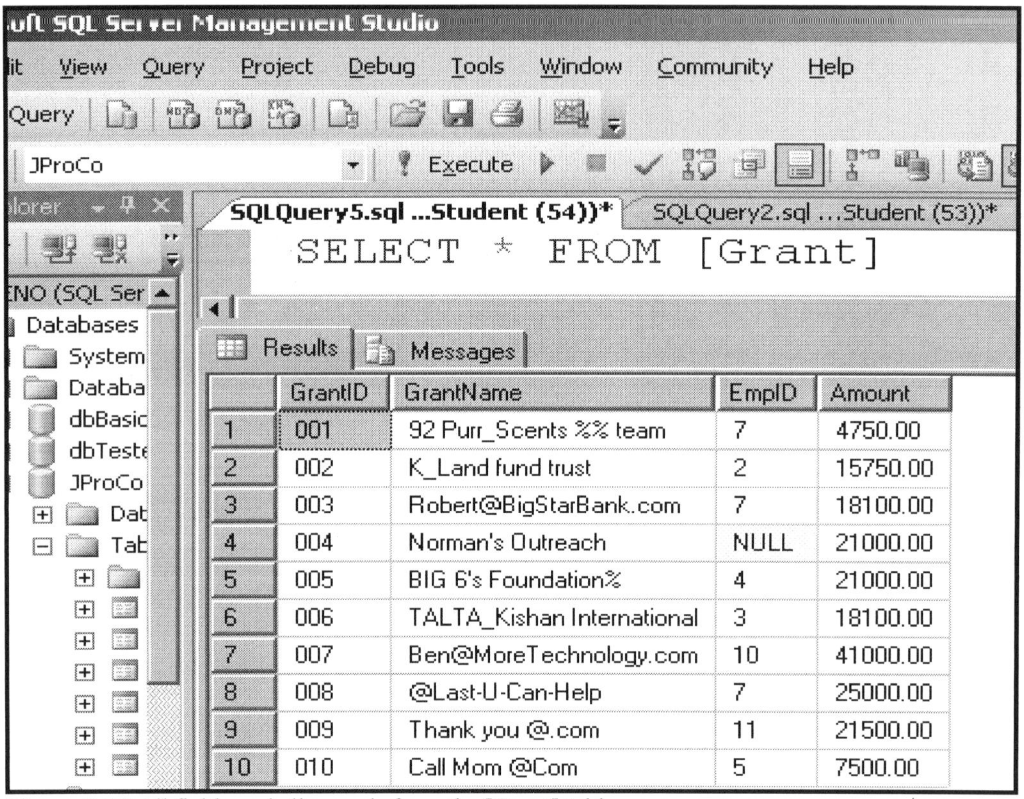

	GrantID	GrantName	EmpID	Amount
1	001	92 Purr_Scents %% team	7	4750.00
2	002	K_Land fund trust	2	15750.00
3	003	Robert@BigStarBank.com	7	18100.00
4	004	Norman's Outreach	NULL	21000.00
5	005	BIG 6's Foundation%	4	21000.00
6	006	TALTA_Kishan International	3	18100.00
7	007	Ben@MoreTechnology.com	10	41000.00
8	008	@Last-U-Can-Help	7	25000.00
9	009	Thank you @.com	11	21500.00
10	010	Call Mom @Com	5	7500.00

Figure 2.16 All fields and all records from the [Grant] table.

We have multiple grants that are over $20,000 in the Amount field. In the following query we use the “greater than” operator to find amounts over 20000:

```
SELECT *
FROM [GRANT]
WHERE Amount > 20000
```

We have multiple grants that are under $20,000 in the Amount field. The following query uses the “less than” operator to find amounts under 20000:

```
SELECT *
FROM [GRANT]
WHERE Amount < 20000
```

We need to be careful when looking for amounts over $21,000 (Figure 2.17) because we have some grants that are exactly $21,000. Using greater than > will not include this amount, but greater than or equal to >= will include the matching amount of $21,000.

```
SELECT *
FROM [Grant]
WHERE Amount > 21000
```

GrantID	GrantName	EmpID	Amount
007	Ben@MoreTechnology.com	10	41000.00
008	www.@Last-U-Can-Help.com	7	25000.00
009	Thank you @.com	11	21500.00

```
SELECT *
FROM [Grant]
WHERE Amount >= 21000
```

GrantID	GrantName	EmpID	Amount
004	Norman's Outreach	NULL	21000.00
005	BIG 6's Foundation%	4	21000.00
007	Ben@MoreTechnology.com	10	41000.00
008	www.@Last-U-Can-Help.com	7	25000.00
009	Thank you @.com	11	21500.00

Figure 2.17 Result sets for "greater than" vs. "greater than" or "equal to" operators.

When someone asks you to pick a number between one and ten, what are valid answers? Zero would be out of range. How about an edge case answer of one? Is one betweenone and ten? Yes! When you use the word between in everyday life the numbers on the edge are considered inclusive. The same is true with the BETWEEN operator in SQL Server.

After the WHERE, you can use the BETWEEN operator with the AND operator to specify two numbers that define your range. When we look for amounts between 21000 and 30000, we get four records in our result set (Figure 2.18).

```
SELECT *
FROM [Grant]
WHERE Amount BETWEEN 21000 AND 30000
```

	GrantID	GrantName	EmpID	Amount
1	004	Norman's Outreach	NULL	21000.00
2	005	BIG 6's Foundation%	4	21000.00
3	008	www.@-Last-U-Can-Help.com	7	25000.00
4	009	Thank you @.com	11	21500.00

Figure 2.18 Using BETWEEN with AND to get a range.

Notice that two of our results are exactly 21,000. BETWEEN offers you results that are inclusive of the numbers in your predicate.

Querying Special Characters

We learned about two special characters earlier called wildcards. When using the percentage sign % or the underscore _ we can do relative searches. We have a grant called "92 Purr_Scents %% team" which has a percentage symbol in the name. We have other grants with percentages in their names. How do you search for a percentage sign with two wildcards on either side? It would appear to SQL that you're looking for three wildcards as seen in the query below:

```
--Bad query pattern logic (finds all records)
SELECT *
FROM [GRANT]
WHERE GrantName LIKE '%%%'
```

We have three special characters and no literal percent symbol. Help is on the way again with the square brackets. Take the wildcard you want to use as a literal percentage symbol and surround it with square brackets. You see two grants having a percentage symbol within their names (Figure 2.19). In this example the square brackets give you the literal percentage symbol.

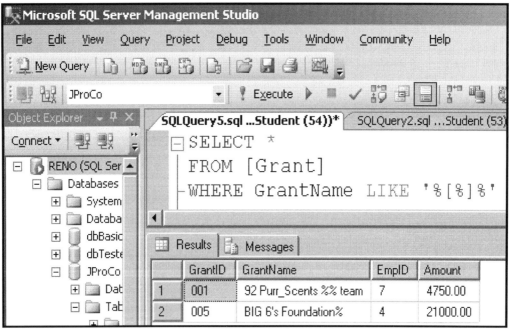

Figure 2.19 Finding a literal % sign in a relative search predicate.

We have a grant called "K_Land fund trust" with an actual underscore in the name. We have other grants with underscores as well. How do you search for an underscore sign with a wildcard on each side? The ineffective query below gets all records that are at least one character long:

```
--Bad query logic finds all records with one or more
characters
SELECT *
FROM [GRANT]
WHERE GrantName LIKE '%_%'
```

We have three special characters and no literal percent sign. Again, we take the wildcard that you want to evaluate and put it inside square brackets.
You see three grants having underscores in their names (Figure 2.20). In this example the square brackets tell SQL you are looking for a literal underscore character.

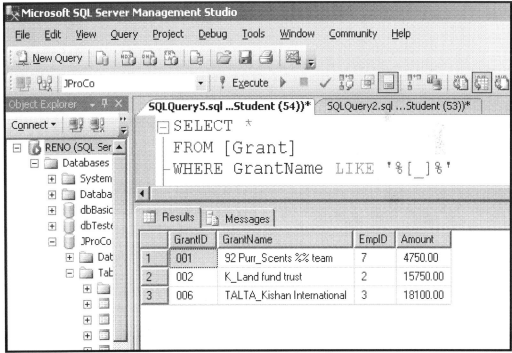

Figure 2.20 Finding a literal _ sign using a relative search predicate.

What if you want to find grants that have an apostrophe (single quote) in their names such as Norman's Outreach? Everything inside single quotes after the LIKE evaluates every record to give you your final result set.

The first single quote starts the string and it ends with the second single quote. Everything between the single quotes is part of the search string. Everything before the first single quote and after the second single quote is not part of the search string. The single quote encompasses or delimits the pattern you are searching. A new challenge arises here. The following query produces a syntax error.

```
--Bad query results in an error.
SELECT *
FROM [GRANT]
WHERE GrantName LIKE '%'%'
```

The problem lies in the fact that SQL Server assumes the predicate is done after the second single quote. SQL Server sees everything after the second single quote as an error in your SQL code. Your intentions were lost or misunderstood. To forego the special meaning of the single quote, precede it with another single quote (Figure 2.21).

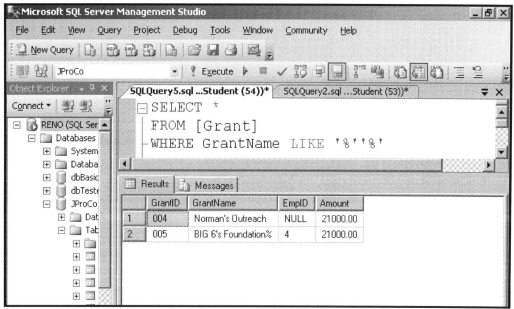

Figure 2.21 Using two single quotes filters your result set for a grant name with an apostrophe.

You now have two records with a single quote in your result set. To view all names without a single quote you would simply change the LIKE to NOT LIKE in the WHERE clause.

Field Selection Lists

So far all of our queries have used the asterisk * symbol right after the SELECT clause. This is both handy and common for looking at information. The asterisk frees you from knowing the names of the fields. One drawback to this method is you get all fields. Sometimes you only want a few specific fields in your result set.

The Employee table has seven fields (Figure 2.22). A few more fields and you would need to scroll right or left to view all your information.

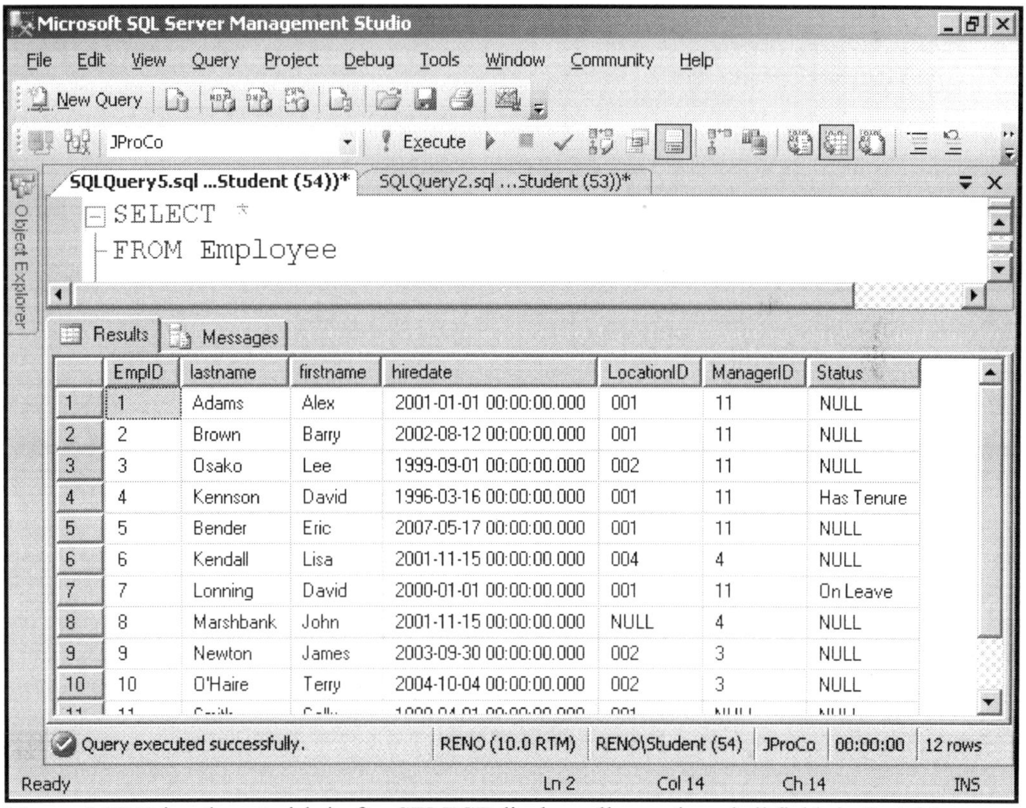

Figure 2.22 Using the asterisk * after SELECT displays all records and all fields in the table.

Tables can have up to 1024 fields. That is a lot of data to view. If you wanted just some of those fields, you can pick them. Simply itemize the field list after the SELECT clause. To do this you need to know the names of the available fields.

By listing the Firstname and LastName fields separated by a comma, we get just two fields in our result set (Figure 2.23).

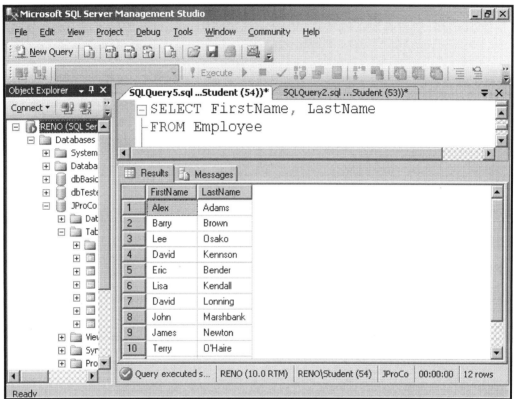

Figure 2.23 Changing your field select list to show just the Firstname and LastName fields.

Until now, we have been using SELECT * in all of our queries. This displays all available fields in a table. However, we can choose to display only the fields we wish to view by naming them, separated by commas, after the SELECT. You can list one, many or all the fields available from the tables listed in the FROM clause. Of course, it's easier to type * than to know and type out all those names separated by commas.

Optionally, you can use the two-part name of the field by listing the table identifier and then the field identifier separated by a period. This requires extra typing, which we show you how to avoid in Chapter 4.

Using two-part names for fields uses the *TableName.FieldName* syntax. Employee.FirstName and Employee.LastName (Figure 2.24) gives us the same results as just specifying FirstName and LastName (Figure 2.23).

Figure 2.24 Field select list using the two-part naming convention of *TableName.FieldName*.

Field names can clash with an existing keyword. For example, the Location table has a field named State. You can put the square brackets around the [State] field to tell SQL Server you're referring to the object and not the keyword command. The following example demonstrates a query that gets street, city and state.

```
SELECT Street, City, [State]
FROM Location
```

Anatomy of a SQL Query

Remember that query keyword order must be followed in your SQL code. Here is the full breakdown of the anatomy of a basic query.

```
USE JProCo                    --Choose your database
GO                            --GO finishes the USE statement
SELECT Firstname,Lastname     --Choose your field(s)
FROM  Employee                --Choose your table(s)
WHERE Firstname = 'Lisa'      --Filter the result set
```

Lab 2.2: Using Criteria

Lab Prep: Before you can begin the lab you must have SQL Server installed and run the Chapter2.2SetupAll.sql script. Since this is one of your first labs please make sure you have viewed the video on how to set up a typical lab called BookSetupLabSteps.wmv. This video shows you the steps involved in setting up all the labs in this book. It is recommended that you view the lab video instructions for this specific lab named Lab2.2_UsingCriteria.wmv.

Skill Check 1: Write a query on the CurrentProducts table of JProCo. Display a result set of all records that have the letter X somewhere in the ProductName field. When you are done, your result should resemble Figure 2.25.

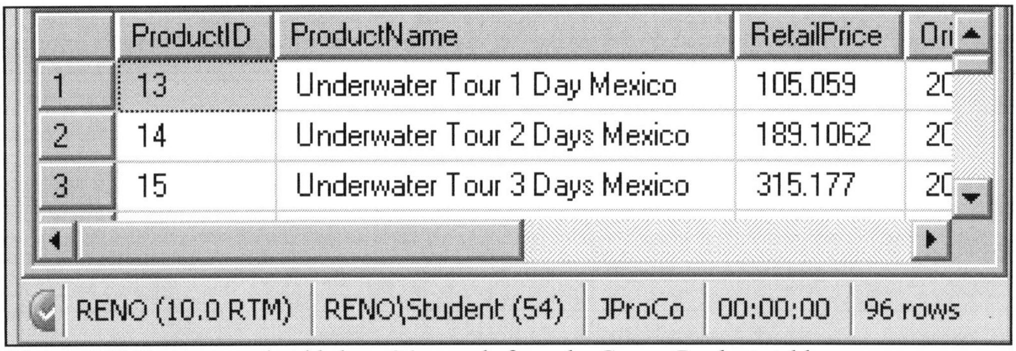

Figure 2.25 Your query should show 96 records from the CurrentProducts table.

Skill Check 2: Write a query to show all records from the CurrentProducts table of the JProCo database with a retail price more than $1,100.00. When you're done, your result should resemble Figure 2.26.

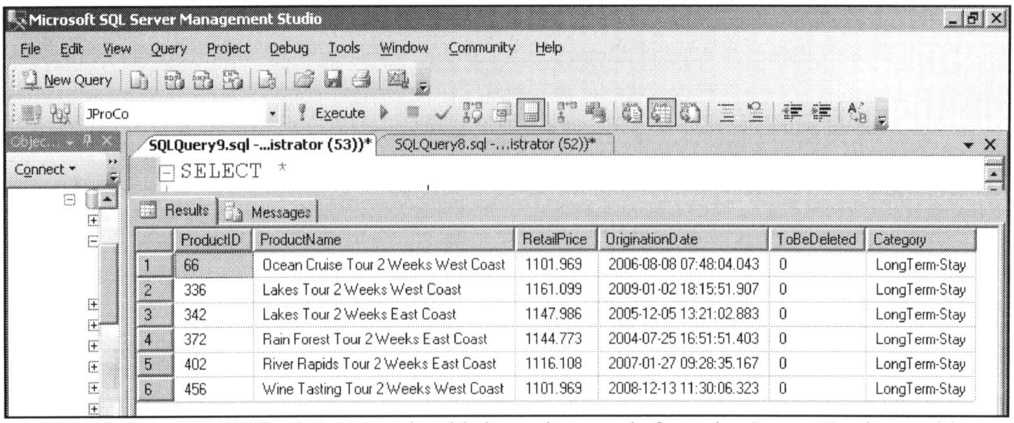

Figure 2.26 Your Skill Check 2 query should show six records from the CurrentProducts table.

Skill Check 3: Write a query from the CurrentProducts table of the JProCo database with the following specifications:
- Show only the ProductName, RetailPrice and Category fields.
- Show the records where the first letter of the product name starts with the letters A to C.

When you're done, your screen should resemble Figure 2.27.

	ProductName	RetailPrice	Category
1	Acting Lessons Tour 1 Day West Coast	111.366	No-Stay
2	Acting Lessons Tour 2 Days West Coast	200.4588	Overnight-Stay
3	Acting Lessons Tour 3 Days West Coast	334.098	Medium-Stay
4	Acting Lessons Tour 5 Days West Coast	445.464	Medium-Stay
5	Acting Lessons Tour 1 Week West Coast	556.83	LongTerm-Stay
6	Acting Lessons Tour 2 Weeks West Coast	1002.294	LongTerm-Stay
7	Acting Lessons Tour 1 Day East Coast	52.67	No-Stay
8	Acting Lessons Tour 2 Days East Coast	94.806	Overnight-Stay
9	Acting Lessons Tour 3 Days East Coast	158.01	Medium-Stay
10	Acting Lessons Tour 5 Days East Coast	210.68	Medium-Stay

Query executed s... | RENO (10.0 RTM) | RENO\Administrator (53) | JProCo | 00:00:00 | 60 rows

Figure 2.27 Your query in Skill Check 3 should show 60 records.

Skill Check 4: Write a query from the [Grant] table of the JProCo database with the following specifications:
- Show all fields.
- Show the four records that have an amount between 7,500 and 20,000.

When you're done, your screen should resemble Figure 2.28.

	GrantID	GrantName	EmpID	Amount
1	002	K_Land fund trust	2	15750.00
2	003	Robert@BigStarBank.com	7	18100.00
3	006	TALTA_Kishan International	3	18100.00
4	010	Call Mom @Com	5	7500.00

Figure 2.28 Your query in Skill Check 4 should show four records.

Skill Check 5: Write a query from the [Grant] table of the JProCo database with the following specifications:
- Show all fields.
- Show the three records that have an underscore in their grant names.

When you're done, your screen should resemble Figure 2.29.

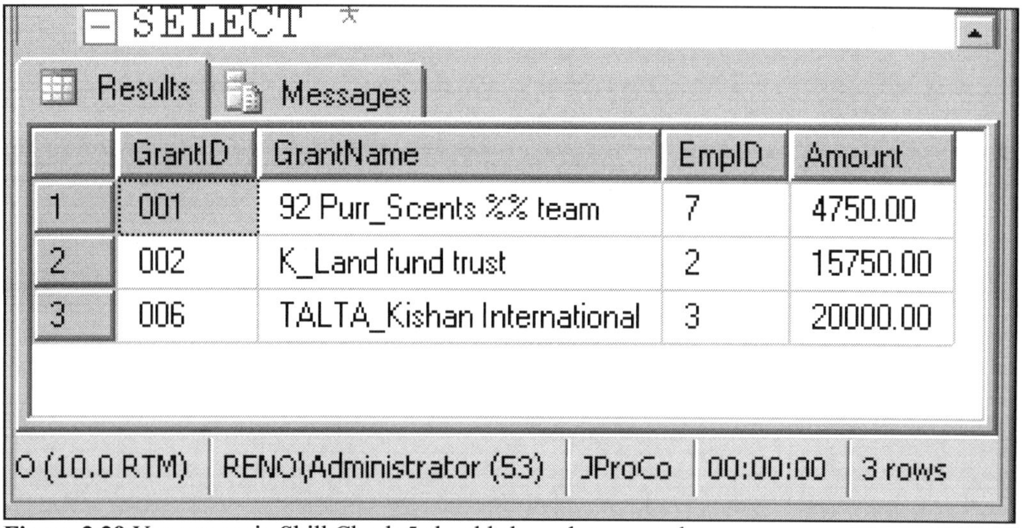

	GrantID	GrantName	EmpID	Amount
1	001	92 Purr_Scents %% team	7	4750.00
2	002	K_Land fund trust	2	15750.00
3	006	TALTA_Kishan International	3	20000.00

O (10.0 RTM) | RENO\Administrator (53) | JProCo | 00:00:00 | 3 rows

Figure 2.29 Your query in Skill Check 5 should show three records.

Skill Check 6: Write a query from the Employee table of the JProCo database with the following specifications:
- Show all fields.
- Show the three employee records having a first name of David or James.

When you're done, your screen should resemble Figure 2.30.

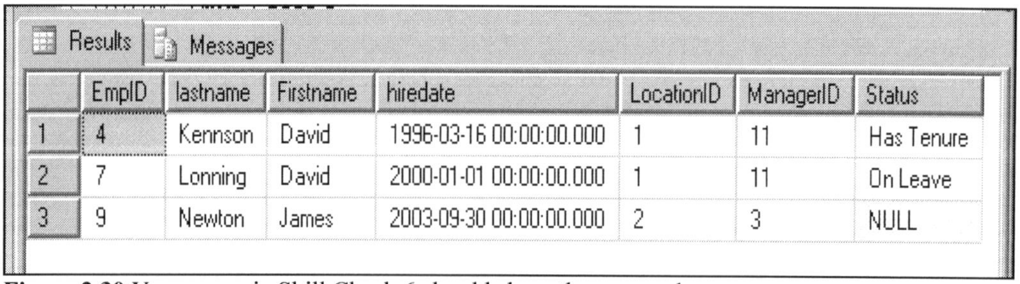

	EmpID	lastname	Firstname	hiredate	LocationID	ManagerID	Status
1	4	Kennson	David	1996-03-16 00:00:00.000	1	11	Has Tenure
2	7	Lonning	David	2000-01-01 00:00:00.000	1	11	On Leave
3	9	Newton	James	2003-09-30 00:00:00.000	2	3	NULL

Figure 2.30 Your query in Skill Check 6 should show three records.

Skill Check 7: Write a query from the [Grant] table of the JProCo database with the following specifications:
- Show all fields.
- Show the two grant records that have the character "O" as the second letter in the GrantName field.

When you're done, your screen should resemble Figure 2.31.

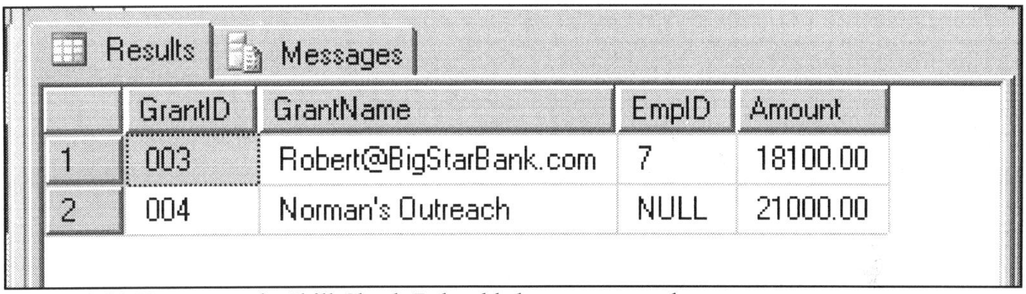

	GrantID	GrantName	EmpID	Amount
1	003	Robert@BigStarBank.com	7	18100.00
2	004	Norman's Outreach	NULL	21000.00

Figure 2.31 Your query in Skill Check 7 should show two records.

Skill Check 8: Write a query from the Employee table of the JProCo database with the following specifications:
- Show all fields.
- Show the two employee records with a status equal to "Has Tenure."

When you're done, your screen should resemble Figure 2.32.

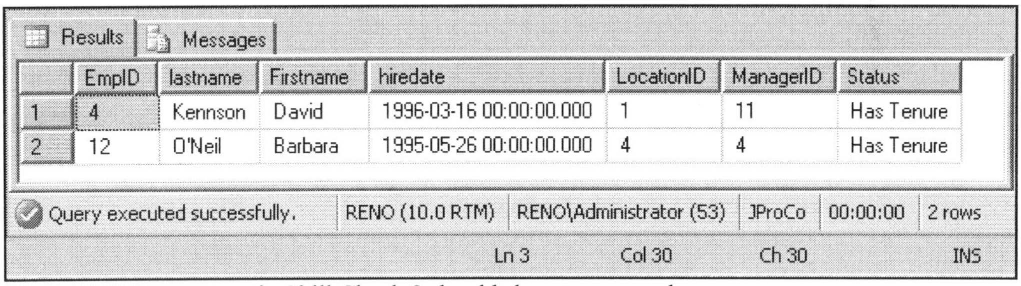

	EmpID	lastname	Firstname	hiredate	LocationID	ManagerID	Status
1	4	Kennson	David	1996-03-16 00:00:00.000	1	11	Has Tenure
2	12	O'Neil	Barbara	1995-05-26 00:00:00.000	4	4	Has Tenure

Query executed successfully. RENO (10.0 RTM) RENO\Administrator (53) JProCo 00:00:00 2 rows

Ln 3   Col 30   Ch 30   INS

Figure 2.32 Your query in Skill Check 8 should show two records.

Skill Check 9: Imagine you have been asked to create a result set from the JProCo database. You must create a record set showing all grants that were funded by someone with a valid .com email address. To succeed, you will need to use wildcards with the following information:

- Look for the @ symbol somewhere in the name.
- The e-mail address name should end in .com
- Make sure at least one character exists before the @ symbol.
- Make sure at least one character exists between the @ and the .com
- Ensure there are no spaces in the GrantName.

When you're done, your screen should resemble Figure 2.33.

GrantID	GrantName	EmpID	Amount
003	Robert@BigStarBank.com	007	18100.00
007	Ben@MoreTechnology.com	010	41000.00

Figure 2.33 Your query should show two records.

Answer Code: The SQL code to this lab can be found in the downloadable file named Lab2.2_UsingCriteria.sql.

Using Criteria - Points to Ponder

1. Always maintain the following query keyword order: SELECT, FROM, and WHERE.

2. An asterisk * coming directly after the SELECT clause means you want to view all available fields.

3. If you want to see only a subset of fields in your query, make sure to itemize each field name, separated by commas, after the SELECT clause.

4. The WHERE clause is handy. It filters records so you just see what you are interested in viewing.

5. The WHERE clause in a SELECT statement is optional. If you omit the WHERE clause, you will get all related records in your record set.

6. Changing the WHERE clause affects the records you see in your query results.

7. Following the WHERE keyword is a logical expression. This logical expression is called a predicate.

8. Using the equal "=" sign finds exact criteria matches.

9. You can use wildcard characters in your WHERE clause.

10. The percent % symbol is the most common wildcard. This symbol represents any number of characters. For example, **WHERE Firstname like '%N'** would find a name that ends in N regardless of how long the name is. Examples may include Ann, MaryAnn and Dean among others.

11. The % sign can even represent zero characters. For example, **'%A%'** would find Alex and Lisa.

12. The SQL operator LIKE can be used to return a range of names, such as those beginning with a letter ranging from A to M. For example, **WHERE Firstname LIKE '[a-m]%'**

13. If you want to "exact match" a % symbol, like the name R%per!est and all other names with a percent symbol in them, surround the wildcard with square brackets. For example, **LastName LIKE '%[%]%'**

Chapter Glossary

BETWEEN Operator: An operator used in SQL selects a range of data between two values.

Clause: A type of keyword used for a query. SELECT is both a clause and a keyword.

Database Context: Refers to which database you are running the current query against.

Delimiter: A character which separates one object or entity from another.

Filter: A clause that limits the records in your query results.

From: A keyword which chooses the table you're querying for the information.

In Operator: An operator used to enumerate a set of exact matches in your query.

Keyword: A word built into the SQL language.

Like: An operator that allows you to do special relative searches to filter your result set for a specified pattern in a column.

Operator: Words or symbols used by SQL to make calculations or evaluations. Some commonly used operators are "AND," "OR," (<), (>) and (=).

Predicate: A logical statement used to evaluate to TRUE, FALSE, or UNKNOWN for each record.

Select: A SQL command used to choose which fields to return in your query results.

Where (clause): The most common optional keyword used to filer query result sets.

Wildcard: Used in SQL match patterns used in conjunction with the LIKE keyword.

Review Quiz

1.) Which SQL clause helps you to limit the number of records you see in a query from a single table?

O a.   FROM
O b.   WHERE
O c.   IF
O d.   SELECT

2.) Which wildcard usage will help you find all last names starting with R?

O a.   WHERE LastName = 'R%'
O b.   WHERE LastName = '%R'
O c.   WHERE LastName LIKE 'R%'
O d.   WHERE LastName LIKE '%R'

3.) The SELECT clause in a query on a single table is…

O a.   Optional
O b.   Required

4.) Which keyword filters or reduces the number of fields in your query?

O a.   ON
O b.   WHERE
O c.   IF
O d.   SELECT

5.) What comes right after the SELECT clause?

O a.   The predicate
O b.   The list of fields
O c.   The list of records

6.) What comes right after the FROM clause?

O a.   The predicate
O b.   The list of fields
O c.   The list of records
O d.   The table or tables
O e.   The data type

7.) You want to find all first names that start with the letters A-M in your Customer table. Which SQL code would you use?

O a.　SELECT * FROM Customer
　　　WHERE Firstname <= 'm%'

O b.　SELECT * FROM Customer
　　　WHERE Firstname = 'a-m%'

O c.　SELECT * FROM Customer
　　　WHERE Firstname like 'a-m%'

O d.　SELECT * FROM Customer
　　　WHERE Firstname = '[a-m]% '

O e.　SELECT * FROM Customer
　　　WHERE Firstname like '[a-m]%'

8.) What comes right after the WHERE clause?

O a.　The predicate
O b.　The list of fields
O c.　The list of records
O d.　The table or tables
O e.　The data type

9.) You want to find all scores for contestants who scored in the range of 20-30 points. Which SQL code would you use?

O a.　SELECT * FROM contestant
　　　WHERE score BETWEEN 20 OR 30
O b.　SELECT * FROM contestant
　　　WHERE score BETWEEN 20 AND 30
O c.　SELECT * FROM contestant
　　　WHERE score IS BETWEEN 20 AND 30
O d.　SELECT * FROM contestant
　　　WHERE score MIDDLE RANGE (20,30)

10.) You want to find all first names that have the letter A as the second letter and do not end with the letter Y. Which SQL code would you use?

O a.   SELECT * FROM Employee
         WHERE Firstname like '_A% ' AND Firstname NOT LIKE 'Y%'

O b.   SELECT * FROM Employee
         WHERE Firstname like '_A% ' AND Firstname NOT LIKE '%Y'

O c.   SELECT * FROM Employee
         WHERE Firstname like 'A_% ' AND Firstname NOT LIKE 'Y%'

11.) You work for a commercial certificate authority (CA) to track safe internet business. You have a table named ApprovedWebSites. Some are ftp:// sites and some are http:// sites. You want to find all approved .org sites listed in the URLName field of the ApprovedWebSites table. All URL names will have the :// with at least one character before them. All sites will have at least one character after the :// and before the .org at the end. What code will give you all .org records?

O a.   SELECT * FROM ApprovedWebSites
         WHERE URLName like '%://%[.org]'

O b.   SELECT * FROM ApprovedWebSites
         WHERE URLName like '_%org'

O c.   SELECT * FROM ApprovedWebSites
         WHERE URLName like '%://%.org'

O d.   SELECT * FROM ApprovedWebSites
         WHERE URLName like '_%://_%.org'

Answer Key

1.) The FROM clause lists the table or tables you are using but does not limit its records so (a) is incorrect. The IF keyword is used for finding running conditions and not inside of queries (see chapter 5), therefore (c) is also incorrect. SELECT limits the number of fields (not records) returned so it's not (d). The WHERE clause creates criteria and limits the records in your result set so (b) is the right answer.

2.) The = sign does not use wildcards so both (a) and (b) are incorrect. Putting the % before the 'R' would give you a name ending in R, so (d) is also incorrect. R% means a string where the first character is 'R' followed by any number of characters (even zero) so (c) would be the correct answer.

3.) Because every query starts with SELECT, it is not an optional word; therefore (a) is incorrect. Given that all queries start with SELECT, it must be required; making (b) the correct answer.

4.) ON is used to define the criteria on which to join two tables, so (a) is incorrect. The WHERE clause creates criteria that limits the *records* in your result set so (b) is also wrong. The IF keyword is used for finding running conditions and not inside of queries (see chapter 5), therefore (c) is also incorrect. Since you list the specific fields you would like displayed in your result immediately following the SELECT keyword, it is limiting the number of fields returned so (d) is the correct answer here.

5.) 'The predicate' is the equation following the WHERE keyword which defines criteria for filtering records so (a) is wrong. 'The list of records' makes up our result set which is usually displayed on screen thus making (c) wrong too. The correct answer is (b) since the SELECT keyword filters the number of fields.

6.) 'The predicate' is the equation following the WHERE keyword which defines criteria for filtering records so (a) is wrong. The SELECT keyword is followed by 'The list of fields' which makes (b) wrong too. 'The list of records' makes up our result set which is usually displayed on screen thus making (c) wrong too. 'The data type' is used when defining fields while creating tables so (e) is also incorrect. FROM lists 'the table or tables' you are using making (d) the correct answer.

7.) Wildcards (%) only work with the LIKE keyword so (a), (b) and (d) are all incorrect. LIKE 'a-m%' would only match strings where the first three characters are 'a-m' so (c) is also wrong. The correct answer is (e) because the predicate uses the LIKE keyword and ends in %, meaning zero or more characters following the first character, which has its range defined correctly with [a-m].

8.) 'The list of fields' follows the SELECT keyword so (b) is incorrect. 'The list of records' makes up our result set making (c) wrong too. 'The table or tables' follows the FROM clause to determine which tables to look in so (d) is also incorrect. 'The data type' is used when defining fields while creating tables so (e) is also incorrect. 'The predicate' is the equation immediately following the WHERE keyword which defines criteria for filtering records so (a) is correct.

9.) BETWEEN uses the AND operator so (a) is incorrect because it used the OR operator. The IS operator is not used with the BETWEEN operator so (c) is also incorrect. There is no such operator as MIDDLE RANGE so (d) is wrong too. The BETWEEN operator requires the AND operator but does not need the IS operator so (b) is correct.

10.) When pattern matching, the use of NOT LIKE 'Y%' only ensures that the first character in the string is not 'Y' so it does not check to see what the string ends in so (a) and (c) are both wrong. The use of LIKE '_A%' will match strings with any character in the first position followed by 'A' followed by zero or more characters; the use of NOT LIKE '%Y' ensures that the last character in the string is not 'Y' so (b) is correct.

11.) The wildcard '%' can match zero characters so (a) is wrong because it would match a string starting with '://'. The pattern we need to match must include '://' and (b) doesn't include this so it is wrong too. The wildcard '%' can match zero characters so (c) is wrong because it would also match a string starting with '://'. The two wildcards '_' and '%' used side by side ensure that a pattern contains at least one character immediately followed by zero or more characters; therefore (d) is the correct answer.

Bug Catcher Game

To play the Bug Catcher game, run the BugCatcher_Chapter2.pps from the BugCatcher folder of the companion files. You can obtain these files from the www.Joes2Pros.com web site.

Chapter 3. Viewing Combined Information

Have you ever had to look something up? Maybe you had a person's name, but not their phone number. When you have part of the information, but you need more related information, you are in effect joining data. When you join data you are putting the information into one viewable location. The data may even physically reside in a separate area. For example, the phone number is still in the phone book even after you write it down on your memo pad. Joining data leaves the original data where it started, but shows you the information all together as one consolidated report. This chapter explores how to select data from two related tables into one result set.

It is common to use two or more tables in a single query. No matter how many tables are in your query, it appears as one result set. Joining tables is one of the most common ways to turn separated data into consolidated information for reports. This chapter will show you how to discern the relationships between tables and query them into one report.

READER NOTE: *Please run the script Chapter3.0SetupAll.sql in order to follow along with the examples in the first section of this chapter. The setup scripts for this book are posted at Joes2Pros.com.*

Database Complexity

There are two types of database complexity. The first type is a *flat file database*. It is a single list that does not relate to any other list. A flat file database cannot go beyond a single table of data.

The second type is called a *relational database*. If you had a list of students at school and wanted to keep track of their parents and legal guardians, you might add a second list. These lists relate to one another. This allows the school to look up the student's parental information. Tables that relate to one another and reside on one managing system are part of a relational database.

As you may recall from the Geek Speak chapter, lists are really called tables. SQL Server thrives by allowing you to query one table or look at a result set that may have relationships between several tables.

Relational Data

Have you ever been given a vague answer to a question? Let's say you asked someone where they worked. You are looking for perhaps a city name or address and they tell you, "I work at headquarters." It's an accurate answer, but not the detailed answer you wanted to know.

After detecting a slight New England accent from James Newton, you look him up in the Employee table and see that he works at LocationID 2. In what city or state is this mysterious LocationID 2 located? A quick query to the Location table shows us the following data (Figure 3.1).

```
SELECT *
FROM Location
```

	LocationID	street	city	state
1	1	111 First ST	Seattle	WA
2	2	222 Second AVE	Boston	MA
3	3	333 Third PL	Chicago	IL
4	4	444 Ruby ST	Spokane	WA

Figure 3.1 The Location table of JProCo.

Now, each time you see an employee listed for LocationID 2 you know his work place street, city and state.

Why not just store city, state, and street information all in the Employee table? In fact why not put all of your data in on giant table so you only have one place to go and get your information? That is a common interview question about database design. Let's give you several reasons for your interviewing arsenal.

One reason is this saves us lots of space by not replicating all three data items for each employee. Another reason for having location fields only in the Location table is that it would save us time as well. What would happen if LocationID 2 moved from Boston to a new building in nearby Cambridge? You would have to update every street, city and state for every employee. Leaving the LocationID field only in the Location table means all employees with LocationID 2 map to an update you make just once.

So, how do we find an employee's address if the information is spread between two tables? Each table has the LocationID field. Stated in a two-part identifier (from Chapter 2), we can say that the Employee.LocationID field corresponds to the Location.LocationID field.

Refer to Figure 3.2 for a look at Alex Adams and Barry Brown. Both these employees work in LocationID 1. If you were new and only had access to the Employee table, you would not have enough detailed information to send a parcel to Alex Adams. What if we put two tables next to one another on our screen? By physically drawing a line from the Employee.LocationID field to the Location.LocationID field we can get more location details for each employee. LocationID 1 is located at 111 First ST. in Seattle, WA.

Employee Table

	EmpID	lastname	firstname	hiredate	LocationID	ManagerID	Status
1	1	Adams	Alex	2001-01-01 00:00:00.000	1	11	NULL
2	2	Brown	Barry	2002-08-12 00:00:00.000	1	11	NULL
3	3	Osako	Lee	1999-09-01 00:00:00.000	2	11	NULL
4	4	Kennson	David	1996-03-16 00:00:00.000	1		
5	5	Bender	Eric	2007-05-17 00:00:00.000	1		
6	6	Kendall	Lisa	2001-11-15 00:00:00.000	4		
7	7	Lonning	David	2000-01-01 00:00:00.000	1		
8	8	Marshbank	John	2001-11-15 00:00:00.000	NULL		
9	9	Newton	James	2003-09-30 00:00:00.000	2		
10	10	O'Haire	Terry	2004-10-04 00:00:00.000	2		

Location Table

	LocationID	street	city	state
1	1	111 First ST	Seattle	WA
2		222 Second AVE	Boston	MA
3	3	333 Third PL	Chicago	IL
4	4	444 Ruby ST	Spokane	WA

Figure 3.2 The Employee and Location tables are correlated on the LocationID field.

What about a global company with locations in all 50 states and over 100 different countries? We will have many records in our Location table and probably will not be able to look at both tables very efficiently on one screen.

How can we effectively see information in two different tables? Our ultimate goal is to show the Employee and Location information in one result set (Figure 3.3). Since we have not shown you the code on how to do this, we have hidden that part of the figure so you can just see what the goal of the upcoming example is.

	EmpID	lastname	Firstname	hiredate	LocationID	ManagerID	Status	LocationID	street	city	state
1	1	Adams	Alex	2001-01-01...	1	11	NULL	1	111 First ST	Seattle	WA
2	2	Brown	Barry	2002-08-12...	1	11	NULL	1	111 First ST	Seattle	WA
3	3	Osako	Lee	1999-09-01...	2	11	NULL	2	222 Second AVE	Boston	MA
4	4	Kennson	David	1996-03-16...	1	11	Has Tenure	1	111 First ST	Seattle	WA
5	5	Bender	Eric	2007-05-17...	1	11	NULL	1	111 First ST	Seattle	WA
6	6	Kendall	Lisa	2001-11-15...	4	4	NULL	4	444 Ruby ST	Spokane	WA
7	7	Lonning	David	2000-01-01...	1	11	On Leave	1	111 First ST	Seattle	WA
8	9	Newton	James	2003-09-30...	2	3	NULL	2	222 Second AVE	Boston	MA
9	10	O'Haire	Terry	2004-10-04...	2	3	NULL	2	222 Second AVE	Boston	MA
10	11	Smith	Sally	1989-04-01...	1	NULL	NULL	1	111 First ST	Seattle	WA
11	12	O'Neil	Barbara	1995-05-26...	4	4	Has Tenure	4	444 Ruby ST	Spokane	WA

Query executed successfully.   Reno (10.0 RTM) RENO\Student (51) JProCo 00:00:00 11 rows

Ready   Ln 1   Col 1   INS

Figure 3.3 Two related tables showing as one result set.

Inner Joins

Each query has only one result set and allows only one FROM clause. How can you put two tables in one FROM clause? You can include many tables in one FROM clause if you use joins. (Prior to SQL Server 2008, the limit was 256 tables. The number of tables you can now join is limited only by available resources.) The most common type of join is called the *inner join*.

The inner join allows you to join multiple tables in one query, but it requires a specific condition in order to do its work. You must ensure that the join statement has two tables with at least one common or overlapping field. We already know the Employee and Location tables share a common LocationID field. The relationship is between Employee.LocationID and Location.LocationID, so just tell SQL Server that the join is on this field and voila! You will combine two tables into one result set.

Employee Table

	EmpID	lastname	firstname	hiredate	LocationID	ManagerID	Status
1	1	Adams	Alex	2001-01-01 00:00:00.000	1	11	NULL
2	2	Brown	Barry	2002-08-12 00:00:00.000	1	11	NULL
3	3	Osako	Lee	1999-09-01 00:00:00.000	2	11	NULL
4	4	Kennson	David	1996-03-16 00:00:00.000	1		
5	5	Bender	Eric	2007-05-17 00:00:00.000	1		
6	6	Kendall	Lisa	2001-11-15 00:00:00.000	4		
7	7	Lonning	David	2000-01-01 00:00:00.000	1		
8	8	Marshbank	John	2001-11-15 00:00:00.000	NULL		
9	9	Newton	James	2003-09-30 00:00:00.000	2		
10	10	O'Haire	Terry	2004-10-04 00:00:00.000	2	3	NULL
11	11	Smith	Sally	1989-04-01 00:00:00.000	1	NULL	NULL
12	12	O'Neil	Barbara	1995-05-26 00:00:00.000	4	4	Has Tenure

Location Table

	LocationID	street	city	state
1	1	111 First ST	Seattle	WA
2	2	222 Second AVE	Boston	MA
3	3	333 Third PL	Chicago	IL
4	4	444 Ruby ST	Spokane	WA

Figure 3.4 The inner join connects two or more tables in the same FROM clause.

Every time a value is found in Employee.LocationID, the inner join searches for the matching record in the Location.LocationID field. If a match is found, data from both tables are displayed as a single record. Both tables will show all their fields if we type SELECT * at the beginning of our query.

In looking at the Grant table we can see Ben@MoreTechnology.com was the largest amount at $41,000 (Figure 3.5).

```
SELECT *
FROM [Grant]
```

	GrantID	GrantName	EmpID	Amount
1	001	92 Purr_Scents %% team	7	4750.00
2	002	K_Land fund trust	2	15750.00
3	003	Robert@BigStarBank.com	7	18100.00
4	004	Norman's Outreach	NULL	21000.00
5	005	BIG 6's Foundation%	4	21000.00
6	006	TALTA_Kishan International	3	18100.00
7	007	Ben@MoreTechnology.com	10	41000.00
8	008	@Last-U-Can-Help	7	25000.00
9	009	Thank you @.com	11	21500.00
10	010	Call Mom @Com	5	7500.00

Figure 3.5 All records from the Grant table.

The employee who made that procurement was EmpID 10. What if we wanted to find more information about this employee? Is this employee a man or woman? When was this employee hired?

To answer detailed questions about this employee, we need to go beyond the Grant table.

For visual purposes, let's put these two tables next to one another. We can see that the EmpID field correlates data between these two tables. Grant.EmpID equates to Employee.EmpID. If we look at EmpID 10 on both tables, we can see Terry O'Haire is the employee who found the $41,000 grant (Figure 3.6).

	EmpID	lastname	firstname	hiredate		GrantID	GrantName	EmpID	Amount
1	1	Adams	Alex	2001-01-01 00:00:00	1	001	92 Purr_Scents %% team	7	4750.00
2	2	Brown	Barry	2002-08-12 00:00:00	2	002	K_Land fund trust	2	15750.00
3	3	Osako	Lee	1999-09-01 00:00:00	3	003	Robert@BigStarBank.com	7	18100.00
4	4	Kennson	David	1996-03-16 00:00:00	4	004	Norman's Outreach	NULL	21000.00
5	5	Bender	Eric	2007-05-17 00:00:00	5	005	BIG 6's Foundation%	4	21000.00
6	6	Kendall	Lisa	2001-11-15 00:00:00	6	006	TALTA_Kishan International	3	18100.00
7	7	Lonning	David	2000-01-01 00:00:00	7	007	Ben@MoreTechnology.com	10	41000.00
8	8	Marshbank	John	2001-11-15 00:00:00	8	008	@Last-U-Can-Help	7	25000.00
9	9	Newton	James	2003-09-30 00:00:00	9	009	Thank you @.com	11	21500.00
10	10	O'Haire	Terry	2004-10-04 00:00:00	10	010	Call Mom @Com	5	7500.00
11	11	Smith	Sally	1989-04-01 00:00:00.000	1		NULL	NULL	
12	12	O'Neil	Barbara	1995-05-26 00:00:00.000	4		4	Has Tenure	

Employee Table / **Grant Table**

Figure 3.6 The Grant table relates to the Employee table on Grant.EmpID to Employee.EmpID.

Again, placing these two small tables side by side and analyzing them can work, but it's time-consuming and not very efficient, especially if we have two very large tables. Instead, we can use SQL Server to put both tables into one result set. Putting information into one report is of great value to businesses.

The tables in Figure 3.6 share the common field of EmpID. Knowing this is a key step.

To put all these records into one result set, you need both tables in the FROM clause. The joins require field(s) that correspond to both tables. The ON clause after the INNER JOIN shows this relationship.

If you looked closely at Figures 3.6 and 3.7 you may see a reason for caution. There are ten grants, but the INNER JOIN only returned nine records. Thus, inner joins can produce what seem to be a data loss. We will explore how to know when this will happen.

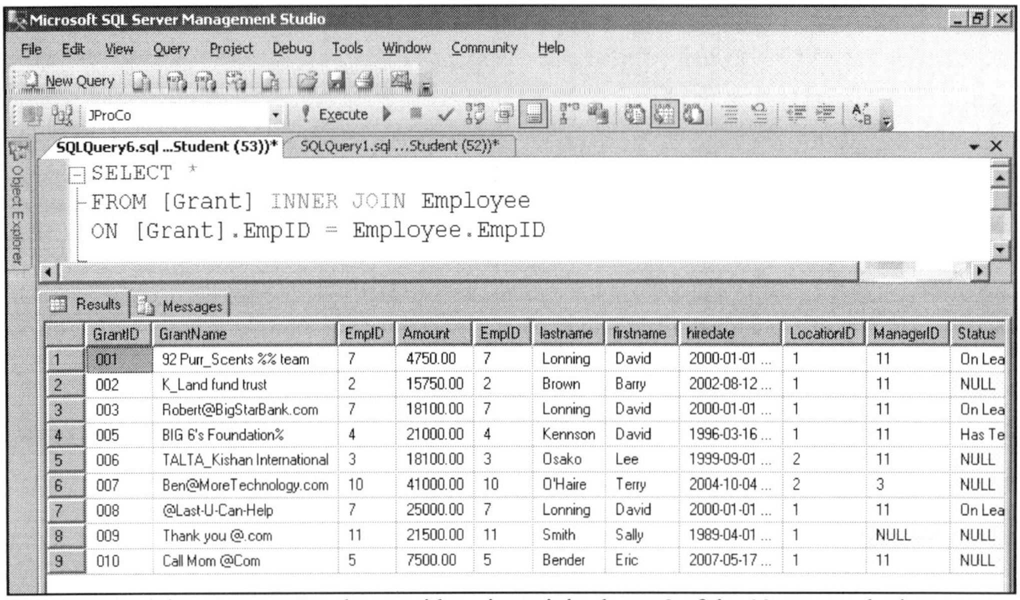

Figure 3.7 Joining Grant to Employee with an inner join shows 9 of the 10 grants who have a matching EmpID in the Employee table.

The Grant called "Norman's Outreach" was an online registration, so no employee is listed as receiving credit. (See Figure 3.6 where EmpID is NULL.) This is the NULL value we talked about in Chapter 1. Nulls will never match records in another table. Since no match was found, the record containing the Norman's Outreach grant was not included in the result set.

The core behavior of inner joins is to only include records when a match is found in both tables. Unmatched records are left out of the query result set.

Lab 3.1: Inner Joins

Lab Prep: Before you can begin the lab you must have SQL Server installed and run the Chapter3.1SetupAll.sql script. It is recommended that you view the Lab video instructions for Lab3.1_InnerJoins.wmv.

Skill Check 1: In one query you want to see the employees and cities where they work. You know the two tables share a common LocationID field. From JProCo, query both tables by joining them on this field. Your field select list should only include Firstname, LastName, City and State. When you are done, your screen should resemble Figure 3.8. Your Result set should have 11 records.

FirstName	LastName	City	State
Alex	Adams	Seattle	WA
Barry	Brown	Seattle	WA
Lee	Osako	Boston	MA
David	Kennson	Seattle	WA
Eric	Bender	Seattle	WA
Lisa	Kendall	Spokane	WA
David	Lonning	Seattle	WA
James	Newton	Boston	MA
Terry	O'Haire	Boston	MA
Sally	Smith	Seattle	WA
Barbara	O'Neil	Spokane	WA

Figure 3.8 Result of Skill Check 1.

Skill Check 2: The Grant table has an EmpID field. List all Employees' first and last names next to the grants they have found. Show the FirstName, LastName, GrantName and Amount fields. When you are done, your screen should resemble Figure 3.9 below. Your Result set should have 9 records.

FirstName	LastName	GrantName	Amount
David	Lonning	92 Purr_Scents %% team	4750.00
Barry	Brown	K_Land fund trust	15750.00
David	Lonning	Robert@BigStarBank.com	18100.00
David	Kennson	BIG 6's Foundation%	21000.00
Lee	Osako	TALTA_Kishan International	18100.00
Terry	O'Haire	Ben@MoreTechnology.com	41000.00
David	Lonning	@Last-U-Can-Help	25000.00
Sally	Smith	Thank you @.com	21500.00
Eric	Bender	Call Mom @Com	7500.00

Figure 3.9 Result screen of Skill Check 2.

Skill Check 3: Change your database context from the JProCo database to the dbBasics database. The Activity tables show the books which have been checked out and the Library card number of the library patron who checked it out. Join the Activity table to the Members table to see the books and the member details of who checked it out. When you're done, your result should resemble the figure you see here. Your Result set should contain 7 records.

	LibraryCardNo	Book	LibraryCardNo	fName	lName	Address	Gender	DOB
1	1001	Dust Bowl	1001	Tom	Larson	312 Costa Ave	M	1971-08-16 00:00:00.000
2	1001	How to Fix Things	1001	Tom	Larson	312 Costa Ave	M	1971-08-16 00:00:00.000
3	1003	Yachting for dummies	1003	Susan	Pederson	4515 Tolo Rd	F	1942-04-04 00:00:00.000
4	1005	How to marry a millionaire	1005	Larry	Kimball	1908 S Huson	M	1966-03-05 00:00:00.000
5	1005	Spice world	1005	Larry	Kimball	1908 S Huson	M	1966-03-05 00:00:00.000
6	1005	Juice Master tells all	1005	Larry	Kimball	1908 S Huson	M	1966-03-05 00:00:00.000
7	1006	Doctor Doctor	1006	Phil	Coleman	655 Rubber Rd	M	1940-07-09 00:00:00.000

Figure 3.10 Result screen of Skill Check 3.

Skill Check 4: In the dbBasics database, join the PurchaseActivity and the Customer table. Show just the Date, Item, Price and CustomerName fields. Your Result set should contain 11 records.

	Date	Item	Price	CustomerName
1	2001-12-08 00:00:00.000	747-400	175000000.00	Japan Air Lines JAL
2	2002-01-16 00:00:00.000	777	120000000.00	KittyHawk Air Cargo
3	2002-02-24 00:00:00.000	777	120000000.00	Air Canada
4	2002-04-04 00:00:00.000	747-400	175000000.00	Japan Air Lines JAL
5	2002-05-13 00:00:00.000	767	105000000.00	Japan Air Lines JAL
6	2002-06-21 00:00:00.000	727-200	90000000.00	Frontier
7	2002-07-30 00:00:00.000	747-400	175000000.00	Southwest Airlines
8	2002-09-07 00:00:00.000	747-400	175000000.00	KittyHawk Air Cargo
9	2002-10-16 00:00:00.000	767	105000000.00	Southwest Airlines
10	2002-11-24 00:00:00.000	727-200	90000000.00	Air Canada
11	2002-12-08 00:00:00.000	747-400	175000000.00	Japan Air Lines JAL

Figure 3.11 Result screen of Skill Check 4.

Answer Code: The SQL code to this lab can be found from the downloadable files named Lab3.1_InnerJoins.sql.

Inner Joins - Points to Ponder

1. Tables with related fields can be used together in a single query using a join.

2. An inner join only returns a result set with perfectly matched values from fields in two or more tables.

3. An inner join is the default join type. If inner is omitted from the join clause of a query, SQL Server will assume it to be an inner join.

Outer Joins

If you understand inner joins, understanding *outer joins* is an easy progression. They both look for and display every match they find between two tables. Both joins require that you specify the matching field(s) in the ON clause. Outer joins can show the records that inner joins omit.

The Employee table has 12 records; the Location table has 4 records. The query using the full outer join shows 13 records. Notice with a full outer join you can sometimes get more records than either table contains individually. Here, the result set has thirteen records. The Employee table has twelve records and the Location table has four. Full outer joins show all matches and unmatched records from both tables.

Left Outer Joins

Before we fire up an outer join, we need to state our goal. There is an employee with no location. There is also a location under construction in Chicago that presently has no employees.

Are we looking for an employee report or a location report? In an employee report, it's OK if Chicago does not show in the results. We need to list all employees from the Employee table. Thus, the outer join must favor the Employee table.

```
SELECT *
FROM Employee LEFT OUTER JOIN Location
ON Employee.LocationID = Location.LocationID
```

EmpID	lastname	firstname	hiredate	LocationID	ManagerID	Status	LocationID	street	city
1	Adams	Alex	2001-01-01 00:00:00.000	1	11	NULL	1	111 First ST	Seattle
2	Brown	Barry	2002-08-12 00:00:00.000	1	11	NULL	1	111 First ST	Seattle
3	Osako	Lee	1999-09-01 00:00:00.000	2	11	NULL	2	222 Second AVE	Boston
4	Kennson	David	1996-03-16 00:00:00.000	1	11	Has Tenure	1	111 First ST	Seattle
5	Bender	Eric	2007-05-17 00:00:00.000	1	11	NULL	1	111 First ST	Seattle
6	Kendall	Lisa	2001-11-15 00:00:00.000	4	4	NULL	4	444 Ruby ST	Spokane
7	Lonning	David	2000-01-01 00:00:00.000	1	11	On Leave	1	111 First ST	Seattle
8	Marshbank	John	2001-11-15 00:00:00.000	NULL	4	NULL	NULL	NULL	NULL
9	Newton	James	2003-09-30 00:00:00.000	2	3	NULL	2	222 Second AVE	Boston
10	O'Haire	Terry	2004-10-04 00:00:00.000	2	3	NULL	2	222 Second AVE	Boston
11	Smith	Sally	1989-04-01 00:00:00.000	1	NULL	NULL	1	111 First ST	Seattle
12	O'Neil	Barbara	1995-05-26 00:00:00.000	4	4	Has Tenure	4	444 Ruby ST	Spokane

Figure 3.12 A left outer join favors the Employee table listed to the left of the join.

In Figure 3.12 from the JProCo database, the Employee table is on the left. Since you want all employees included, you will make this a *left outer join*. Notice John Marshbank appears. This left outer join will find all employees from the table on the left. It then tries to find matches with the table on the right. All employees are shown and matches are filled in and displayed.

Right Outer Joins

If OSHA came to inspect all buildings, your goal would be to find all locations. They want to see all locations and who works at those locations. They have no interest in John Marshbank since he does not occupy a building. They want to see the buildings even if they are under construction and no employees work there.

To show all records from the table on the right, you need a *right outer join* (Figure 3.13). Since the right outer join favors the Location table, all locations will be displayed. The Employees list for Chicago is NULL. However, Chicago still appears as a location.

```
SELECT *
FROM Employee RIGHT OUTER JOIN Location
ON Employee.LocationID = Location.LocationID
```

Results | Messages

EmpID	lastname	firstname	hiredate	LocationID	ManagerID	Status	LocationID	street	city
1	Adams	Alex	2001-01-01 00:00:00.000	1	11	NULL	1	111 First ST	Seattle
2	Brown	Barry	2002-08-12 00:00:00.000	1	11	NULL	1	111 First ST	Seattle
4	Kennson	David	1996-03-16 00:00:00.000	1	11	Has Tenure	1	111 First ST	Seattle
5	Bender	Eric	2007-05-17 00:00:00.000	1	11	NULL	1	111 First ST	Seattle
7	Lonning	David	2000-01-01 00:00:00.000	1	11	On Leave	1	111 First ST	Seattle
11	Smith	Sally	1989-04-01 00:00:00.000	1	NULL	NULL	1	111 First ST	Seattle
3	Osako	Lee	1999-09-01 00:00:00.000	2	11	NULL	2	222 Second AVE	Boston
9	Newton	James	2003-09-30 00:00:00.000	2	3	NULL	2	222 Second AVE	Boston
10	O'Haire	Terry	2004-10-04 00:00:00.000	2	3	NULL	2	222 Second AVE	Boston
NULL	NULL	NULL	NULL	NULL	NULL	NULL	3	333 Third PL	Chicago
6	Kendall	Lisa	2001-11-15 00:00:00.000	4	4	NULL	4	444 Ruby ST	Spokane
12	O'Neil	Barbara	1995-05-26 00:00:00.000	4	4	Has Tenure	4	444 Ruby ST	Spokane

Figure 3.13 The right outer join shows all locations, even if nobody works there.

Notice the EmpID values are no longer in order. The LocationID values go from one to four in order. The Location table is showing all records in order and any matching values it finds in the join. Location is on the right side of this right outer join.

Full Outer Joins

If you wanted to see all employees, even if they have no location, a left outer join works great! What about seeing all locations, even without employees? The right outer join is your ticket for the location report.

If you wanted to see all employees and all locations regardless of whether each employee matches to a location and regardless of whether each location matches to an employee, you want a *full outer join* (Figure 3.14).

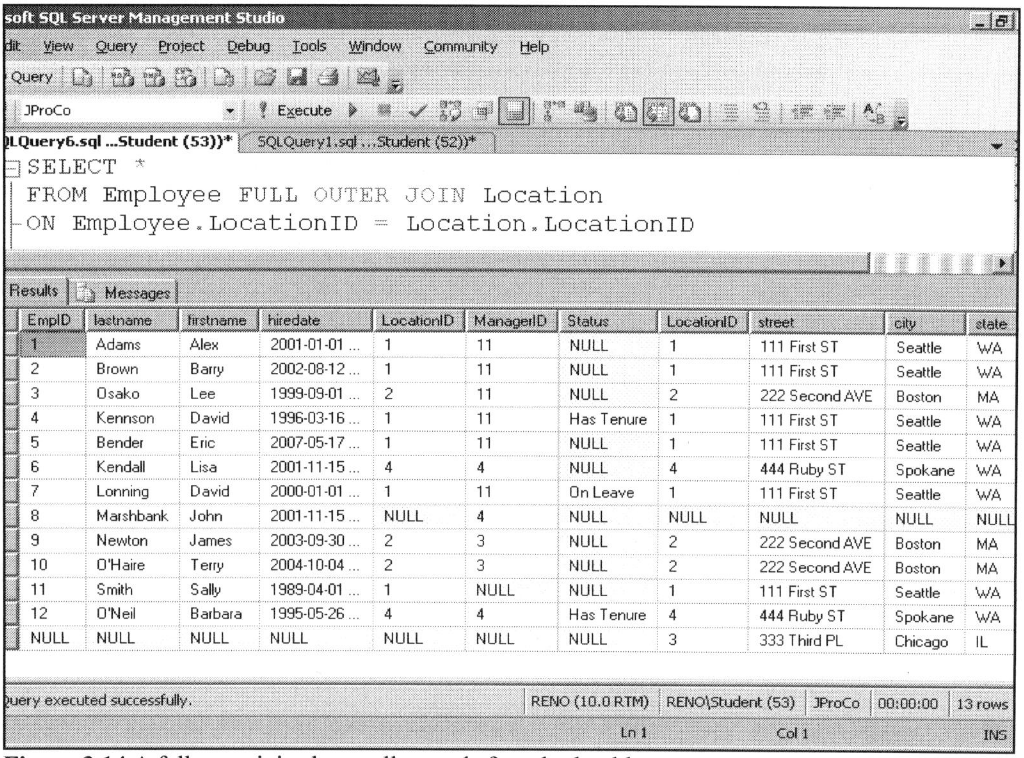

Figure 3.14 A full outer join shows all records from both tables.

Notice with a full outer join you get can get more records than either table contains. Here, the result set has thirteen records. The Employee table has twelve records and the Location table has four. Full outer joins show all matches and unmatched records from both tables.

Here is another example of the full outer join with all records from both tables. You want to find all employees with no grants and all grants with no employees. Use the full outer join seen in Figure 3.15.

As we can see, the full outer join finds all matches and unmatched records. All our joins so far have not used the WHERE clause, so we got all possible records. With a WHERE clause you would get only the records that satisfied the WHERE criteria. For example, we could add the clause WHERE LocationID = 1 to the code shown above (Figure 3.14). This WHERE clause would filter the records down to just the Seattle location and the records that remain will display. Without the WHERE clause, you get all matches and unmatched records in your result set. Unmatched records between the tables show up as NULL.

```
SELECT *
FROM [Grant] FULL OUTER JOIN [Employee]
ON [Grant].EmpID = [Employee].EmpID
```

Results | Messages

GrantID	GrantName	EmpID	Amount	EmpID	lastname	firstname	hiredate	LocationID	ManagerID	Status
001	92 Purr_Scents %% team	007	4750.00	007	Lonning	David	2000-01-01 00:00:00.000	001	011	On Leave
002	K_Land fund trust	002	15750.00	002	Brown	Barry	2002-08-12 00:00:00.000	001	011	NULL
003	Robert@BigStarBank.com	007	18100.00	007	Lonning	David	2000-01-01 00:00:00.000	001	011	On Leave
004	Norman's Outreach	NULL	5500.00	NULL	NULL	NULL	NULL	NULL	NULL	NULL
005	BIG 6's Foundation%	004	21000.00	004	Kennson	David	1996-03-16 00:00:00.000	001	011	Has Tenure
006	TALTA_Kishan International	003	18100.00	003	Osako	Lee	1999-09-01 00:00:00.000	002	011	NULL
007	Ben@MoreTechnology.com	010	41000.00	010	O'Haire	Terry	2004-10-04 00:00:00.000	002	003	NULL
008	@Last-U-Can-Help	007	25000.00	007	Lonning	David	2000-01-01 00:00:00.000	001	011	On Leave
009	Thank you @ com	011	21500.00	011	Smith	Sally	1989-04-01 00:00:00.000	001	NULL	NULL
010	Call Mom @Com	005	7500.00	005	Bender	Eric	2007-05-17 00:00:00.000	001	011	NULL
NULL	NULL	NULL	NULL	001	Adams	Alex	2001-01-01 00:00:00.000	001	011	NULL
NULL	NULL	NULL	NULL	006	Kendall	Lisa	2001-11-15 00:00:00.000	004	004	NULL
NULL	NULL	NULL	NULL	008	Marshbank	John	2001-11-15 00:00:00.000	NULL	004	NULL
NULL	NULL	NULL	NULL	009	Newton	James	2003-09-30 00:00:00.000	002	003	NULL
NULL	NULL	NULL	NULL	012	O'Neil	Barbara	1995-05-26 00:00:00.000	004	004	Has Tenure

Figure 3.15 A full outer join between the Grant and Employee tables shows all records.

Filtering Multi-Table Queries

Outer joins show more records than inner joins. Regardless of the type of join you select the WHERE clause trims your record set. Does the JOIN clause filter your records before the WHERE clause or vice versa? What records can you expect from queries with a JOIN clause that also have a WHERE clause? We will explore the multi-table join criteria in the chapter topics that follow.

Filtering with Inner Joins

The following inner join with no criteria produces eleven records:

```
SELECT *
FROM Employee INNER JOIN Location
ON Employee.LocationID = Location.LocationID
```

Of the twelve employees, John Marshbank does not appear in the query result set. John was already filtered out from the inner join. We want to see if the WHERE clause can look for John and bring him back into the result set. In Figure 3.16 we know there is a John working for the company, but we get no records in our result set. Since the join filters him out, there is no John for the WHERE to find. The end result is an empty result set.

```
SELECT *
FROM Employee INNER JOIN Location
ON Employee.LocationID = Location.LocationID
WHERE   FirstName = 'John'
```

Results	Messages
EmpID	Lastname	Firstname	HireDate	LocationID	ManagerID	Status	LocationID	street	city

Figure 3.16 The records for John cannot be found by the inner join, so the WHERE clause has no records to filter.

Filtering with Outer Joins

Changing the query to a left outer join normally shows all records from the Employee table. That makes 12 employees available for the WHERE clause to choose from. The predicate only wants John, so your result set has one record (Figure 3.17).

Filtering with All Types of Joins

To know how filtering in your WHERE clause works with joins, think of it much the same way as a single table query. What you're seeking must be in the table and it must meet the filtering criteria. Think of a joined query as one big table. If he is in the table, the WHERE will take only what the predicate says.
Follow one simple rule: The records must meet both the join and filtering criteria. If either process eliminates a record, it will not appear in your result set.

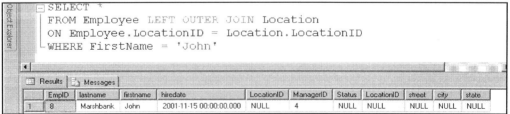

Figure 3.17 The WHERE criteria fetches the only record that matches its expression from the left outer join.

Lab 3.2: Outer Joins

Lab Prep: Before you can begin the lab, you must have SQL Server installed and run the Chapter3.2SetupAll.sql script. It is recommended that you view the Lab video instructions for Lab3.2_OuterJoins.wmv.

Skill Check 1: Open a query window to the JProCo database. Write a query that shows the list of all grants and the first and last names of the employees who acquired them. If the grant was not found by an employee, we still want to see a NULL first and last name. To do this, join the [Employee] and [Grant] tables. Show the FirstName, LastName, GrantName and Amount fields. Your result set should have 10 records. When you are done with the exercise your screen should resemble Figure 3.18.

FirstName	LastName	GrantName	Amount
David	Lonning	92 Purr_Scents %% team	4750.00
Barry	Brown	K_Land fund trust	15750.00
David	Lonning	Robert@BigStarBank.com	18100.00
NULL	NULL	Norman's Outreach	21000.00
David	Kennson	BIG 6's Foundation%	21000.00
Lee	Osako	TALTA_Kishan International	18100.00
Terry	O'Haire	Ben@MoreTechnology.com	41000.00
David	Lonning	@Last-U-Can-Help	25000.00
Sally	Smith	Thank you @.com	21500.00
Eric	Bender	Call Mom @Com	7500.00

Figure 3.18 Result for Skill Check 1.

Skill Check 2: Open a query window to the JProCo database. Write a query so that you see all employees and the list of grants they have found. If they found no grants, a NULL should appear next to their name. Show the FirstName, LastName, GrantName and Amount fields. When you are done with the exercise your screen should resemble Figure 3.19 to the right.

	FirstName	LastName	GrantName	Amount
1	Alex	Adams	NULL	NULL
2	Barry	Brown	K_Land fund trust	15750.00
3	Lee	Osako	TALTA_Kishan International	18100.00
4	David	Kennson	BIG 6's Foundation%	21000.00
5	Eric	Bender	Call Mom @Com	7500.00
6	Lisa	Kendall	NULL	NULL
7	David	Lonning	92 Purr_Scents %% team	4750.00
8	David	Lonning	Robert@BigStarBank.com	18100.00
9	David	Lonning	@Last-U-Can-Help	25000.00
10	John	Marshbank	NULL	NULL
11	James	Newton	NULL	NULL
12	Terry	O'Haire	Ben@MoreTechnology.com	41000.00
13	Sally	Smith	Thank you @.com	21500.00
14	Barbara	O'Neil	NULL	NULL

Figure 3.19 Result screen for Skill Check 2.

Answer Code: The SQL code to this lab can be found in the downloadable files in a file named Lab3.2_OuterJoins.sql

Outer Joins - Points to Ponder

1. Outer joins can allow more records to be seen in your result set than just an equal record match list from the Inner join.

2. There are three types of outer joins: left outer join, right outer join and full outer join.

3. In a left outer join, the table named before the join might have records that appear even if SQL Server finds no matching records in the table listed after the LEFT OUTER JOIN clause.

4. The table listed after the RIGHT OUTER JOIN might have records that appear even if no matching records are found in the table on the left of the join.

5. In full outer joins, all matches and unmatched records are displayed from both tables.

6. Using the word OUTER is optional. LEFT OUTER JOIN means the same thing as LEFT JOIN in a query.

7. Using the word INNER is optional. INNER JOIN means the same thing as JOIN in a query.

8. Regardless of the type of Join you use the records produced from the Join can be filtered by the criteria in the WHERE clause. The WHERE clause filters records after the JOIN clauses.

Chapter Glossary

Data Loss: An activity that you run on your system the deletes data you wanted to keep.

Flat File Database: A database with only one table. A text file or simple list is a flat file database.

Inner Join: Combines records from two or more tables where matching values are found.

Join Clause: The clause used to join tables in SQL.

Outer Join: Combines records from two or more tables and shows matching and unmatched values.

Relational Database: A database containing more than one table.

Review Quiz

1.) Which symbol says you want all fields from a table in a SELECT statement?

O a.   ___
O b.   &
O c.   %
O d.   *

2.) The WHERE clause in a query on a single table is…

O a.   Optional
O b.   Required

3.) The FROM Clause in a query against a single table is…

O a.   Optional
O b.   Required

4.) Which record(s) will not return with the following WHERE clause? WHERE EmpName like '%T' (Choose all correct answers)

☐ a.   Thomas
☐ b.   Atwater
☐ c.   Tompter
☐ d.   TeeTee

5.) Which record will not return with the following WHERE clause? WHERE LastName like 'T%'

O a.   Thomas
O b.   Atwater
O c.   Tompter.
O d.   TeeTee

6.) Which type of join would not show nulls as a match?

O a.   INNER JOIN
O b.   LEFT OUTER JOIN
O c.   RIGHT OUTER JOIN
O d.   FULL OUTER JOIN

7.) Which syntax would create an error?

O a.   JOIN
O b.   INNER JOIN
O c.   INNER OUTER JOIN
O d,   FULL JOIN
O e.   FULL OUTER JOIN

8.) Look at the following SQL statement:

```
SELECT *
FROM Employee LEFT OUTER JOIN Location
ON Location.LocationID = Employee.LocationID
```
What will be displayed in the result set?

O a.   All records where both tables match.
O b.   All records in Employee including matches from Location.
O c.   All records from Location including matches from Employee.
O d.   The superset of both tables.

9.) You have a table named Employee. You write the following query:

```
SELECT *
FROM Employee
```
You plan to join the Location table and fear there may be some employees with no location. You want to make sure that the query returns a list of all employee records. What join clause would you add to the query above?

O a.   LEFT JOIN Location ON employee.LocationID = location.LocationID
O b.   RIGHT JOIN Location ON employee.LocationID = location.LocationID
O c.   INNER JOIN Location ON employee.LocationID = location.LocationID
O d.   FULL JOIN Location ON employee.LocationID = location.LocationID

Answer Key

1.) The _ matches exactly one character when comparing strings so (a) is wrong. & is not a wildcard and would only match another & so (b) is wrong too. % represents zero or more characters when pattern matching so (c) is also wrong. The correct answer is (d) because * represents every field in a table.

2.) The WHERE clause filters records from the result set if used but not every result set needs to be filtered so (b) is not correct. If you want all records returned from a query you would not filter the table with a WHERE clause so (a) is the correct answer.

3.) Running a query without knowing what tables to use is not possible so (a) is not correct. Since the FROM clause tells the query which tables to look in, it is required making (b) the correct answer.

4.) Because % represents zero or more characters and the last character in the pattern to be matched is 'T' the only names that will be returned will end in 'T'. Since none of the names end in 'T' (a)Thomas, (b)Atwater, (c)Tompter and (d) TeeTee are all correct answers.

5.) Because % represents zero or more characters and the first character in the pattern to be matched is 'T' the only names that will be returned will start with 'T'. Since 3 of the names do start with 'T' (a)Thomas, (c)Tompter and (d) TeeTee are all wrong. Since Atwater is the only one that does not start with 'T' (b) is the correct answer.

6.) OUTER JOINs display mismatching records using NULL as a value for fields in records that otherwise would not have been returned so (b), (c) and (d) are incorrect. INNER JOINs only display records where the field from one table contains the same value as the field in the other table so (a) is correct.

7.) Since JOIN is short for INNER JOIN both (a) and (b) are incorrect. Because FULL JOIN is short for FULL OUTER JOIN both (d) and (e) are incorrect too. Because INNER and OUTER are two different types of JOIN you can't use both on the same tables so (c) is the right answer.

8.) An INNER JOIN will return 'All records where both tables match' so (a) is incorrect. RIGHT OUTER JOINing to Location would return 'All records from Location including matches from Employee' making (c) wrong too. A FULL OUTER JOIN would return 'The superset of both tables' so (d) is also wrong. Because Employee is on the left and Location is on the right of the LEFT OUTER JOIN operator (b) is correct and will return 'All records in Employee including matches from Location'

9.) RIGHT JOIN Location ON Employee.LocationID = Location.LocationID will return all location records including any matches from the employee table so (b) is wrong. INNER JOIN Location ON Employee.LocationID = Location.LocationID will only return the employee records that have a matching location so (c) is wrong too. FULL JOIN Location ON Employee.LocationID = Location.LocationID will return the superset of both tables making (d) incorrect. LEFT JOIN Location ON Employee.LocationID = Location.LocationID will return all employee records including any matches from the location table making (a) the correct answer.

Bug Catcher Game

To play the Bug Catcher game, run the BugCatcher_Chapter3.pps from the BugCatcher folder of the companion files. You can obtain these files from the www.Joes2Pros.com web site.

Chapter 4. Query Strategies

The better you get at writing queries, the more people want you to write them. Once you learn all the tricks, you'll get the "Wow" reactions from your managers and teammates. You'll also get to be a part of all the deadlines. Part of the query strategy is to show you how to write robust queries that won't break if the database changes. That usually requires some extra code, but is well worth the effort. Another great query strategy helps you write robust and stable queries using fewer keystrokes. This chapter covers ways to increase your bag of tricks while showing how to make your life easier when writing queries.

READER NOTE: *Please run the script Chapter4.0SetupAll.sql in order to follow along with the examples in the first section of this chapter. The setup scripts for this book are posted at Joes2Pros.com.*

Query Writing Strategy

Here is something I have yet to find in any book. When enthusiastic SQL students do this, they experience a revelation. The number of errors drops significantly and the speed at writing complex queries increases immediately. Knowing how to narrow down what you are looking for amongst a vast list of choices helps immensely. Grabbing the right tables first and then the fields second is like grabbing the right menu before ordering an item from it. In fact, one student named Tim took this back to his team of SQL developers and they immediately implemented this process.

We are all used to following steps. Most of the time, actions are sequential from top to bottom or left to right. Other times we complete things in phases. The two phases you are going to see here apply to joining tables. Just remember to organize first and clean up second.

When you go to a new restaurant, you ask to see the menu. You want to see all they have to offer. The odds are you may like half the items, but only need a few for your party. Looking at the menu is like starting off with a SELECT *. After looking at all the fields, you pick the one(s) you want.

Sometimes restaurants have multiple menus. My favorite restaurant has a kids' menu, an adult menu, a "gluten-free" menu and a drink menu. These menus were gathered at our station. Ultimately, in my head, a selection was narrowed to what was needed.

Phase I: Organize. When you're building a new query from many tables, you'll find yourself wondering, "Where do I start?" First, lay the steps out by identifying which tables contain the essential data. Second, get all your joins working with a SELECT * statement. Third, add any basic filtering criteria.

Phase II. Itemize. Once all joins and criteria, such as SELECT *, FROM and WHERE are working, you are ready for Phase II. This entails going back and changing your SELECT * to an itemized select field list as your final step.

Let's explore how this two-phase process of "Organize then Itemize" is a time-saver. We are going to use one of the challenges from the last lab. In Lab 3.2 (Outer Joins) in Skill Check 2, you needed to get four fields from two different tables. If you list all four desired fields and test one table at time, you get an error as seen on the right side of Figure 4.1.

In Figure 4.1 we write the SELECT statement and part of the FROM clause. The FROM clause will have two tables when we are done, but for now we just want to get the Location table working. When we use the SELECT * it removes any possible errors from line 1. From there, we can focus on our more complicated join logic. We can add tables one at a time until all is working. This is the Organize phase.

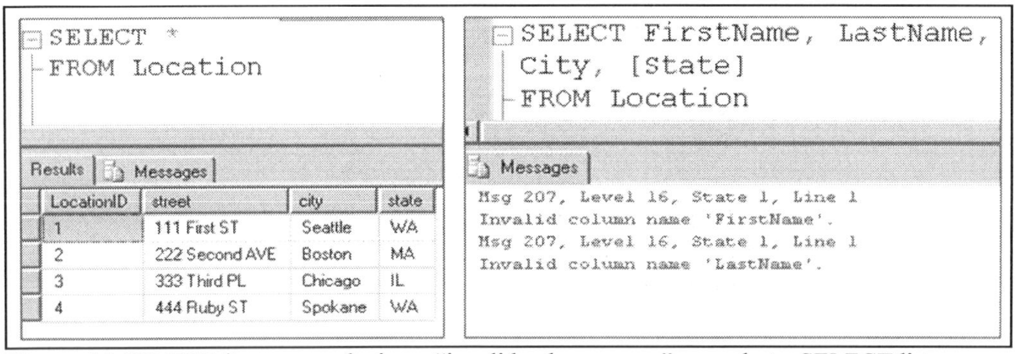

Figure 4.1 SELECT * never results in an "invalid column name" error, but a SELECT list can.

After your query is organized and working, you can go back and itemize the SELECT field list to display just what you want. This is the Itemize phase. These steps are broken down as follows:

```
--ORGANIZE PHASE: Get SELECT * query written.
    -- Test first table logic
    SELECT *
    FROM Location

    --Test second table with join
    SELECT *
    FROM Location INNER JOIN Employee
    ON Location.LocationID = Employee.LocationID

    --Test all tables with criteria
    SELECT *
    FROM Location INNER JOIN Employee
    ON Location.LocationID = Employee.LocationID
    WHERE [State] = 'WA'
```

83

```
--ITEMIZE PHASE: Change to SELECT field list
    --Choose your fields
    SELECT FirstName, LastName, City, [State]
    FROM Location INNER JOIN Employee
    ON Location.LocationID = Employee.LocationID
    WHERE [State] = 'WA'
```

SELECT is always the first statement in a query. It's natural to want to finish your SELECT statement before writing the FROM clause. Start with SELECT * and finish the query. Do your field list when all else is done. Use this method and you will never again get a field selection error while building queries.

Table Aliasing

When people ask me, "How did you do that?" oftentimes they are asking about ordinary work that got done quickly. This is great for deadlines. *Table aliasing* is a big saver of keystrokes. As we know, tables are listed in the FROM clause. We had to retype the table names again in the ON clause as seen in the code below:

```
SELECT *
FROM Location INNER JOIN Employee
ON Location.LocationID = Employee.LocationID
```

Setting Aliases

Our next goal is to get the FROM clause to refer to the Employee table as Emp and the Location table as Loc. It's like giving your friend a nickname. They respond and use it, but their birth certificate still has the original name. In other words, the tables will not change names literally, but your query can use a shorter name. Simply alias the table name as another name in the FROM clause and you then reuse the shorter name. Here is a SQL example:

```
SELECT *
FROM Location AS Loc INNER JOIN Employee AS Emp
ON Loc.LocationID = Emp.LocationID
```

In this example, the payoff is only slightly obvious. Some queries will use the table name in dozens of places. It's far quicker to type "Loc" many times versus "Location."

Using Aliases

At this point, you are probably not a big fan of two-part field names in a query. In fact, the simple name does the same thing with far fewer keystrokes. In comparing the two queries below, we see identical results.

```
--Simple Field Names
SELECT Firstname, LastName, [State]
FROM Location INNER JOIN Employee
ON Location.LocationID = Employee.LocationID

--Two-part Field Names
SELECT Employee.Firstname, Employee.LastName,
Location.[State]
FROM Location INNER JOIN Employee
ON Location.LocationID = Employee.LocationID
```

The truth is we lucked out on all our past queries. The simple field name query from above is looking for Firstname from either table. There is a Firstname field in Employee and none in Location. Firstname must really mean Employee.Firstname so SQL Server implicitly does this behind the scenes for you. The same is true with the [State] field. When SQL Server looks for the [State] field in the Employee table and realizes it isn't present, it does us the courtesy of pulling it in from the Location table.

Please don't do any of the following steps regarding renaming your fields. They are only for demonstration and assume a knowledge level discussed in Chapter 5 and Chapter 6. Enjoy the concept and feel free to come back and experiment after you have finished this book.

So far, we have been lucky. Everything has worked from the simple name. Why? Let's use an example. The Employee table has a Status field as seen in Figure 4.2.

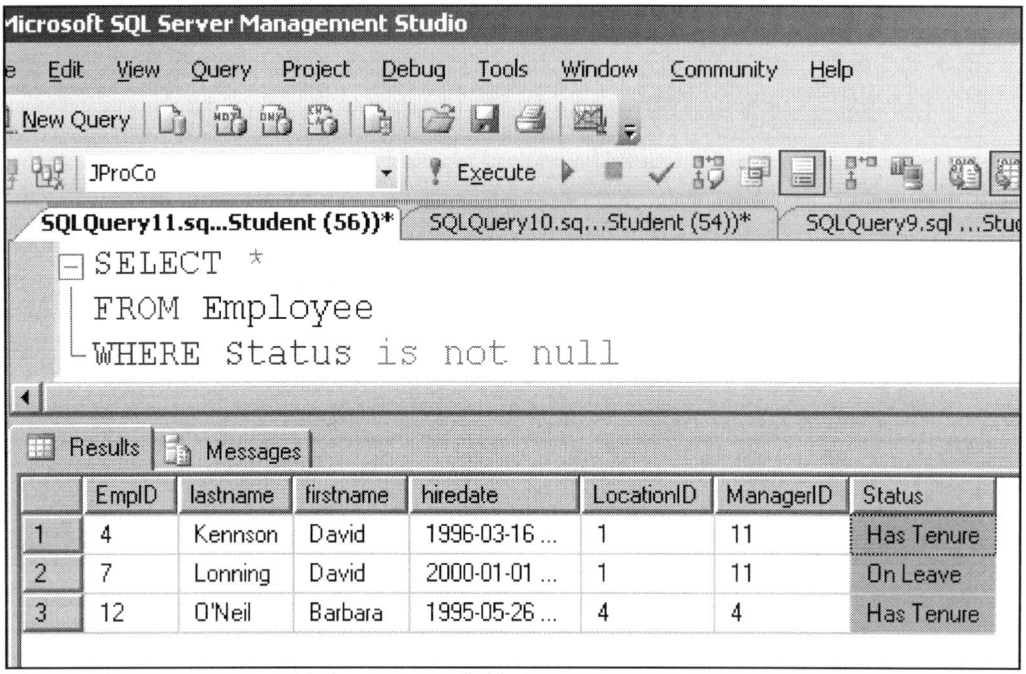

Figure 4.2 The Employee table has a Status field.

What if the Status field was renamed to "State" in the Employee table? You could end up with two table designs like the ones you see in Figure 4.3.

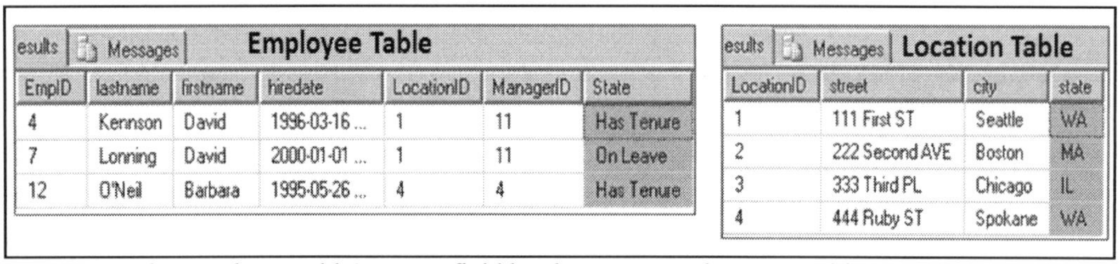

Figure 4.3 The Employee table's status field has been renamed to state. This move could lead to confusion as the Location table already has a state field with an entirely different meaning.

Let's say the Employee. Status field was renamed to the Employee.State field as in Figure 4.4.

```
SELECT * FROM
  Location AS Loc INNER JOIN Employee AS Emp
  ON Emp.LocationID = Loc.LocationID
```

Results | Messages

	LocationID	street	city	state	EmpID	lastname	firstname	hiredate	LocationID	ManagerID	State
1	1	111 First ST	Seattle	WA	1	Adams	Alex	2001-01-01 00:00:00.000	1	11	NULL
2	1	111 First ST	Seattle	WA	2	Brown	Barry	2002-08-12 00:00:00.000	1	11	NULL
3	2	222 Second AVE	Boston	MA	3	Osako	Lee	1999-09-01 00:00:00.000	2	11	NULL
4	1	111 First ST	Seattle	WA	4	Kennson	David	1996-03-16 00:00:00.000	1	11	Has T
5	1	111 First ST	Seattle	WA	5	Bender	Eric	2007-05-17 00:00:00.000	1	11	NULL
6	4	444 Ruby ST	Spokane	WA	6	Kendall	Lisa	2001-11-15 00:00:00.000	4	4	NULL
7	1	111 First ST	Seattle	WA	7	Lonning	David	2000-01-01 00:00:00.000	1	11	On Le
8	2	222 Second AVE	Boston	MA	9	Newton	James	2003-09-30 00:00:00.000	2	3	NULL
9	2	222 Second AVE	Boston	MA	10	O'Haire	Terry	2004-10-04 00:00:00.000	2	3	NULL
10	1	111 First ST	Seattle	WA	11	Smith	Sally	1989-04-01 00:00:00.000	1	NULL	NULL
11	4	444 Ruby ST	Spokane	WA	12	O'Neil	Barbara	1995-05-26 00:00:00.000	4	4	Has T

Figure 4.4 SELECT * displays the State fields from both the Location and Employee tables.

This brings up a question. If the SELECT statement field list includes [State], will SQL Server choose the Employee.State field or the Location.State field? The sheer risk of picking the wrong field means SQL Server will give an error message and request more information. If you do a SELECT * you will get both fields and no error.

When you itemize fields, you must specify exactly which one you want. Suppose you would like to include the State field in your report. If you use just the simple name for a field when two fields with the same name exist, your specification will be ambiguous (Figure 4.5) and SQL Server displays an error.

Microsoft SQL Server Management Studio

File   Edit   View   Query   Project   Debug   Tools   Window   Community   Help

New Query | JProCo | Execute

Object Explorer

Connect ▾

Reno (SQL Server 10.0.16
  Databases
    System Databases
    Database Snapshc
    dbBasics
    dbTester
    JProCo
      Database Diac

SQLQuery1.sql ...Student (52))*

```
SELECT FirstName, LastName, [State]
  FROM Location   AS Loc
  INNER JOIN Employee AS Emp
  ON Loc.LocationID = Emp.LocationID
```

Messages

```
Msg 209, Level 16, State 1, Line 1
Ambiguous column name 'State'.
```

Figure 4.5 SQL Server can't tell which [State] field you wish to see.

Notice the error message is coupled with an explanation that SQL Server does not guess what information you want to see. The only time it allows simple field names in a multiple table query is when that is the only field with that name. Another good tip is the SELECT * does not give you ambiguous column name errors since it pulls in all fields.

We wanted the City and State fields displayed from the Location table. We can fix this error by using the two-part field name. In your field selection list, specify the Location.City and the Location.State fields with the table aliases (Figure 4.6). We used the Loc alias for the Location table in this query. Doing so allows us to use a shorter name each time we reference that table. This allows the State field to work in our query. We did not need to prefix the City field to get this query to work. Can you guarantee that tomorrow someone will not add a City field to the Employee table in your database to denote where the employee resides? This would break some of your queries.

You want to ensure that your queries will work today and into the future. A good way to do this is to use two-part names for all fields listed in your SELECT statement. This seems like extra typing which can be significantly reduced by using aliases.

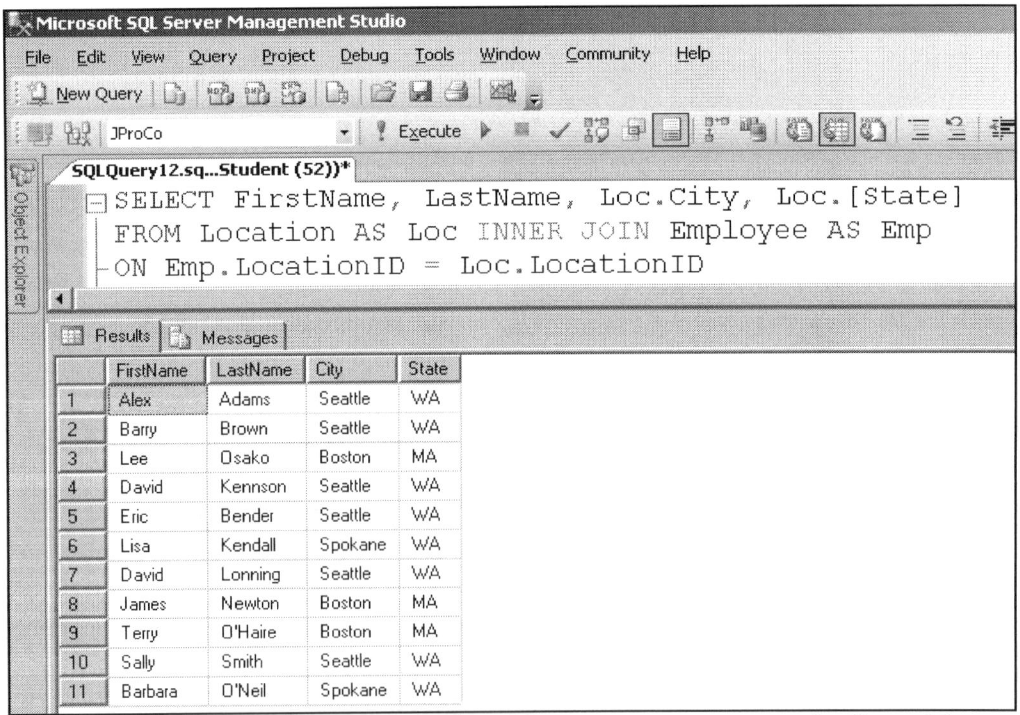

Figure 4.6 Using the Loc alias for the Location table to create two-part names for City and State.

In Figure 4.7 we have changed every listed field to use the two-part name. The aliasing we did in our FROM clause allowed us to use the shorter names. Aliasing is a time-saving way to allow you to create robust and durable code more easily.

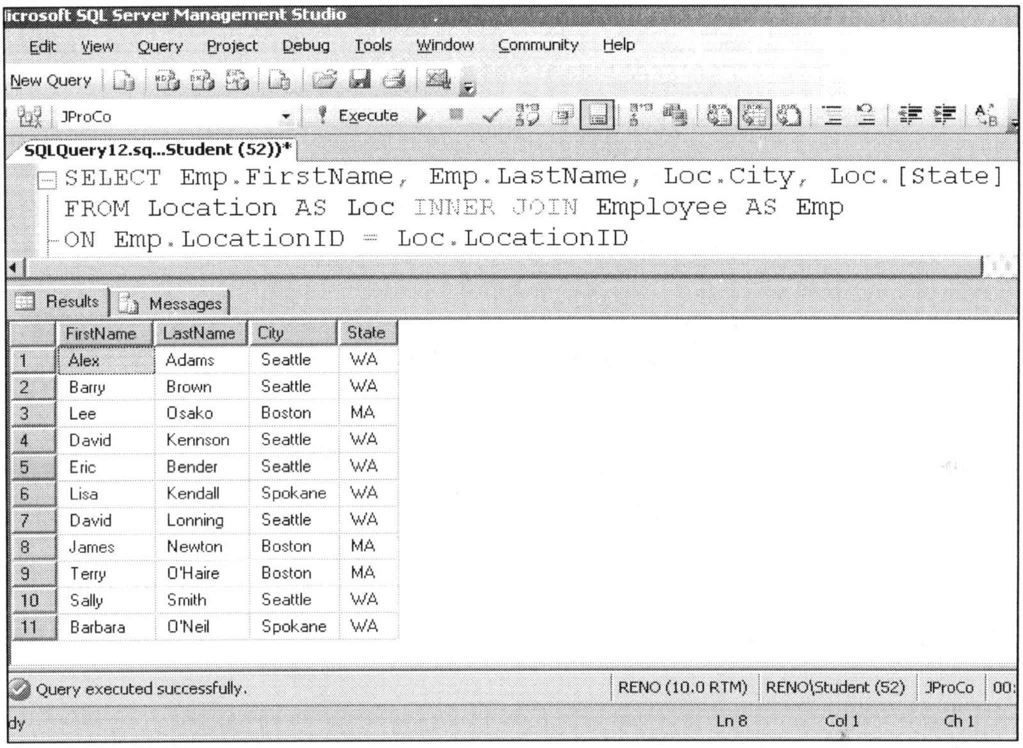

Figure 4.7 All four fields in the select list are using two-part names.

Lab 4.1: Table Aliasing

Lab Prep: Before you can begin the lab, you must have SQL Server installed and run the Chapter4.1SetupAll.sql script.

Skill Check 1: In JProCo you want to see the employees who found grants. You want to just view the Firstname and LastName fields from the Employee table and the GrantName and Amount fields from the Grant table. The Employee table should be aliased as E and the Grant table as G. All four fields must use the two-part field name identifier. When you are done, your screen should resemble Figure 4.8.

```
SELECT E.FirstName, E.LastName,
G.GrantName, G.Amount
```

FirstName	LastName	GrantName	Amount
David	Lonning	92 Purr_Scents %% team	4750.00
Barry	Brown	K_Land fund trust	15750.00
David	Lonning	Robert@BigStarBank.com	18100.00
David	Kennson	BIG 6's Foundation%	21000.00
Lee	Osako	TALTA_Kishan International	18100.00
Terry	O'Haire	Ben@MoreTechnology.com	41000.00
David	Lonning	@Last-U-Can-Help	25000.00
Sally	Smith	Thank you @.com	21500.00
Eric	Bender	Call Mom @Com	7500.00

Figure 4.8 Skill Check 1 uses table aliases.

Skill Check 2: In JProCo you want to see a list of employees and where they work only if they work at one of the four locations. Show just the FirstName, LastName, City and State fields. Alias the Employee table as emp and the Location table as loc. Your result set should contain eleven records.

Answer Code: The SQL code to this lab can be found from the downloadable files named Lab4.1_TableAliasing.sql.

Table Aliasing - Points to Ponder

1.   Databases and tables have names. These names are called Identifiers. In JProCo there is a table named Employee. Table is the object and Employee is this object's Identifier.

2.   When you alias a table, you use an abbreviation. SQL aliasing usually means using a shorter name than the original identifier.

3.   Aliases must be declared immediately after the table's name in the FROM clause.

4.   When you alias a table, you must use the alias wherever you refer to that table in your query.

5.   The process of qualifying fields with two part names makes your queries unambiguous.

6.   The extra work of qualifying your fields is reduced by using the shortened alias instead of the complete table name.

7.   Using the keyword AS when specifying an alias is optional. It is recommended because it makes your code easier to read.

Cartesian Result Sets

Sometimes you will find tables that have no field relatable to any other table. There is no way to perform a meaningful inner or outer join for reporting. Sometimes you are really looking for combinations between tables rather than exact matches. The Cartesian combination of data coupled with the cross join will be explored in this section.

Inner and outer joins are useful for finding records you have in related tables. These join types reflect the reality of your data. In contrast, a *cross join* does not need related data to execute. You can personally use a cross join to explore future possibilities. For example, at the beginning of a college semester, students may want to know what courses are required of them. Perhaps they have already satisfied some of those requirements. The requirements apply to all students regardless of the coursework they have done so far. A cross join simply returns all possible combinations of the record set data from the tables listed.

By cross-joining the list of students with the list of course requirements, you get all combinations. If 10 students need to take three required courses each, then the Cartesian result is 30 records. Each student will be listed three times in the result set, once for each required class.

The cross join list details the courses each student must complete before graduation. This list has nothing to do with what they have actually done. The cross join result set is a combination of the information freshman students need to know to ensure their futures.

Let us suppose that employees Alex Adams and Barry Brown from the JProCo database want to become managers. In JProCo, there is a list of management classes aspiring managers must complete. This list is located in the JProCo MgmtTraining table.

A query of the Employee table using the EmpID numbers for Alex and Barry, and a separate SELECT query of the MgmtTraining table shows both employees and the three required classes as seen in Figure 4.9.

```
SELECT *
FROM Employee WHERE EmpID IN (1,2)

SELECT * FROM mgmtTraining
```

Results | Messages

EmpID	Lastname	FirstName	HireDate	LocationID	ManagerID	Status
1	Adams	Alex	2001-01-01 00:00:00.000	1	11	NULL
2	Brown	Barry	2002-08-12 00:00:00.000	1	11	NULL

ClassID	ClassName	ClassDurationHours
1	Embracing Diversity	12
2	Interviewing	6
3	Difficult Negotiations	30

Figure 4.9 Two employees are in the first result set while three classes are in the second.

We don't know how many classes Alex or Barry have already taken. A third-party company stored all registrations. We are more interested right now in supplying them with a list of requirements for their benefit. A cross join shows the entire list of classes each aspiring employee must complete before being considered for JProCo management.

If Alex must complete three classes and Barry must complete the same three, combining the result sets from both queries would give us six records (2 * 3 = 6 records) as seen in Figure 4.10.

```
SELECT * FROM Employee
CROSS JOIN MgmtTraining
WHERE EmpID in (1,2)
```

Results | Messages

	EmpID	lastname	firstname	hiredate	LocationID	ManagerID	State	ClassID	ClassName	Class
1	1	Adams	Alex	2001-01-01 ...	1	11	NULL	1	Embracing Diversity	12
2	1	Adams	Alex	2001-01-01 ...	1	11	NULL	2	Interviewing	6
3	1	Adams	Alex	2001-01-01 ...	1	11	NULL	3	Difficult Negotiations	30
4	2	Brown	Barry	2002-08-12 ...	1	11	NULL	1	Embracing Diversity	12
5	2	Brown	Barry	2002-08-12 ...	1	11	NULL	2	Interviewing	6
6	2	Brown	Barry	2002-08-12 ...	1	11	NULL	3	Difficult Negotiations	30

Figure 4.10 A cross join with three records from one table and two from another gives us six records in our result set.

A cross join does not show us the actual relationship between the tables. This list in Figure 4.10 does not show us what classes Barry and Alex have taken. Instead, a cross join shows all possible record combinations between two record sets and combines them into one record set. These tables often have nothing in common. They may have no common field upon which to join. Because of this trait, you do not need to specify an ON clause in a cross join query.

Lab 4.2: Cross Joins

Lab Prep: Before you can begin the lab you must have SQL Server installed and run the Chapter4.2SetupAll.sql script.

Skill Check 1: You have twelve Employees and four locations. Each Employee has one location, but they could visit all of them. Write a query to show the combinations of every employee and every location. Select only the Firstname, LastName, City and State fields. The final result should reveal 48 records. Alias the Employee table as E and the Location table as L. When you are done, your screen should resemble Figure 4.11.

Answer Code: The SQL code to this lab can be found from the downloadable files named Lab4.2_CrossJoins.sql.

FirstNAme	LastNAme	City	State
Alex	Adams	Seattle	WA
Barry	Brown	Seattle	WA
Lee	Osako	Seattle	WA
David	Kennson	Seattle	WA
Eric	Bender	Seattle	WA
Lisa	Kendall	Seattle	WA
David	Lonning	Seattle	WA
John	Marshbank	Seattle	WA
James	Newton	Seattle	WA
Terry	O'Haire	Seattle	WA
Sally	Smith	Seattle	WA
Barbara	O'Neil	Seattle	WA
Alex	Adams	Boston	MA
Barry	Brown	Boston	MA
Lee	Osako	Boston	MA
David	Kennson	Boston	MA
Eric	Bender	Boston	MA
Lisa	Kendall	Boston	MA

Figure 4.11 Skill Check 1 has 48 records.

Cross Joins - Points to Ponder

1. A cross join creates or finds all possible entity combinations.

2. The cross join does not need to use an ON clause.

3. The size of the result set created from a cross join is the number of records in the first table multiplied by the number of records in the second table.

4. A cross join gives you every combination of both tables. It is known as a Cartesian product or Cartesian result.

5. If one table had 12 records and the other had four, then the Cartesian result of these tables would be 48 records.

6. Use a cross join when you need a Cartesian result from your tables.

Unmatched Records Queries

You may remember that our JProCo database has a related table with some unmatched records. For example, John Marshbank has no LocationID at JProCo. It's the LocationID field of the Employee table that is used to map to the LocationID field of the Location table. Without even looking at the Location table we can tell which Employee records would be not be matched up to records in the Location table. All we need to do is find the NULL in the LocationID field.

With a single table query we can easily see that John Marshbank is the only employee without a location (Figure 4.12).

```
SELECT FirsTName,
  LastName,
  LocationID
FROM Employee
```

	FirsTName	LastName	LocationID
1	Alex	Adams	1
2	Barry	Brown	1
3	Lee	Osako	2
4	David	Kennson	1
5	Eric	Bender	1
6	Lisa	Kendall	4
7	David	Lonning	1
8	John	Marshb...	NULL
9	James	Newton	2
10	Terry	O'Haire	2
11	Sally	Smith	1
12	Barbara	O'Neil	4

Figure 4.12 The Employee table shows who has a LocationID of NULL.

Whenever you have relatable fields like LocationID that allows nulls, you need to be on the lookout for possible unmatched records in related tables.

Looking at the Location table in Figure 4.13 we see all the data. In fact, this table does not allow nulls for the LocationID field.

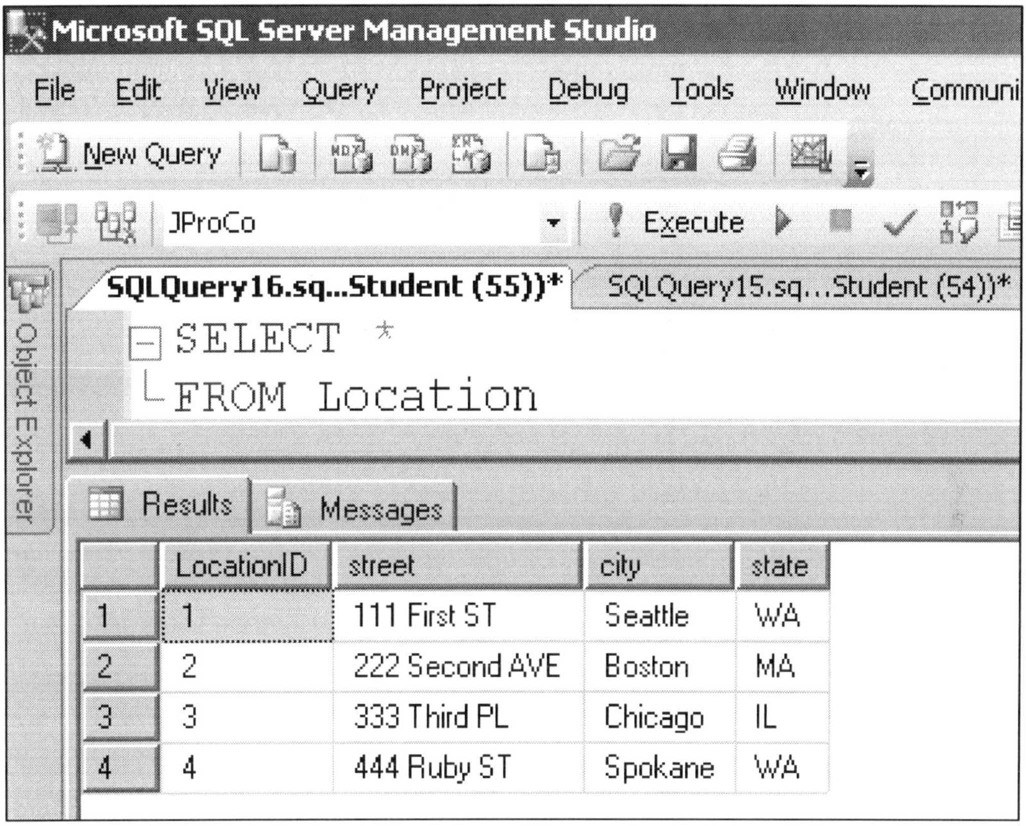

Figure 4.13 Location table has no nulls, but may still have unmatching LocationID values in the Employee table.

Looking further, there are no nulls anywhere in the Location table. So does this mean that all locations have at least one employee? Perhaps that is not the case. You may remember that Chicago has no employees. If you wanted to find all locations with no employees, you would run an unmatched records query.

In this case, we have to join the Location table with the Employee table to determine the location where nobody yet works. What type of join will tell us this? Since nulls don't map through a join, the INNER JOIN drops the record from the result set and we won't see Chicago. The outer join will show both the matches and the unmatched records, so we see every location (Figure 4.14).

97

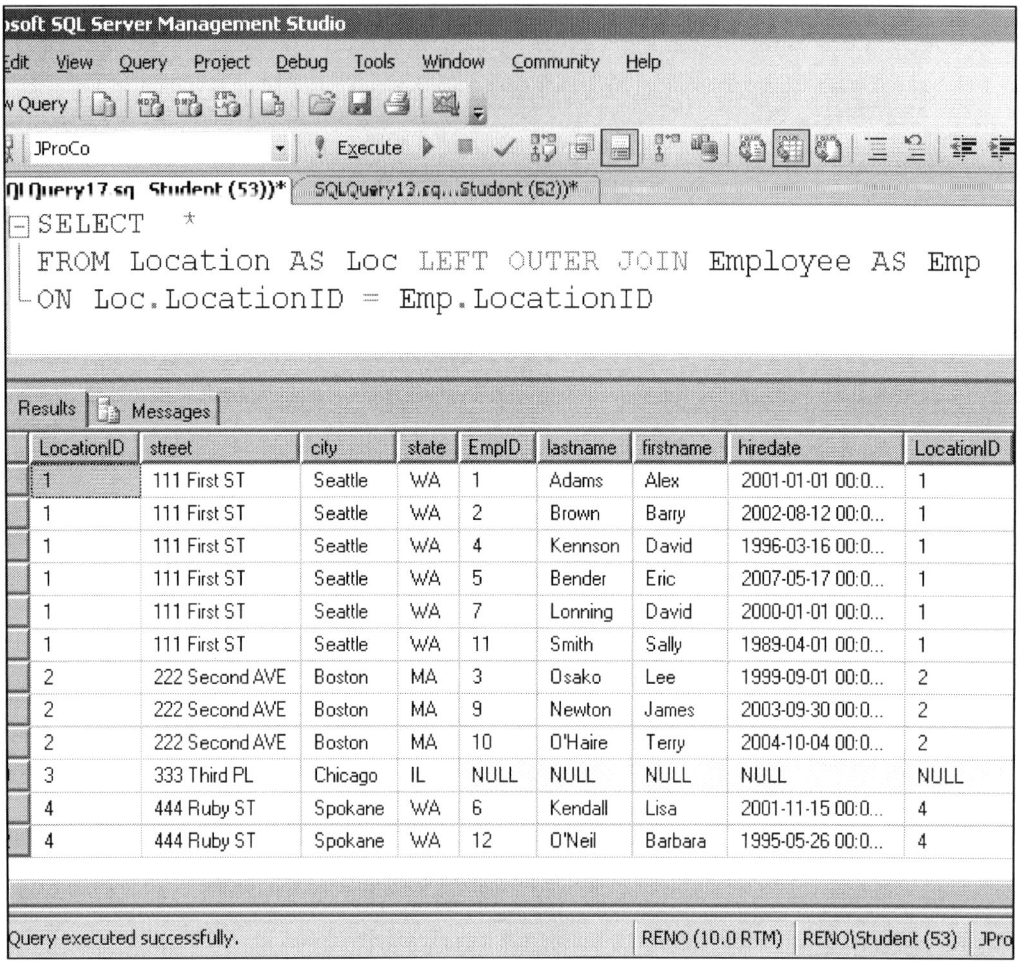

Figure 4.14 The left outer join favors the Location table and Chicago appears with a null employee.

Seattle is listed many times. Chicago is listed once with no employee found. A NULL appears in the fields from the Employee table for Chicago. With the Location table on the left and the NULL on the right, we have part of an unmatched records query. To find just the records that don't match, we look for null records on the table that the outer join does not favor. In this case, it's the Employee table.

The outer join will show us the unmatched records with null location details if you set the WHERE clause to look for nulls on a field in the non-dominant table. Unmatched record queries use SQL to return a result set displaying only the unmatched records between the two tables.

When our query criterion specifies NULL, only Chicago shows up in our result set. By doing a LEFT OUTER JOIN and using a NULL value from the Employee table (or "RIGHT" table) as our search condition criteria, our unmatched records query shows us one record. (Figure 4.15)

```
SELECT *
FROM Location as Loc LEFT OUTER JOIN Employee as Emp
ON Loc.LocationID = Emp.LocationID
WHERE Emp.EmpID IS NULL
```

Results | Messages

	LocationID	street	city	state	EmpID	LastName	FirstName	HireDate	LocationID	ManagerID	Status
1	3	333 Third PL	Chicago	IL	NULL	NULL	NULL	NULL	NULL	NULL	NULL

Figure 4.15 A mismatch query where records from the left table find no records from the right table.

Lab 4.3: Unmatched Records Queries

Lab Prep: Before you can begin the lab, you must have SQL Server installed and run the Chapter4.3SetupAll.sql script.

Skill Check 1: David Lonning and a few other employees have been great about finding grants. Some employees have found none at all. Write an unmatched records query to show all employees who have never found a grant. Show the FirstName, LastName and GrantName fields. When you are done, your screen should resemble Figure 4.16.

Answer Code: The SQL code to this lab can be found from the downloadable files named Lab4.3_UnmatchedRecordsQueries.sql.

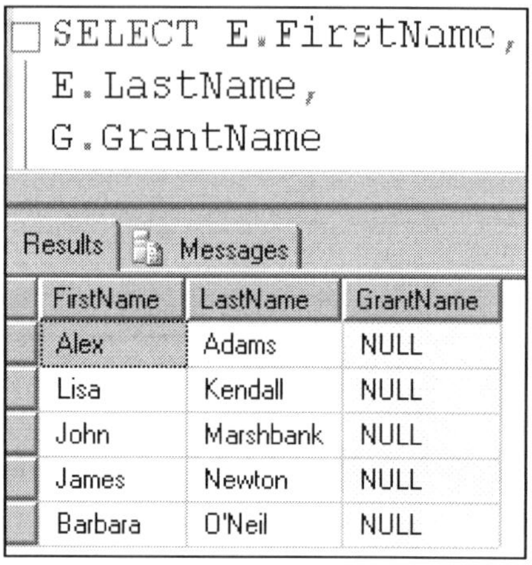

```
SELECT E.FirstName,
  E.LastName,
  G.GrantName
```

Results | Messages

FirstName	LastName	GrantName
Alex	Adams	NULL
Lisa	Kendall	NULL
John	Marshbank	NULL
James	Newton	NULL
Barbara	O'Neil	NULL

Figure 4.16 Skill Check 1 has five records.

Unmatched Records Queries - Points to Ponder

1. Left joins and right joins are useful for finding records when two sets of table records have unmatched values on the joined field.

2. When looking for null values, use the IS NULL operator phrase rather than the comparison operator symbol equal sign = NULL.

3. Using a WHERE clause adds search criteria to your query. WHERE clauses filter the records. The correct SQL syntax for a WHERE clause is: WHERE <column name> search condition. In our unmatched records query example the clause read **WHERE FirstName IS NULL**.

4. If all values in your joined fields match, the unmatched records query result set will return no records.

Chapter Glossary

Alias: An abbreviated name for a database object to save keystrokes while writing queries.

Cartesian result: All combinations of records from all tables. If table A has five records and table B has 10 records, the Cartesian result set would be 50 records.

Cross Join: A type of join that produces a Cartesian result set.

Unmatched records query: A technique used to find the records between tables that don't match.

Review Quiz

1.) You want to change the database context to your JProCo database. Which code accomplishes this?

O a. GOTO JProCo
O b. USE JProCo
O c. GO JProCo
O d. SELECT JProCo

2.) You have two tables. Which type of join would produce the most number of records?

O a. INNER JOIN
O b. LEFT OUTER JOIN
O c. RIGHT OUTER JOIN
O d. FULL OUTER JOIN
O e. CROSS JOIN

3.) What is the correct way to alias the sales table?

O a. FROM Sales AS sl
O b. FROM sl AS Sales sl
O c. SELECT Sales AS sl

4.) Square brackets are required when…

O a. The table name conflicts with a keyword
O b. The table name is the same as another table.
O c. The table uses the same name as the database.
O d. To alias the table.

5.) What happens when you omit the word INNER from an INNER JOIN?

O a.   You get an error message.
O b.   The join becomes and outer join.
O c.   The join operates as an inner join by default.

6.) Which of the following queries returns a true Cartesian result from the Employee and Location tables?

O a.   SELECT P.EmployeeID, T.[Name]
        FROM Employee P
        FULL OUTER JOIN Location T
        WHERE T.TerritoryID = P.TerritoryID

O b.   SELECT P.EmployeeID, T.[Name]
        FROM Employee P
        CROSS JOIN Location T
        WHERE T.TerritoryID = P.TerritoryID

O c.   SELECT P.EmployeeID, T.[Name]
        FROM Employee P
        CROSS JOIN Location T
        WHERE T.TerritoryID != P.TerritoryID

O d.   SELECT P.EmployeeID, T.[Name]
        FROM Employee P
        CROSS JOIN Location T

Answer Key

1.) GOTO tells SQL Server to jump to a labeled piece of code to execute so (a) is incorrect. GO tells SQL Server to finish processing the preceding code before continuing making (c) incorrect too. SELECT is the first word in a query so (d) is incorrect. USE JProCo will change the database context to the JProCo database so (b) is correct.

2.) INNER JOIN will return only those records that have a matching value in a field common to both tables, limited to the number of records in the larger table, so (a) is wrong. LEFT OUTER JOIN will return every record in the left table and include any matches from the other table, limited to the number of records in the left table so (b) is also wrong. RIGHT OUTER JOIN will return every record in the right table and include any matches from the other table, limited to the number of records in the right table so (c) is wrong too. FULL OUTER JOIN will return every row from both tables including the mismatched records, limited to the sum of the records from each table making (d) wrong also. A CROSS JOIN will return every row in one table for each row in the other table creating a Cartesian result; the number of rows returned is the number of rows from the first table multiplied by the number of rows in the other, so (e) is the right one.

3.) 'FROM sl AS Sales sl' will alias the 'sl' tables as 'Sales' then display a syntax error because of the second 'sl' making (b) wrong. 'SELECT Sales AS sl' will alias the 'Sales' field as 'sl' so (c) is also wrong. 'FROM Sales AS sl' will alias the 'Sales' table as 'sl' so (a) is correct.

4.) If 'The table name is the same as another table' we must fully qualify the name to refer to the correct table but square brackets are not needed so (b) is not correct. If 'The table uses the same name as the database' then the table's fully qualified name will be *DBName*.dbo.*DBName* but square brackets are not needed so (c) is also wrong. When 'The table name conflicts with a keyword' we can use square brackets to tell SQL Server we are referring to an object and not the keyword so (a) is the right choice.

5.) Because JOIN is short for INNER JOIN there will be no error message so (a) is not correct. If OUTER is omitted from LEFT OUTER JOIN or RIGHT OUTER JOIN the join will work as an outer join so (b) is also incorrect. The join operates as an inner join by default when the word INNER is omitted so (c) is correct.

6.) The queries in (a), (b) and (c) all use a WHERE clause to filter the results so even if they had used a CROSS JOIN they still won't return every row in one table for each row in the other making all three of those answers wrong. The query in (d) is correct because it uses a CROSS JOIN and doesn't filter any of the results.

Bug Catcher Game

To play the Bug Catcher game run the BugCatcher_Chapter4.pps from the BugCatcher folder of the companion files. You can obtain these files from the www.Joes2Pros.com web site.

Chapter 5. Data Definition Language (DDL)

From our discussion so far, it probably won't surprise you to know that in the database world, data is king because it's all about data. Databases are impressive tools that can be fun to use. Powerful programs like SQL Server exist because of the need for businesses and organizations to reliably store, organize, access and protect their mission-critical data. In this chapter we won't work with data at all. We will learn to build the two basic structures that contain our valuable data: databases and tables.

__READER NOTE:__ Please run the script Chapter5.0SetupAll.sql in order to follow along with the examples in the first section of this chapter. The setup scripts for this book are posted at Joes2Pros.com.

Creating and Dropping Databases

When you create a new database, it contains no data. In fact, it has no tables to hold data until you create them. Data is like cargo – it needs a container to hold it. The container itself is not really data, but a design or definition.

The Fields within a table define what data they will hold. For example, if the EmpID field only accepts integer data, the table will not allow you to use any other data type. For example, you cannot put your name in that field. When you create a new object you are creating a definition for data. Any statement that starts with the keyword CREATE is known as a Data Definition Language statement (DDL). As the name implies, DDL statements are all about defining the structures you build to hold data. The three DDL keywords are CREATE, DROP and ALTER. (ALTER will be covered in Chapter 7.)

A student will often ask me if you can have two databases on your SQL Server named JProCo. If you already have a database named JProCo and try to create it again, you will get an error. SQL Server will not allow you to create two databases with the same name on the same SQL server instance.

You can have the same database name on many different servers. If you had a SQL Server named Reno and another named Tampa they each could have a JProCo database.

There are two main ways to create a database. You can click through SQL's graphical user interface or you can use SQL code. While you should be aware of the click method, it's far more likely in a business setting and even in your own individual study and use of SQL Server that you will write reusable code to create databases. Clicking is visual and easy to teach, but, unlike code, the click process will not give you a readable path to trace your steps. If you make a mistake, you have to start over. If you need to create the same database on 10 different servers, you need to be extremely careful. One incorrect click would make a large difference. As we've mentioned in previous chapters, this is another case where reusable code is your friend.

Creating Databases with Management Studio

We are going to create a database named db1 with Management Studio. Go to the left side of the Management Studio window to the Object Explorer window. Right-click the Databases folder and select "New Database" as in Figure 5.1.

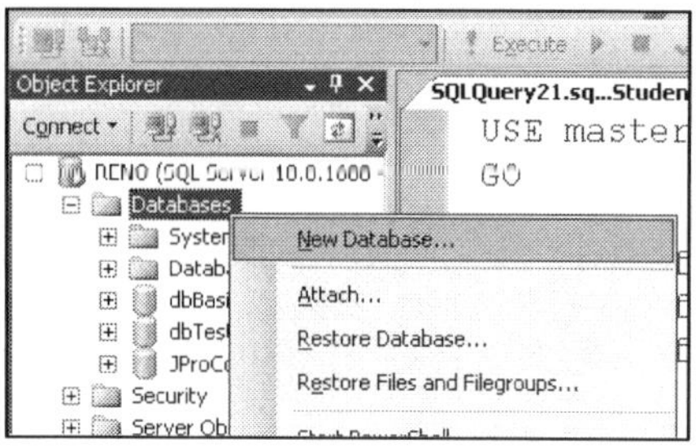

Figure 5.1 Creating a new database from Object Explorer.

The steps from here are pretty simple. Enter the database name and click the OK button. The program executes for a few seconds as your new user database must get registered with the SQL Server that will use it.

Once you're done, you will notice a new yellow cylinder in your Object Explorer with the name of db1. Currently db1 has no tables, but is ready for you to add them at will.

What if you want to get rid of the database? That is called dropping a database. When it comes time to drop the db1 database, it's a simple process. The db1 database is inside the Databases folder of Object Explorer. Simply right-click db1 and select Delete. You confirm with the OK button and the yellow cylinder called db1 disappears from your Object Explorer.

Creating Databases with SQL Code

We know SQL Server keeps track of all its databases. Most of your SQL setup and settings are stored in one location. Some applications like to store settings in a file or registry. Since SQL is a champ at storing data in tables, it has its own private collection of System tables. System tables are storage areas to keep track of what is on the system. When you add a new database like db2, it gets recorded in these special system tables.

Most of the system tables are stored in a System database called Master. In fact, the Object Explorer is talking to the systems databases right now and graphically showing you what it has found. You can talk directly with the Master database. You use the Master database to make major changes on SQL Server or just look around at what has been created or set on your server.

To create a database named db2, you need to first open a new query window to the Master database. You can also add a USE statement to get the master database. Write and execute the following SQL statement you see in Figure 5.2.

You may remember the GO statement from Chapter 2. This separates your code into batches. Each batch finishes entirely before the next batch starts. This means you are in the Master database context before you try to create the db2 database.

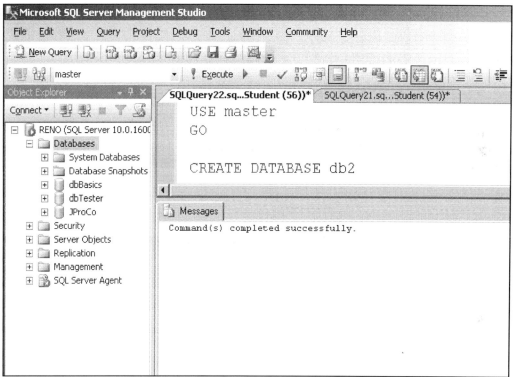

Figure 5.2 SQL Server creates db2 sucessfully, but won't show it in the Object Explorer until you refresh the view.

SQL Server tells us it successfully created db2. The "Command(s) completed successfully" message in Figure 5.3 confirms the new database exists. The Object Explorer just needs to be refreshed. Go to the left side of the Management Studio window to the Object Explorer window. Right-click the Databases folder and select Refresh.

The Object Explorer now shows the db2 database in Figure 5.3. It appears along with your other user databases as a yellow cylinder. This is an easy way to view all the databases on your SQL Server instance.

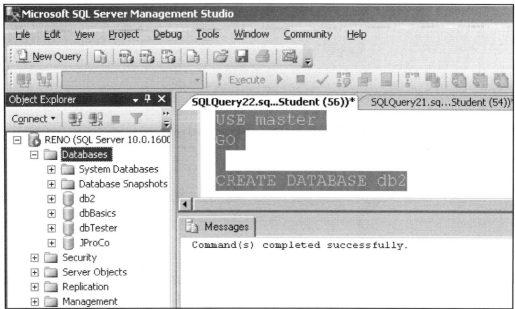

Figure 5.3 The db2 database appears after you refresh the Object Explorer.

Now that we have created a database, let's eliminate or remove it using this SQL statement:

```
USE master
GO


DROP DATABASE db2
GO
```

In your Object Explorer it appears that your db2 database is still present. Once again refresh your screen. Go to the left side of the Management Studio window to the Object Explorer window. Right-click the Databases folder and select Refresh. You will see that SQL Server has dropped or eliminated the database from your system.

SQL uses the keyword DROP to eliminate databases. If you're wondering why DROP is used instead of the keyword DELETE, hang on – you'll find the complete explanation in Chapter 6 on DML statements.

Verifying Which Databases Exist

Databases which you create, change and drop are called *user databases*. They hold all the business data you need on SQL Server. When someone says "database" this tends to be shorthand for User Database.

There are databases that SQL Server itself uses for storing settings and other metadata it needs to operate. These system databases can tell you a lot about what is going on. They are not used to store user-generated information.

Create a new user database named dbMovie and Refresh your screen. After doing this, the system now has five user databases (Figure 5.4).

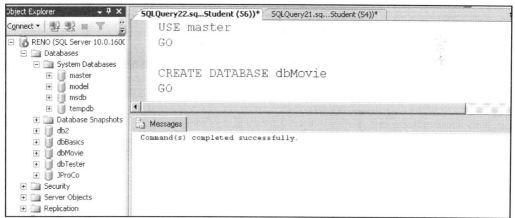

Figure 5.4 This sytem has five user databases and four system databases.

The Object Explorer also shows four system databases for a total of nine. Keep a mental note of this list for the next explanation.

The Object Explorer talks to SQL Server and asks for a list of databases to show the user. You can do the same thing by looking for the data directly. To see how many databases exist on your instance of SQL Server, query the system table directly. Type and run the code below:

```
USE master
GO

SELECT * FROM sys.sysdatabases
```

You get a list of all system and user databases. Notice this list matches the same list you see in the Object explorer.

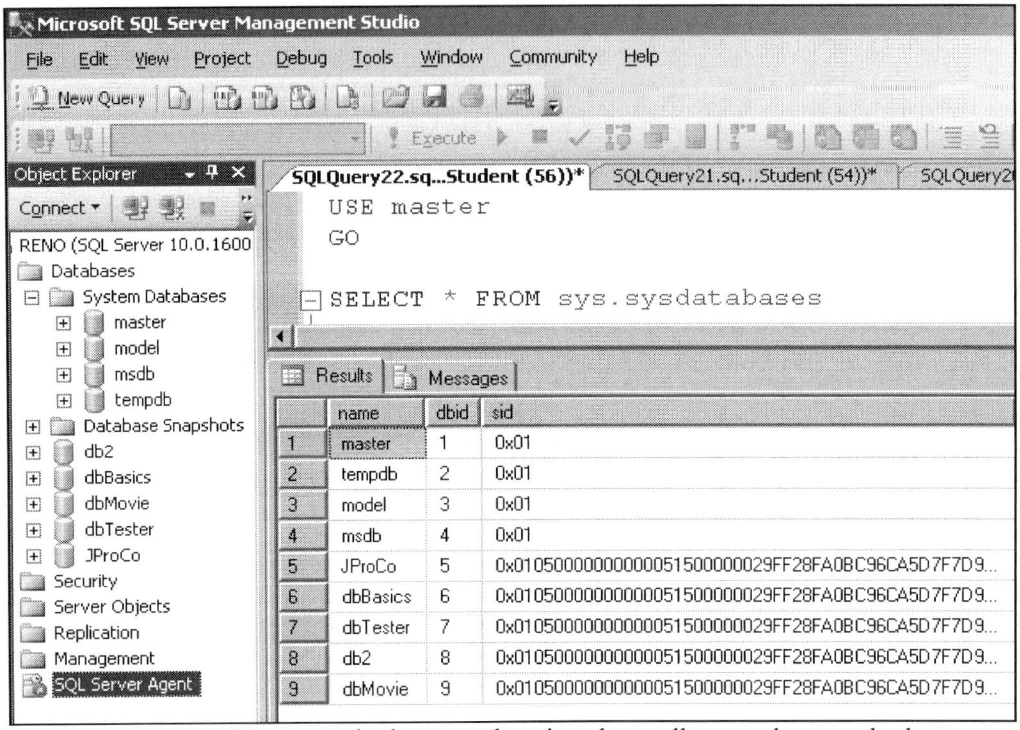

Figure 5.5 A query of the sys.sysdatabases catalog view shows all user and system databases on SQL Server.

Sys.SysDatabases acts like a table, but is actually called a Catalog View. A Catalog is a term that either means database or data storage area. If you wanted to specifically find out whether you have a database named JProCo, you could modify your earlier query as shown below:

```
SELECT *
FROM sys.sysdatabases
WHERE [name] = 'JProCo'
```

If you get one record, then JProCo exists. If you get no records, you don't have a JProCo on your server.

We know you can't create another JProCo database or you would get an error. What if you tried to drop a database that does not exist? There is no dbJoes on our SQL Server. If you try to drop dbJoes and it's not there, you get an error as seen in Figure 5.6.

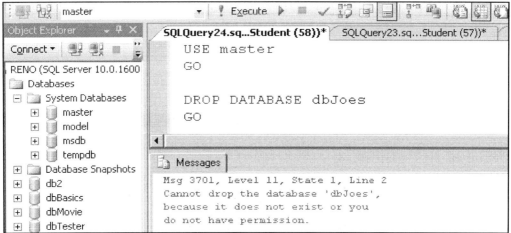

Figure 5.6 You can't drop a database that does not exist.

You can drop a database only if it exists. Trying to affect an object that does not exist will give you an error message.

There is a way to make sure the database is gone: Drop it only if it exists. If it does not exist, there's no need to drop it. The following code will only drop the dbJoes database if it exists:

```
USE master
GO


IF EXISTS(SELECT * FROM sys.sysdatabases
WHERE [name] = 'dbJoes')
DROP DATABASE dbJoes
GO
```

By the time the second GO has been hit, you know there is no dbJoes database on your system. How does it do this? This code first tells SQL Server to use the master database. GO ensures that the "USE master" runs completely before the code to DROP the database starts. IF EXISTS is a conditional statement.

IF EXISTS will evaluate what is inside the parentheses. If it finds any records in the select, then it evaluates to true. If nothing is found, it becomes false. If the dbJoes database exists, the DROP DATABASE statement will drop the dbJoes database. If the IF EXISTS condition is false, then code execution skips the next line and does not run the drop. In this case, there is no dbJoes database to be dropped.

Creating User Databases

You would almost never drop a production database, but when you are building and testing a database to be deployed to production, you are constantly making improvements until you have a finished product. During the development cycle you need to test what happens when you install the database from scratch.

The only way you can install a database is if it's not there already. If you're installing on a brand new system, you simply create the database. If you are installing on a system that already has it, you need to drop and recreate the database. You don't want two different code sets. The following code will work on both systems:

```
USE master
GO


IF EXISTS(SELECT * FROM sys.sysdatabases
WHERE [name] = 'dbMovie')
DROP database dbMovie
GO


CREATE database dbMovie
GO
```

The second batch contains a DROP statement. That second batch will only run if the database exists. Once done, it creates the database. If the database does not exist, only the third batch runs. The end result is the creation of a new database.

Lab 5.1: Creating Databases

Lab Prep: Before you can begin the lab you must have SQL Server installed and run the Chapter5.1SetupAll.sql script.

Skill Check 1: Create a script using four separate batches. Remember batches are separated with the word GO. The first batch will use the master database. The second batch will drop the dbSkillCheck database only if it exists. The third batch will create the dbSkillCheck database. The final batch will set the database context to dbSkillCheck. When you are done, your screen should resemble Figure 5.7.

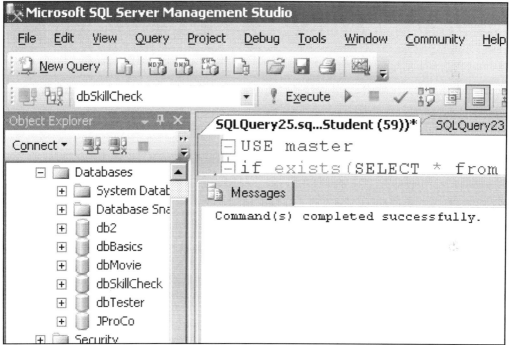

Figure 5.7 dbSkillCheck should be created and the database context set to it.

Answer Code: The SQL code to this lab can be found from the downloadable files named Lab5.1_CreatingDatabases.sql.

Creating Databases - Points to Ponder

1. CREATE is used to make new objects in SQL Server, including a whole database. The CREATE clause is part of a DDL statement.

2. DROP removes objects in SQL Server, including entire databases. The DROP clause is part of a Data Definition Language (DDL) statement.

3. System tables include information that SQL Server uses to define and maintain the database. The traditional abbreviation for database is DB or db.

4. Newer system table names begin with "sys" followed by a dot and then the table name.

5. Sys.SysDatabases, sysdatabases and Sys.Databases let you view information about the databases on your SQL Server. Sys.SysDatabases is the newest version for SQL Server. The others are used to facilitate "backward compatibility" with older SQL code you may encounter.

6. Sys.SysDatabases is a catalog view and the SQL Server recommended way to view metadata. Metadata are information about how your SQL Server is set up. Metadata are contained in the columns or fields of the Sys.SysDatabases table.

7. You cannot drop a database that is already gone. You cannot create a duplicate database if one already exists.

8. An "IF EXISTS" statement will only run the next command if it evaluates as true. If it is false, SQL Server skips the next statement.

9. A batch is a set of SQL statements that are executed in their entirety before continuing on to further commands.

10. Batches are separated by the word GO.

Creating Tables

You have a new dbMovie database. Since it doesn't yet have tables, let's create some and put this database to use.

To build a new table you will use the CREATE keyword. CREATE is a DDL statement. Open your dbMovie database from the last lab with a USE statement as seen in Figure 5.8.

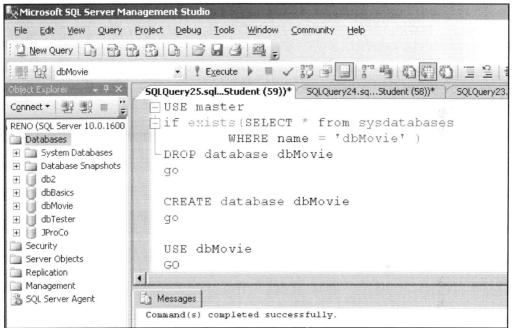

Figure 5.8 The USE statement changes the database context to the dbMovie database.

Remember that whatever your database context is, that is where the next command will attempt to run. If you create a table while in JProCo, that is the new table's home. If you do this in the dbMovie context, the new table will reside in dbMovie. Use the code you see here:

```
CREATE TABLE tblMovie
(    m_id INT primary key,
     m_Title varchar(30) not null,
     m_Runtime int null
)
GO
```

This SQL code will create the tblMovie table. The field names and data types are in the parentheses. The m_id is the primary key for the table which means you can't have two movies with the same ID. (Note: Primary key details are outside of the scope of this book and will be covered in Book#2.) The second field definition shows that the m_Title cannot contain null values. The m_Runtime field will accept integer (Int) data and can be null. You can create a movie name and enter the runtime at a later date when it is known.

SQL Server creates the table definition with the CREATE statement. Query the table with a SELECT clause looking at all records. Since this table is brand new, it has no records. The unpopulated table is seen in Figure 5.9 with the three fields you created.

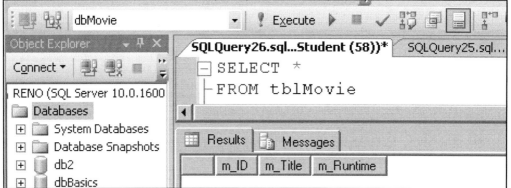

Figure 5.9 This query shows the tblMovie, but is not yet populated with records.

No matter how much data you add, tblMovie will still have just three fields unless you change the table definition later.

We currently have no data in this table. As promised, this chapter is all about the definition of objects and the next chapter will show you many ways to insert, update and delete data from a table.

Lab 5.2: Creating Tables

Lab Prep: Before you can begin the lab you must have SQL installed and run the Chapter5.2SetupAll.sql script.

Skill Check 1: Write a script to create the tblMovie table in the dbMovie database in five batches. Remember batches are separated with the word GO. The first batch will use the master database. The second batch will drop the dbMovie database only if it exists. The third batch will create the dbMovie database. The fourth batch will set the database context to dbMovie. The fifth batch will create the tblMovie table. It should not matter if your system already has the dbMovie database since your batches take care of dropping and creating this database. When you are done, your Object Explorer screen should resemble Figure 5.10.

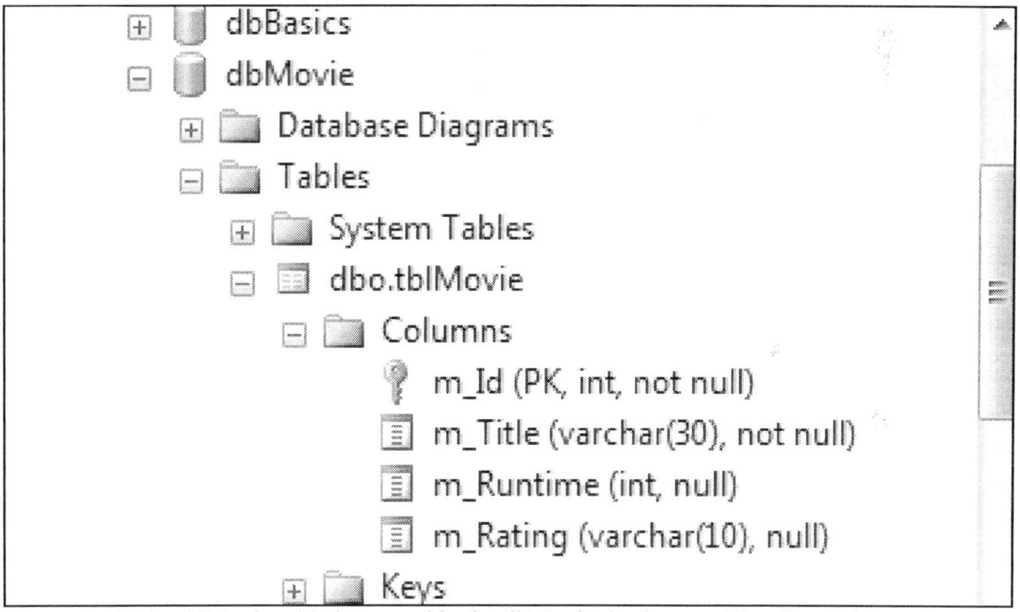

Figure 5.10 The tblMovie table is created in the dbMovie database and has four fields.

Note: Your tblMovie table will now have four fields with the following definitions:

- m_id   int   primary key
- m_Title   varchar(30)   not null
- m_Runtime   int   null
- m_Rating   varchar(10)   null

Skill Check 2: Write a script to create the tblCar table in the dbCar database in five batches. The first batch will use the master database. The second batch will drop the dbCar database only if it exists. The third batch will create the dbCar database. The fourth batch will set the database context to dbCar. The fifth batch will create the tblCar table. When you are done, your Object Explorer screen should resemble Figure 5.11.

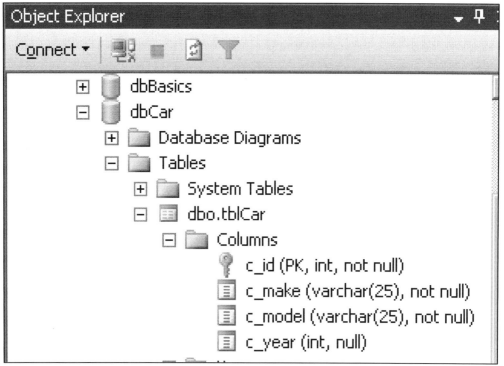

Figure 5.11 The tblCar table is created in the dbCar database and has four fields.

Note: Your tblCar table will now have four fields with the following definitions:

- c_id   int   primary key
- c_make   varchar(25)   not null
- c_model   varchar(25)   not null
- c_year   int   null

Answer Code: The SQL code to this lab can be found from the downloadable files named Lab5.2_CreatingTables.sql.

Creating Tables - Points to Ponder

1. The CREATE TABLE statement is the SQL way of adding a table object to a database.

2. A CREATE TABLE statement is a DDL statement.

3. At the time that you create a table, you should specify the fields you want.

4. When specifying fields you have to specify the field's data type, such as integer, decimal or character.

5. Column names for a table must be unique. You can't have two fields named Hiredate in the same table.

6. You may use the same column name in different tables. The LocationID field may exist in both the Employee and Location table.

7. When a field is defined as "NOT NULL" this means the field value can never be empty. Each time a new row is added, you must enter a value in that field.

8. A table is a collection of fields that can hold data. Each table is contained within a database.

9. A newly created database contains no tables, but you can create as many tables as your company needs.

10. The CREATE TABLE statement is the SQL statement for making a table. A table is one kind of a database object.

11. Once you create a table, you populate it by adding records.

12. A CREATE TABLE statement is a DDL statement. DDL means Data Definition Language. CREATE and DROP are DDL keywords.

Chapter Glossary

Catalog: A database or data storage area.

Catalog View: System information combined by SQL Server into a table-like view which can be queried with a SELECT statement.

Create: A DDL statement that creates an object or database.

DDL Statement: A statement that creates, alters or drops databases or database objects.

Drop: A DDL statement that eliminates an object or database.
Primary Key: Attribute of a field that ensures no 2 records have identical values.
System Table: A table created by SQL Server to track design and settings used by SQL Server.

Review Quiz

1.) You want to see whether your dbMovies database exists. Which SQL code will achieve this?

O a.   IF (select * from sysdatabases WHERE [name] = 'dbMovies')
O b.   WHEN exists (select * from sysdatabases WHERE [name] = 'dbMovies')
O c.   IF EXISTS (select * from sysdatabases WHERE [name] = 'dbMovies')
O d.   WHEN exists(select * from sysdatabases WHERE[name] = 'dbMovies ')

2.) What occurs if you try to DROP a database that is not present on SQL Server?

O a.   You get an error message.
O b.   It indicates you ran, but really did nothing.
O c.   It drops the closest matching name.

3.) What is the purpose of the GO keyword?

O a.   To speed up processing.
O b.   To work with an IF statement when it evaluates to true.
O c.   To run code in separate batches.

4.) Which SQL keyword goes first when you want to make a new database?

O a.   NEW
O b.   CREATE
O c.   UPDATE
O d.   INSERT

5.) At the time of table creation, you should add the fields you want because...

O a.   You cannot add them later.
O b.   It's considered a good practice.

6.) Can you create a table with zero fields?

O a.   Yes – you can create a table with any number of fields including 0.
O b.   No – You need at least one field to create a table.

Answer Key

1.) IF requires a Boolean expression and the select statement within the parenthesis of answer (a) does not return a True or False value so you will get an error message. The code in (b) and (d) will return an error message for incorrect syntax near the keyword WHEN. IF EXISTS (select * from sysdatabases WHERE [name] = 'dbMovies') will return a true value if the dbMovies database is present in the system tables so (c) is correct.

2.) Because you get an error message when you attempt to DROP a database that is not present on SQL Server both (b) and (c) are incorrect. If you attempt to DROP a database that is not present on SQL Server you will get an error message so (a) is the correct choice.

3.) The GO keyword has nothing to do with speeding up processing so (a) is incorrect. IF statements will determine whether the next piece of code is executed or not so (b) is also wrong. The GO keyword tells SQL Server to finish executing the preceding code before continuing making (c) the correct answer.

4.) NEW is not a SQL Keyword so (a) is not the right answer. UPDATE and INSERT both modify records in a table so (c) and (d) are not correct either. CREATE is the first word in a statement when you want to make a new database so (b) is the right answer.

5.) You can add fields later that you did not think of at the time of table creation so (a) is incorrect. It is considered a good practice to add all the fields you want at the time of table creation making (b) the correct answer.

6.) When creating a table you must specify at least one field so (a) is not correct. Since you need at least one field specified at the time of table creation (b) is the correct answer.

Bug Catcher Game

To play the Bug Catcher game run the BugCatcher_Chapter5.pps from the BugCatcher folder of the companion files. You can obtain these files from the www.Joes2Pros.com web site.

Chapter 6. Data Manipulation Language (DML) Scripting

Databases contain tables, and tables contain the actual data. Queries turn data into information, which is what businesses need to see and use for decision-making. Manipulating data involves changing, deleting and viewing your data. So far, all our Data Manipulation Language (DML) examples in the first five chapters use the SELECT keyword. In this chapter we learn the other DML statements. Besides selecting data, DML statements allow us to INSERT, UPDATE and DELETE data from tables.

READER NOTE: *Please run the script Chapter6.0SetupAll.sql in order to follow along with the examples in the first section of this chapter. The setup scripts for this book are posted at Joes2Pros.com.*

Inserting Data

Tables were created for the purpose of holding data. Every table begins its life as an unpopulated table. The only way to populate a table is by inserting data. SQL coding that starts with the INSERT keyword are DML statements that add new records to tables.

Currently, the dbMovie database has only one table: tblMovie. Assuming you finished lab 5.2 then the tblMovie table is unpopulated, meaning it has no records. How much data you need to add depends on how many fields the table has. If the table has three fields you would likely need to add three pieces of information. A quick look at the tblMovie table shows we have four fields as in Figure 6.1.

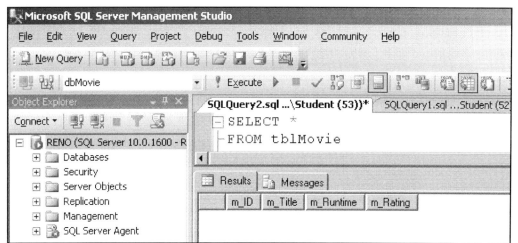

Figure 6.1 The tlbMovie table has no records in its four fields.

To fill the first record we need to supply four values. In an insert statement you separate each entity value with a comma. To add movie 1 called "AList Explorers," which is a PG-13 movie 96 minutes long, you use the following code:

```
INSERT INTO tblMovie
VALUES (1,'AList Explorers',96,'PG-13')
```

If you want to insert two records at the same time, you always have the option to run multiple INSERT INTO statements. We can insert movie 2 and movie 3 at the same time as in Figure 6.2.

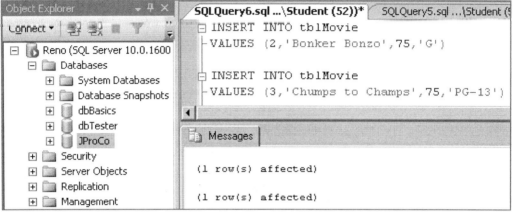

Figure 6.2 Two INSERT INTO statements each inserted a record.

There was no need to run these INSERT INTO statements in separate batches with a GO statement. DML statements like INSERT INTO use Transaction Control Language (TCL) instead of batches. More about TCL will be discussed in Chapter 10.

Each statement ran its records once, resulting in two additional records in the tblMovie table. The old familiar DML statement that starts with the keyword SELECT will show the result set containing the records you inserted. A quick look at all records for the tblMovie table can confirm how many records you have as seen in Figure 6.3.

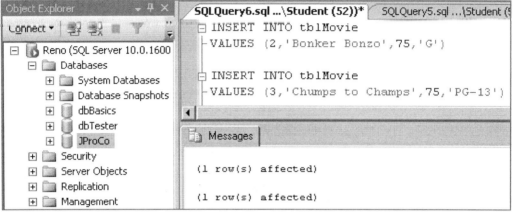

Figure 6.3 All three insert statements give you three new records.

Row Constructors

New features are invented so we may discover and use them. Since many of my students work or contract at Microsoft, homework is often done on beta software. One student was tasked to do a double insert like the one in Figure 6.2. She did a great innovative job and humbly I had to change her grade from zero to a perfect 100.

That day the student taught me a new feature for SQL Server 2008 called *row constructors*. You can do a double insert of data with one INSERT INTO statement using row constructors. Simply separate each group of values with a comma. The row constructor looks exactly like the double INSERT INTO except that you replace the INSERT with a comma (Figure 6.4).

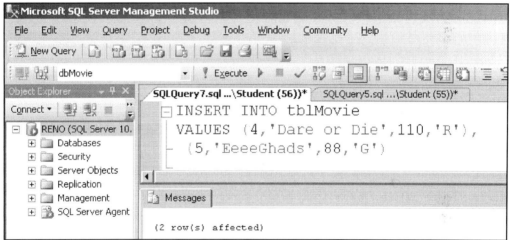

Figure 6.4 Two inserts are done with a comma separating each value. Row constructors are a brand new SQL Server 2008 feature.

The two records m_id 4 and 5 were successfully inserted into tblMovie and appear just the same as m_id 2 and 3. As you can see in Figure 6.4, they were done all at once using the new SQL 2008 feature called row constructors. The first advantage of using row constructors is obvious. You save time by not having to type an additional INSERT INTO statement. The second advantage is that SQL Server uses only one lock instead of two when using the row constructors feature. SQL Server confirms a single transaction of two rows as seen in the "2 row(s) affected" message in the Figure 6.4. SQL Server confirms two transactions with one row each as seen in Figure 6.2. Each transaction gobbles up a bit of time by issuing a lock. You will learn why this is important later in Chapter 10.

Lab 6.1: Inserting Data

Lab Prep: Before you can begin the lab you must have SQL Server installed and run the Chapter6.1SetupAll.sql script.

Skill Check 1: Create a table named Customer in the JProCo database. The table should contain the five fields you see below:

- CustomerID int primary key
- CustomerType varchar(30) not null
- Firstname varchar(20) null
- LastName varchar(30) null
- CompanyName varchar(30) null

Once the table is created, write five insert statements to add the customers you see listed in Figure 6.5.

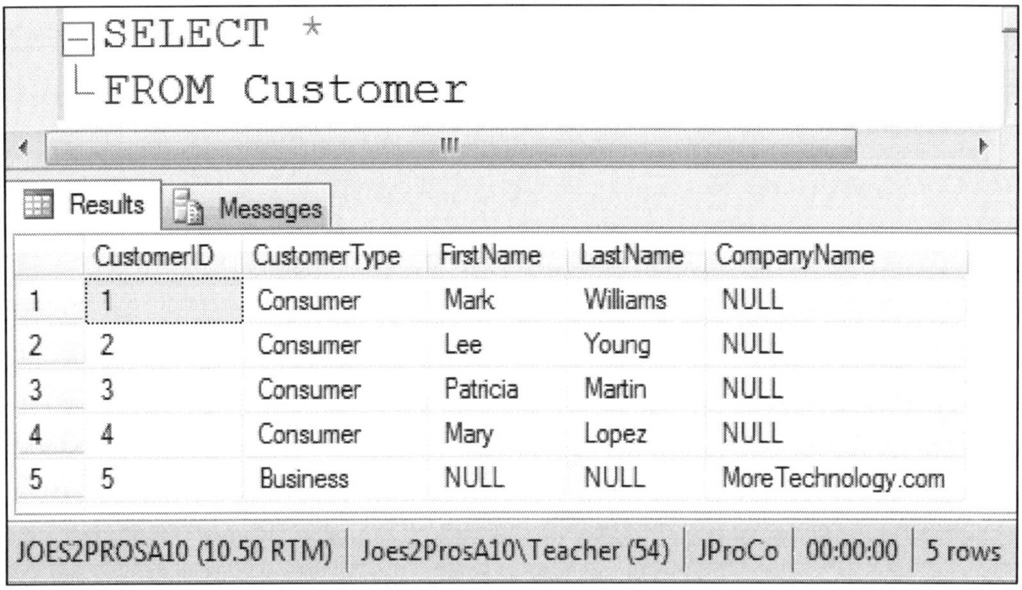

```
SELECT *
FROM Customer
```

	CustomerID	CustomerType	FirstName	LastName	CompanyName
1	1	Consumer	Mark	Williams	NULL
2	2	Consumer	Lee	Young	NULL
3	3	Consumer	Patricia	Martin	NULL
4	4	Consumer	Mary	Lopez	NULL
5	5	Business	NULL	NULL	MoreTechnology.com

Figure 6.5 The Customer table of JProCo is created and populated.

Lab Self Checker 1: Skill Check 1 has a self-checker to see if all DML and DDL statements ran correctly. Open a query window and type the following code:

EXEC dbTester.dbo.Lab61SelfChecker

This will show you all the items in the lab you did correctly. A perfect score is 1,000 points.

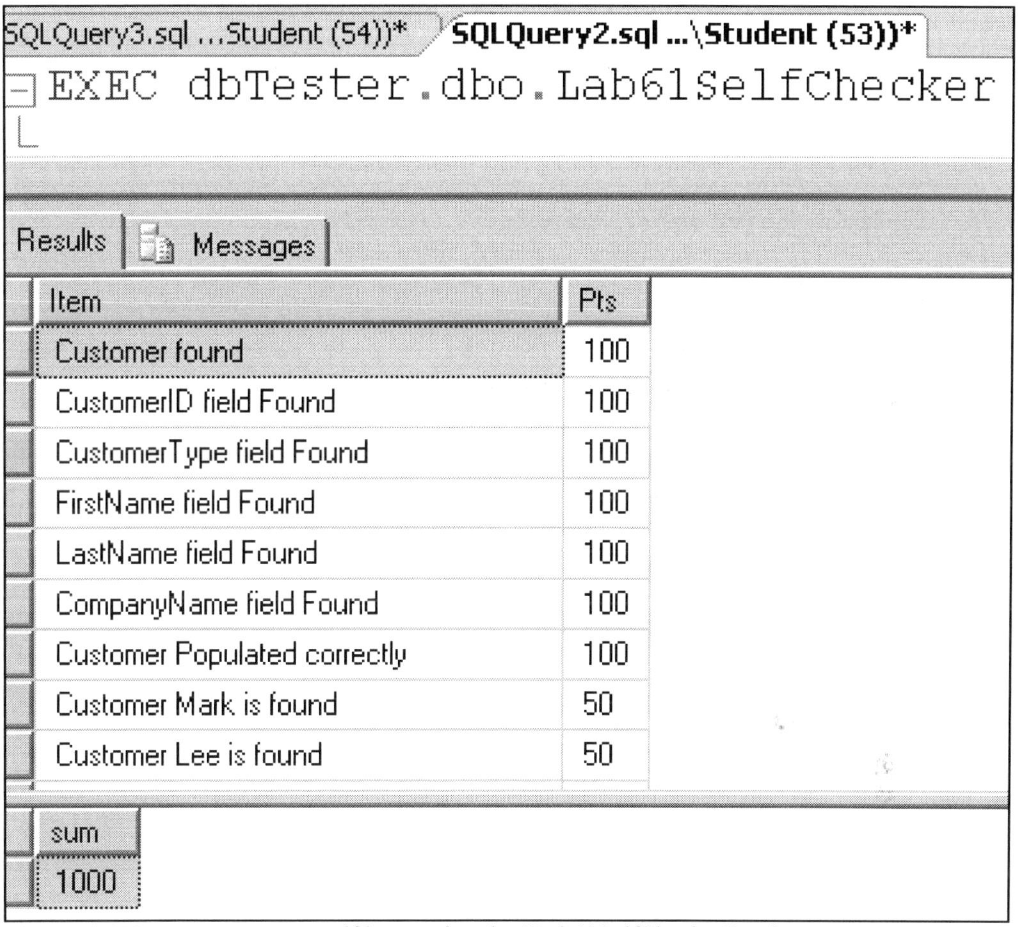

```
SQLQuery3.sql ...Student (54))*   SQLQuery2.sql ...\Student (53))*
EXEC dbTester.dbo.Lab61SelfChecker
```

Item	Pts
Customer found	100
CustomerID field Found	100
CustomerType field Found	100
FirstName field Found	100
LastName field Found	100
CompanyName field Found	100
Customer Populated correctly	100
Customer Mark is found	50
Customer Lee is found	50

sum
1000

Figure 6.6 You can score yourself by running the "Lab61SelfChecker" script.

Answer Code: The SQL code to this lab can be found from the downloadable files named Lab6.1_InsertingData.sql.

Inserting Data - Points to Ponder

1. You can add records to a table by using an INSERT statement.

2. An INSERT statement is a DML statement.

3. Before SQL 2008 you could only insert 1 record with one insert statement.

New to SQL 2008 is a feature called Row Constructors where you can insert many records at once with one insert statement.

Updating Data

Whenever you move, you normally notify your bank or credit card providers of your new address. Somewhere among their databases are tables that hold customer names and addresses. What if the address fields need to be updated? Changes over time mean Relational Database Management Systems (RDBMS) like SQL Server need the power to update existing data.

Think of an update as a statement that changes – or *manipulates* – existing data without adding any new records. Often, updates are needed so changes in your data, such as a new address, can be reflected. Sometimes changes happen because you found an error that must be corrected. In either case, the language of SQL offers you the *UPDATE* keyword. Any statement starting with the keyword UPDATE is a DML statement.

Before we make updates, it's a good idea to examine the existing data in Figure 6.7. In this example, we have five records showing five different movie names.

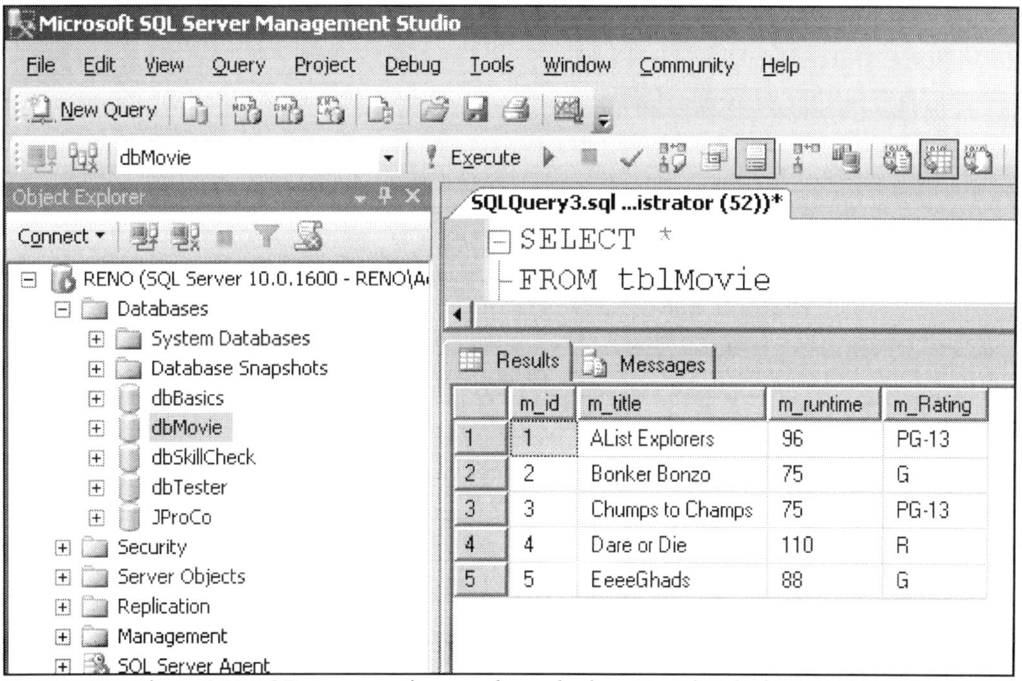

Figure 6.7 Using a SELECT statement is a good way look at your data before making changes.

Single Table Updates

Your tblMovie table needs the "AList Explorers" movie title revised to have a hyphen in it so it appears as "A-List Explorers." You can make this modification without adding any new records by using an update statement.

Update statements offer lots of power because you can update one or more records with one statement. A common attempt to fix this might result in the code you see below:

```
UPDATE tblMovie
SET m_Title = 'A-List Explorers'
```

This may have worked a little too well. As Figure 6.8 reveals, field m_Title is now set to "A-List Explorers." However, there is a big problem when you don't specify which record you want updated. Now all movies have their titles set to "A-List Explorers."

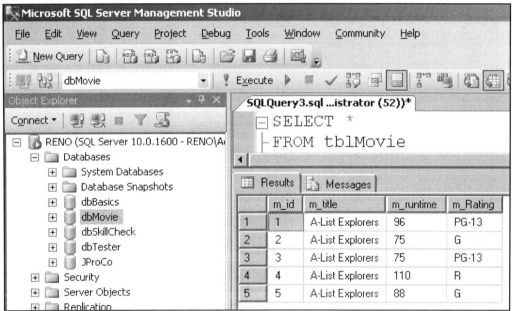

Figure 6.8 An update statement without specific criteria changes all records.

If you do this you may have a problem. With your data gone, the only way to get it back is from a backup or script. Since our database has only one table, we can easily recreate it. The following code should get you back to the point just before you made your update statement:

```
USE master
GO

IF exists(SELECT * FROM Sys.SysDatabases WHERE
[name] = 'dbMovie' )
DROP database dbMovie
go

CREATE database dbMovie
go

USE dbMovie
GO

CREATE TABLE tblMovie
(
m_id int primary key,
m_Title varchar(30) not null,
m_Runtime int null,
m_Rating varchar(10)
)

INSERT INTO tblMovie
VALUES (1,'A-List Explorers',96,'PG-13')

INSERT INTO tblMovie
VALUES (2,'Bonker Bonzo',75,'G')

INSERT INTO tblMovie
VALUES (3,'Chumps to Champs',75,'PG-13')

INSERT INTO tblMovie
VALUES (4,'Dare or Die',110,'R')

INSERT INTO tblMovie
VALUES (5,'EeeeGhads',88,'G')
```

Note: The previous code works just fine if you have permissions to drop the
dbMovie database and nobody else is using that database. If you have multiple
query windows open and any one of them has the database context set to
dbMovie, the DROP DATABASE statement will fail.

Now it's time to do just what we intended. The record with m_id set to 1 should
have its m_Title set to the hyphenated "A-List Explorers" name.

```
UPDATE tblMovie
SET m_Title = 'A-List Explorers'
WHERE m_id = 1
```

The criteria you use in an update statement utilize the same syntax and rules you
already learned in the queries. DML statements have a standard way of using
criteria.

We can now take a look at our handiwork. In looking at all records of your
tblMovie table you can see five different records. You also see from Figure 6.9
that a change was only made to the first movie.

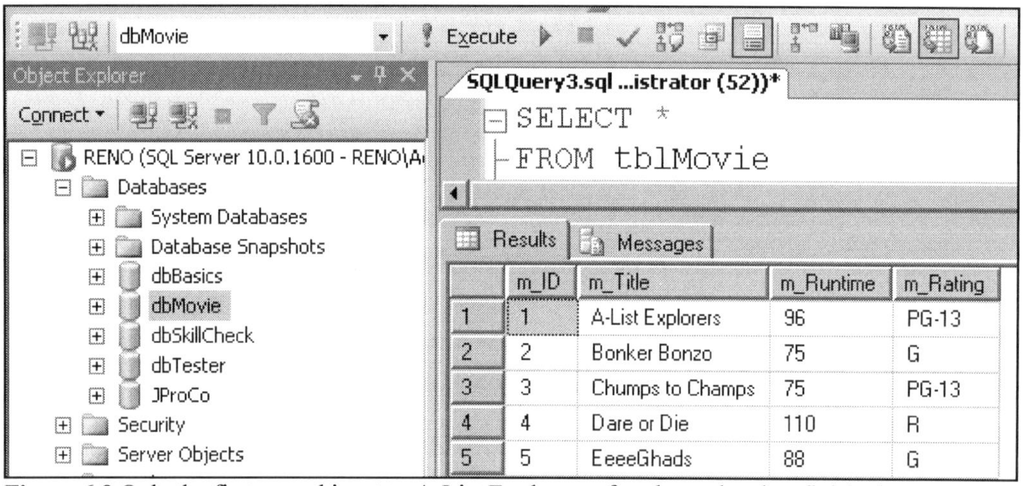

Figure 6.9 Only the first record is set to A-List Explorers after the update has finished.

Setting all records to the same value is very rare. Therefore, using an update
statement with criteria using the WHERE clause is an essential database
development skill. Doing this correctly ensures you change only the records that
need to be updated.

Multiple Table Updates

Updating only the necessary records with filtering criteria is vital to ensure you change the right records. The WHERE clause always takes care of this. Your criteria can query on any available field. Let's change the database context back to JProCo and look again at the data we are about to update in Figure 6.10.

Employee Table

```
QLQuery13.sq...Student (55))*
SELECT * FROM Employee
```

Results | Messages

EmpID	lastname	firstname	hiredate	LocationID	ManagerID	Status
1	Adams	Alex	2001-01-...	1	11	NULL
2	Brown	Barry	2002-08-...	1	11	NULL
3	Osako	Lee	1999-09-...	2	11	NULL
4	Kennson	David	1996-03-...	1	11	Has Tenure
5	Bender	Eric	2007-05-...	1	11	NULL
6	Kendall	Lisa	2001-11-...	4	4	NULL
7	Lonning	David	2000-01-...	1	11	On Leave
8	Marshbank	John	2001-11-...	NULL	4	NULL
9	Newton	James	2003-09-...	2	3	NULL
10	O'Haire	Terry	2004-10-...	2	3	NULL
11	Smith	Sally	1989-04-...	1	NULL	NULL
12	O'Neil	Barbara	1995-05-...	4	4	Has Tenure

PayRates Table

```
QLQuery13.sq...Student (55))*
SELECT * FROM PayRates
```

Results | Messages

EmpID	YearlySalary	MonthlySalary	HourlyRate
1	75000.00	NULL	NULL
2	78000.00	NULL	NULL
3	NULL	NULL	45.00
4	NULL	6500.00	NULL
5	NULL	5800.00	NULL
6	5200.00	NULL	NULL
7	NULL	6100.00	NULL
8	NULL	NULL	32.00
9	NULL	NULL	18.00
10	NULL	NULL	17.00
11	115000.00	NULL	NULL
12	NULL	NULL	21.00

Figure 6.10 The PayRates table (right) shows five hourly Employees. We learn the names of those hourly employees by examining the EmpID field in the Employee table (left).

Sally Smith is a member of management at JProCo. Sally has the EmpID of 11. There are six employees that report directly to Sally. Another way to say this is six employee records have ManagerID of 11. To find all Employees who report to Sally, we can filter on just her ManagerID. The following query shows six records in the query result set:

```
SELECT *
FROM Employee
WHERE ManagerID = 11
```

Sally has decided that all of her yearly salaried employees will get a raise of $1,000 per year. How many of the employees reporting to Sally are on a yearly salary and how many are hourly? You may see the challenge here goes a bit beyond the last update example. We need to update a field in the PayRates table based on criteria (ManagerID) in the Employee table. To do this update, we can use an inner join queries from both tables.

In Figure 6.11 we see all the detailed information about the employees and their income information. Only the employees working for Sally appear in the result set. Two of Sally's six employees are paid yearly. To look at just those two employees, we need to find all records that have data for YearlySalary.

```
SELECT *
FROM Employee as E INNER JOIN PayRates AS PR
ON E.EmpID = PR.EmpID
WHERE ManagerID = 11
```

	EmpID	lastname	firstname	hiredate	LocationID	ManagerID	Status	EmpID	YearlySalary	MonthlySalary	HourlyRate
1	1	Adams	Alex	2001-01-01 ...	1	11	NULL	1	75000.00	NULL	NULL
2	2	Brown	Barry	2002-08-12 ...	1	11	NULL	2	78000.00	NULL	NULL
3	3	Osako	Lee	1999-09-01 ...	2	11	NULL	3	NULL	NULL	45.00
4	4	Kennson	David	1996-03-16 ...	1	11	Has Tenure	4	NULL	6500.00	NULL
5	5	Bender	Eric	2007-05-17 ...	1	11	NULL	5	NULL	5800.00	NULL
6	7	Lonning	David	2000-01-01 ...	1	11	On Leave	7	NULL	6100.00	NULL

Figure 6.11 Joining the Employee and PayRates tables for Manager 11 shows the pay for all of Sally's workers.

A slight change to the code in Figure 6.11 will give you the records you need. A query with a join and an update statement with a join are very similar. The good news is your work is almost done. Just change the first line of your SELECT. Your first line will be an update as you see in the code below:

```
UPDATE PR SET YearlySalary = YearlySalary +
1000
FROM Employee as E INNER JOIN PayRates AS PR
ON E.EmpID = PR.EmpID
WHERE ManagerID = 11
AND YearlySalary IS NOT NULL
```

This update statement takes the existing value of the YearlySalary and adds $1,000 dollars to that amount. If you were making 75,000 before you ran this update, you would now have a value of 76,000. Using the query from the prior

134

example, we can now see Alcx Adams and Barry Brown each have salaries $1000 higher than before. Figure 6.12 reflects this annual increase.

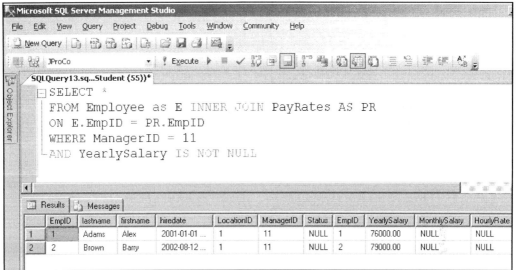

Figure 6.12 The two employees with YearlySalary values $1000 higher than in Figure 6.11.

You use a multi-table update statement anytime your SET value is in a different table than some of your criteria. Using the join syntax you learned from Chapter 3 allows you to run an update statement based on multiple tables.

Lab 6.2: Updating Data

Lab Prep: Before you can begin the lab, you must have SQL Server installed and run the Chapter6.2SetupAll.sql script. The updates in this lab are for practice and future chapters will use the original data.

Skill Check 1: One of the movies in your tblMovie table was named incorrectly. M_ID 4 should be titled "Dare the World to Try." Write an update statement that makes the change you see in Figure 6.13.

```
SELECT * FROM tblMovie
```

Results	Messages		
m_id	m_title	m_runtime	m_Rating
1	A-List Explorers	96	PG-13
2	Bonker Bonzo	75	G
3	Chumps to Champs	75	P-13
4	Dare the World to Try	110	R
5	EeeeGhads	88	G

Figure 6.13 m_id 4 has a new m_Title value.

Skill Check 2: JProCo employee 11 (Sally Smith) is getting married and wants her last name changed to Green.

Skill Check 3: All JProCo employees from LocationID 4 (Spokane) are contractors. Change the value of the status field to "External" for all employee records of LocationID 4.

Skill Check 4: In the dbMovie database the tblMovie table needs a correction. The movie "EeeeGhads" should be hyphenated to "Eeee-Ghads" for m_id 5.

Skill Check 5: In the JProCo database, you need to correct a typo in the Location table for Seattle. There is no First Street in Seattle. In the Street field of the Location table, change street address from "111 First ST" to "111 1st Ave" for LocationID 1.

Skill Check 6: The Boston location manager of JProCo has called you to request an update to correct some discovered errors. Boston has a standard form for all grants written to be in the amount of $20,000. In looking at all grants written by employees from LocationID 2 you see two grants have an incorrectly entered amount.

SQLQuery6.sql ...Student (52))*	SQLQuery2.sql ...Student (53))*

```
SELECT E.FirstName, E.LastName, E.LocationID,
G.GrantName, G.Amount
FROM [Grant] G INNER JOIN Employee E
ON G.EmpID = E.EmpID
WHERE LocationID = 2
```

Results | Messages

	FirstName	LastName	LocationID	GrantName	Amount
1	Lee	Osako	2	TALTA_Kishan International	18100.00
2	Terry	O'Haire	2	Ben@MoreTechnology.com	41000.00

Figure 6.14 There are two employees from Boston with grants.

Your challenge is to correctly UPDATE all Boston employees by making sure any grants found by them are set to $20,000. When you are done, your update should produce the result set you see in Figure 6.15.

```
SELECT E.FirstName, E.LastName, E.LocationID,
G.GrantName, G.Amount
FROM [Grant] G INNER JOIN Employee E
ON G.EmpID = E.EmpID
WHERE LocationID = 2
```

Results | Messages

FirstName	LastName	LocationID	GrantName	Amount
Lee	Osako	2	TALTA_Kishan International	20000.00
Terry	O'Haire	2	Ben@MoreTechnology.com	20000.00

Figure 6.15 All Boston employees now have grant amount values of $20,000.

Answer Code: The SQL code to this lab can be found from the downloadable files named Lab6.2_UpdatingData.sql.

Updating Data - Points to Ponder

1. The UPDATE statement modifies existing data for columns in tables.

2. Statements starting with the word UPDATE are Data Manipulation Language (DML) statements.

3. Most queries pull data from multiple tables that relate to each other. You can join many tables in one query. Prior to SQL Server 2008, the limit was 256 tables in one query. The number of tables you can now join is limited only by available resources.

4. DML statements begin with the keywords SELECT, INSERT, UPDATE and DELETE.

5. During an update, the SET keyword assigns values to records in the selected columns. Remember to use the WHERE clause to limit the SET value changes to just the record you wish to target for an UPDATE.

6. You will almost always use the WHERE clause with the SET clause to limit the number of rows updated. Rarely will you update an entire table with the same value.

7. The SET command in the UPDATE statement assigns a new value to fields in the selected table rows.

Deleting Data

Knowing how to delete data is an essential skill you want to do carefully and correctly. With a little practice you can make sure you delete the records you want without deleting too many. We will practice our deletes on the dbMovie database. That way no harm comes to JProCo and you can experience deleting data without fear on a small sample database.

The tblMovie table is just the way you need it. However, the data in there is pretend data you used for testing before signing off for official company use. When you decide you need to delete all records, but the table must remain intact, you are depopulating the table. A DELETE statement with no criteria like the code below achieves this result.

```
DELETE tblMovie
```

Executing the code shows exactly how many records you have deleted. Any time you run a DML statement, the confirmation shows as "row(s) affected" (Figure 6.16).

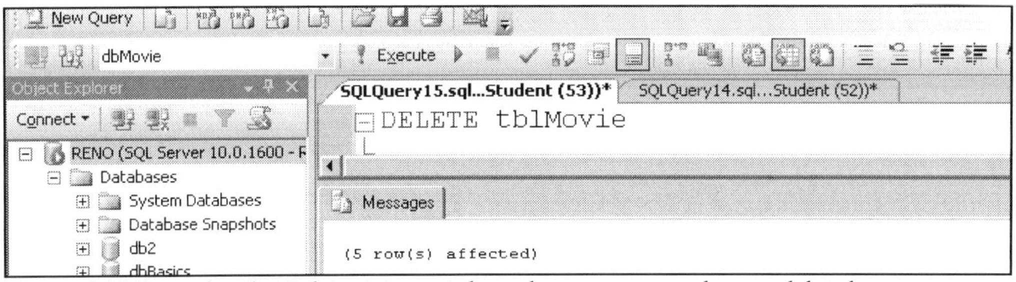

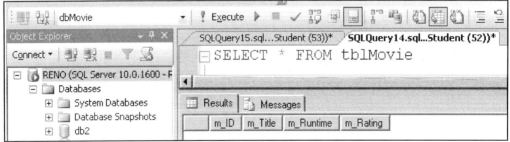

Figure 6.16 Executing the Delete statement shows how many records were deleted.

After you run this code check your records by querying tblMovie. This result set returns no records (Figure 6.17).

Figure 6.17 All records have been deleted from this table (tblMovie).

This is common when you are working with test data and actual table design. OK, let's Geek it up a notch. You may be working on prototype databases soon to be used by your company. Just to test them you might fill these databases with pretend DML data. This is known as your testing environment. You could say the DDL code is identical to production DDL code and the DML code is for testing the data flow.

Delete gets rid of all records that fit your criteria. If you have no criteria, all records of that table disappear. If you want to delete just some records, you can use a WHERE clause in the same way as all other DML statements. For example, let me put all the movie data back with the following code:

```
DELETE tblMovie

INSERT INTO tblMovie
VALUES (1,'A-List Explorers',96,'PG-13')

INSERT INTO tblMovie
VALUES (2,'Bonker Bonzo',75,'G')

INSERT INTO tblMovie
VALUES (3,'Chumps to Champs',75,'PG-13')

INSERT INTO tblMovie
VALUES (4,'Dare or Die',110,'R')

INSERT INTO tblMovie
VALUES (5,'EeeeGhads',88,'G')
```

After deleting all the records, we re-populate the table with the code you see above. Now we have movies one to five in the databases. This time we want to delete some of the records.

Our next goal is to delete every movie that is over 90 minutes long. To do this we find any m_Runtime that is greater than 90 minutes. Using the code in Figure 6.18 will achieve this result.

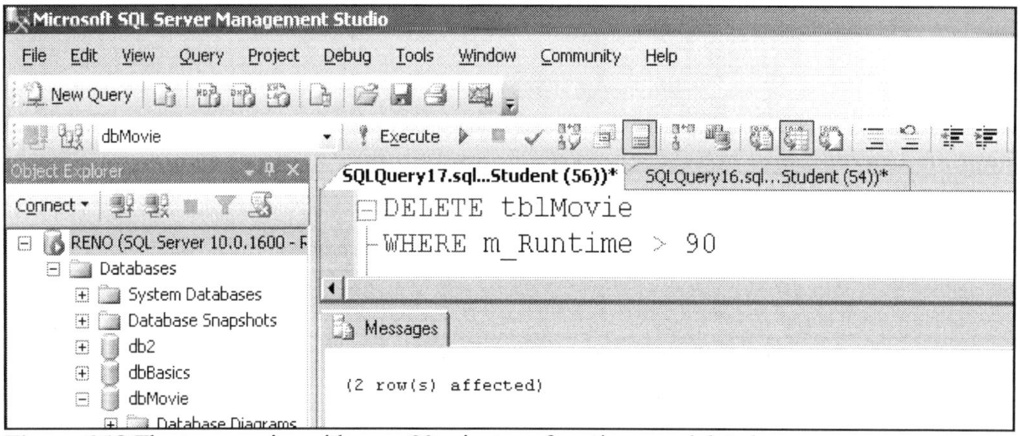

Figure 6.18 The two movies with over 90 minutes of runtime are deleted.

The affected records are "A-List Explorers" at 96 minutes and "Dare or Die" at 110 minutes. Two rows were affected (see the message in the lower half of Figure 6.18). If you had five movie records and deleted two, then three records remain. The number of rows listed as affected (two rows in this case) will be the same number of records removed from a populated table.

It will be easy to check the remaining records in your table. The most common DML statement is a select query to view your records. The select statement from Figure 6.19 shows we now have three records remaining.

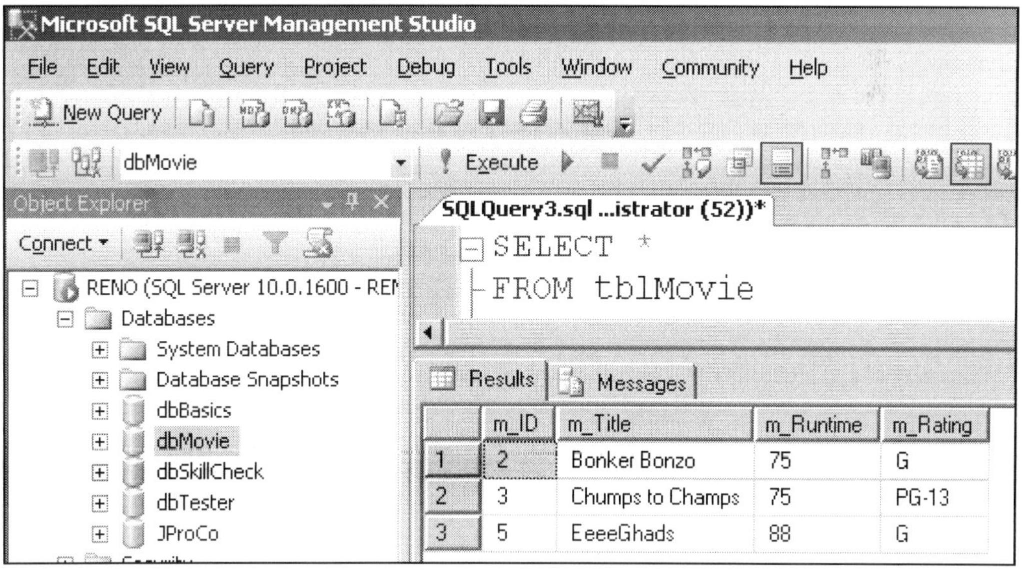

Figure 6.19 After deleting two of your five movies, you have three records left in your table.

Like any other DML statement (SELECT, INSERT, UPDATE and DELETE), you can isolate the data you want by using joins and criteria. If you use the DELETE keyword without criteria, all records are deleted.

Multiple Table Deletes

Let us save our deleting practice for the upcoming lab. In the meantime, we can fix this damage with the following code:

```
DELETE tblMovie

INSERT INTO tblMovie
VALUES (1,'A-List Explorers',96,'PG-13')

INSERT INTO tblMovie
VALUES (2,'Bonker Bonzo',75,'G')

INSERT INTO tblMovie
VALUES (3,'Chumps to Champs',75,'PG-13')

INSERT INTO tblMovie
VALUES (4,'Dare or Die',110,'R')

INSERT INTO tblMovie
VALUES (5,'EeeeGhads',88,'G')
```

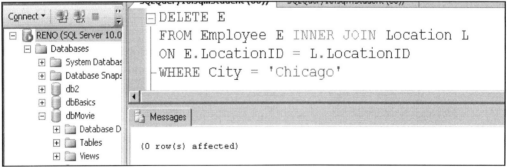

Figure 6.20 Deletes can be used with joins and criteria to affect only the records you want.

You can also use joins to do a DELETE. Let's move back to JProCo. If, for example, you wanted to delete all employees from Chicago, you would run the query from Figure 6.20. Since Chicago has no employees, this statement ran without affecting any records. All join records that meet your criteria will be affected. Make sure you have tested your code before running the delete.

Lab 6.3: Deleting Data

Lab Prep: Before you can begin the lab you must have SQL Server installed and run the Chapter6.3SetupAll.sql script.

Skill Check 1: Open a query window to your dbMovie database. Your movies with a G rating are being tracked in a Kids' Movies database. You are told to delete all records from your tblMovie table that have an m_Rating of G. Write a delete statement that deletes all such movies. When you are done, your table should contain only the three records you see in Figure 6.21.

```
SELECT *
FROM tblMovie
```

Results	Messages			
m_id	m_title		m_runtime	m_Rating
1	A-List Explorers		96	PG-13
3	Chumps to Champs		75	PG-13
4	Dare or Die		110	R

Figure 6.21 Skill Check 1 deletes all G-rated movies.

Skill Check 2: Open a query window to your JProCo database. Delete all records from the MgmtTraining table that have a ClassDurationHours value of greater than 20. This should delete one record.

Answer Code: The SQL code to this lab can be found from the downloadable files named Lab6.3_DeletingData.sql.

Deleting Data - Points to Ponder

1. Data Definition Language (DDL) statements handle the structure or design of database objects (e.g., databases and tables) whereas Data Manipulation Language (DML) statements affect the actual data content. SELECT, INSERT, UPDATE and DELETE are four key DML keywords.

2. Statements starting with the word DELETE are DML statements.

3. DELETE is used to remove records from a table, but not the table itself. Statements starting with DELETE are DML statements.

4. The table and the table's structure remain intact when the data is removed using the DELETE statement without criteria.

5. All Data Manipulation Language (DML) statements start with SELECT, INSERT, UPDATE or DELETE.

DML Syntax

A big thank you goes to the loving pushback from the weekend spring VTE class of 2009 (VTE stands for Volt Technical Education). They reviewed this chapter and noticed the table below was removed. People told me how useful it was and so now it's back. When students tell me what works, future students benefit.

Because of them you have the table below at your fingertips. This is a quick reference summary of what was covered in this chapter. If this makes sense, you have a solid grasp of this topic. Table 6.1 shows the different DML statements and coding examples.

Table 6.1 Shows uses of the DML statements INSERT, UPDATE and DELETE.

Task	Explanation and code sample
Inserting data	This example shows how two records are added to the Location table. The table is in the JProCo database. INSERT INTO Location VALUES (5 , '523 Elm', 'Portland', 'OR') INSERT INTO Location VALUES (6 , '678 Front', 'Yakima', 'WA')
Updates based on one table	This example shows the data getting updated. You will change the street for Yakima to be 699 Mead Street UPDATE Location SET Street = '699 Mead Street' WHERE LocationID = 6
Updates based on many tables	In the following example, the Vacation time in the Benefits table is being updated to 40 hours vacation based on the ManagerID in the Employee table. UPDATE B SET VacationTime = 40 FROM Employee as E INNER JOIN Benefits AS B ON E.EmpID = B.EmpID WHERE ManagerID = 11
Delete based on a single table	This code shows the record for Yakima is deleted from the Location table. DELETE Location WHERE City = 'Yakima'
Deletes based on many tables	In the following example, all records are deleted for Employees who work in the Yakima Location. DELETE Emp FROM Employee AS Emp INNER JOIN Location AS Loc ON Emp.LocationID = Loc.LocationID WHERE Loc.City = 'Yakima'

Creating SQL Scripts

In combining all the skills we have learned to create and populate the tblMovie, we get the code below. Note: the code here uses row constructors to insert values. If you are not using SQL Server 2008, you may wish to refer to a prior example for the precise code syntax.

```
USE master
GO

IF EXISTS(SELECT * FROM sys.sysdatabases
          WHERE [name] = 'dbMovie')
DROP DATABASE dbMovie
GO

CREATE DATABASE dbMovie
GO

USE dbMovie
GO

create table tblMovie
(m_id int primary key,
m_Title varchar(30) not null,
m_Runtime int,
m_Rating varchar(10))

INSERT INTO tblMovie
VALUES (1,'A-List Explorers',96,'PG-13'),
       (2,'Bonker Bonzo',75,'G'),
       (3,'Chumps to Champs',75,'PG-13')

INSERT INTO tblMovie
VALUES (4,'Dare or Die',110,'R'),
       (5,'EeeeGhads',88,'G')
```

This code starts off with the DDL statement that drops and creates objects. Once the database is created, we need to populate the table with some DML statements starting with the INSERT keyword. When you write this much code, you have probably worked on it over time. You are likely going to have someone run this code so they benefit from your work. In either case, you want to save this code as a file. When you save code as a file it has a .sql extension. SQL code saved as a file is called a *script*.

For the Joes2Pros practices, we're going to need to have the Joes2Pros folder on your C drive to store your work. If you don't have this already then make sure this the folder exists in your Windows Explorer (Figure 6.22).

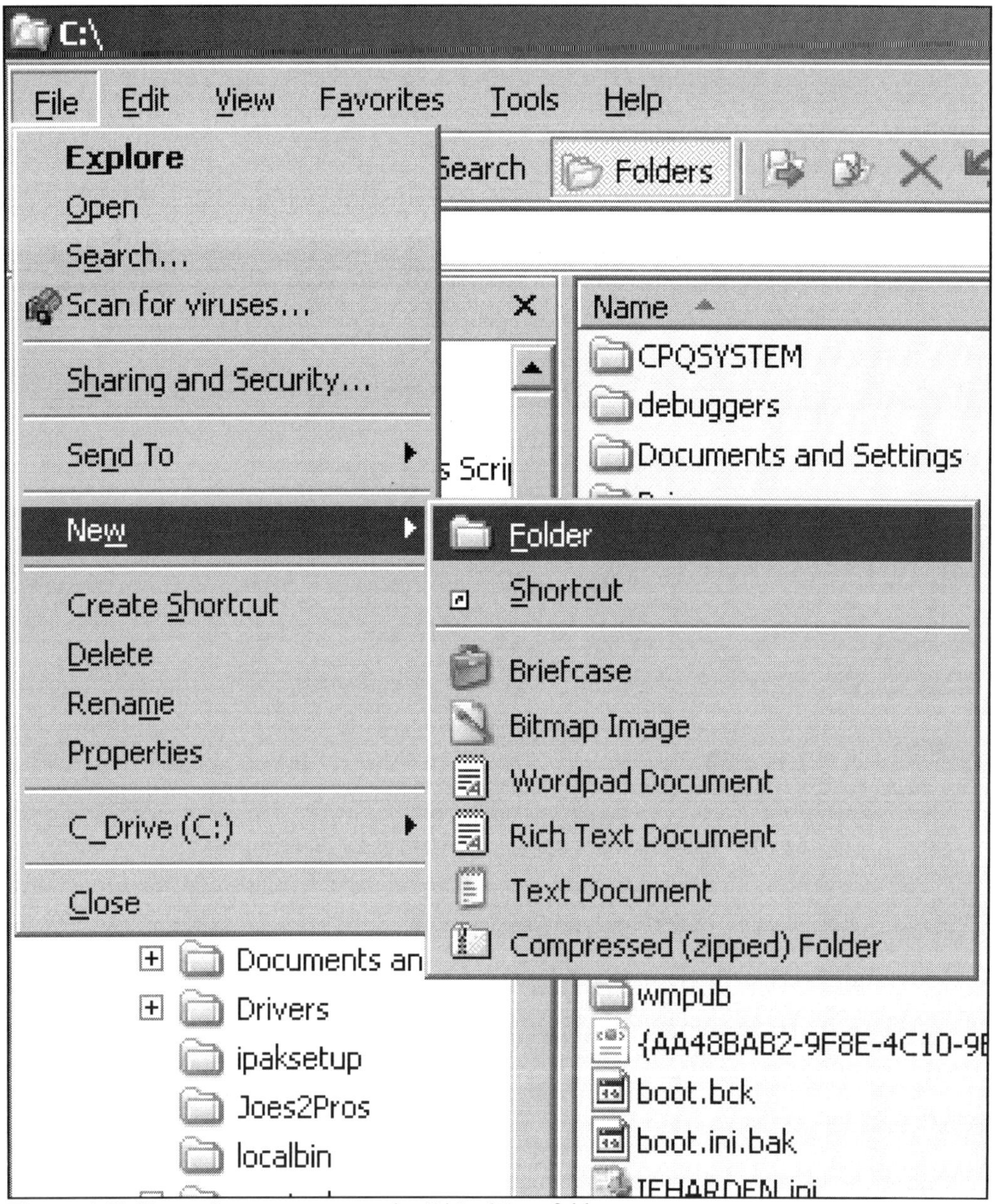

Figure 6.22 Shows the steps to create the C:\Joe2Pros folder.

After naming the folder "Joes2Pros," you have an empty folder ready to hold anything you wish to save. Once you test your code, save the file as CreateDBMovie.sql in your C:\Joes2Pros folder (Figure 6.23).

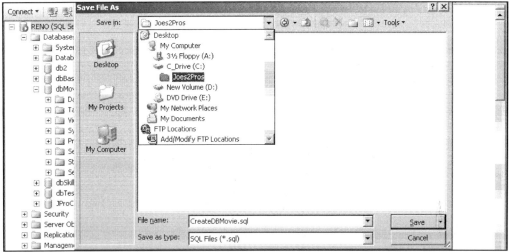

Figure 6.23 Saving your T-SQL code as a SQL script to the C:\Joes2Pros folder.

As soon as you save the SQL statements, they are SQL scripts (Figure 6.24). Scripts have the .sql extension. In our example we have one script saved. Our C:\Joes2Pros folder has the CreateDBMovie.sql script. Scripts eliminate the need to re-create SQL code that is used repeatedly. This script can be re-executed in your testing environment. Scripts are also useful for sharing with others.

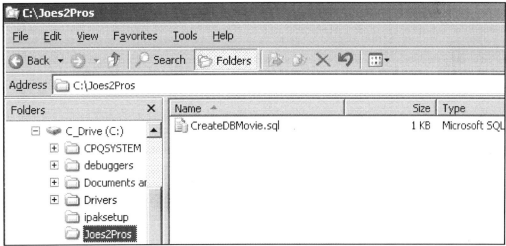

Figure 6.24 Verify your SQL script has been saved.

Executing SQL Scripts

Your work is done and you saved it as a script so you can demo this the next day. A quick way to get your demo started is to open Management Studio and get the query window open with your script loaded. Choose File > Open > File as shown in Figure 6.25.

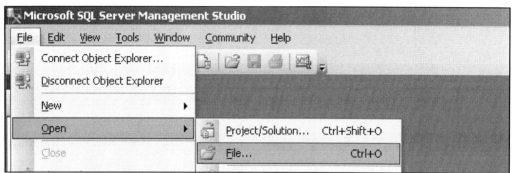

Figure 6.25 You can open a script from Management Studio from the File menu.

Choose your file location and click the Open button. The end result is your script is loaded in a query window (Figure 6.26). All you need to do now is execute the code with F5 or the Execute button.

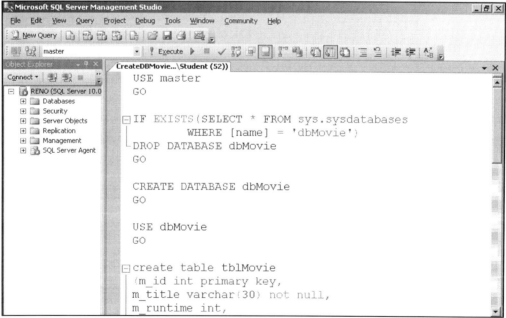

Figure 6.26 The CreateDBMovie script is open in a query window of Management Studio.

From Management Studio you can open a script. First, close completely out of Management Studio to a blank desktop. You will see how to open the script in Management Studio in one step. You open the script through a process known as invocation.

Open your Windows Explorer. Find the CreateDBMovie.sql script and double-click the file. The SQL Server Management Studio opens with your script inside. You hit the connect button and you are ready to run the script. You may notice when you open SQL Server with this process, you don't see an Object Explorer on the left, just a big query window (Figure 6.27).

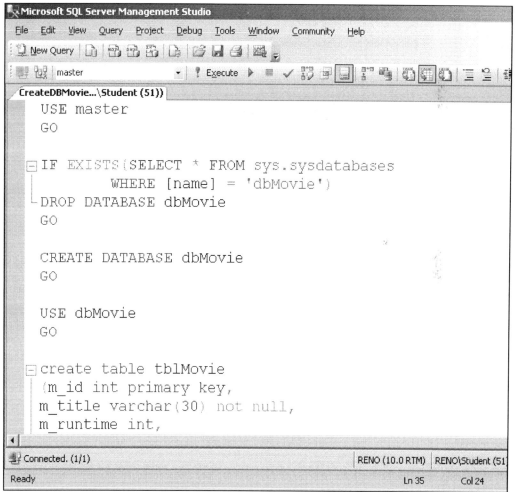

Figure 6.27 Your script opens in Management Studio by double-clicking the file in Windows Explorer.

149

SQLCMD Utility

There is another way to invoke a script without touching Management Studio. You will use a command utility called *SQLCMD*. Since our script creates a database, a good demonstration of this method will be to first drop our dbMovie database. Highlight just the first two batches of the script and execute. Notice in Figure 6.28 that your code ran and the dbMovie database is gone.

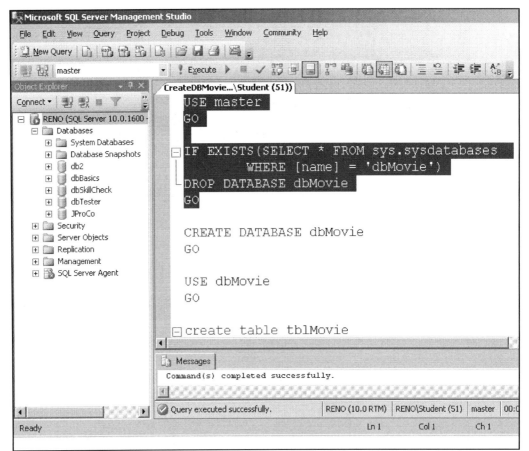

Figure 6.28 Run just the DROP portion of your script by highlighting the first two batches.

Now that the database is completely gone, close back to your desktop. Click Run. Type in the letters CMD in the Run box and hit OK (Figure 6.29).

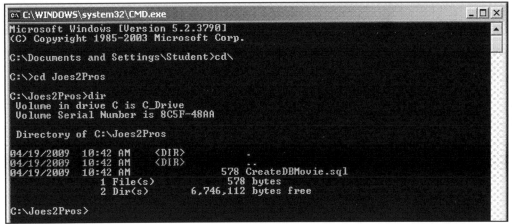

Figure 6.29 Type CMD from the Run command.

If you have SQL Express please keep reading but don't do any of the steps until you get to Figure 6.34. If you have any other edition then change the directory to the C:\ Drive root directory by typing the change directory acronym "cd\"at the end of the line. Go into your folder by typing "cd" followed by a space and then "Joes2Pros" to locate that folder. Once you are in your Joes2Pros folder, you can see its directory listing by typing "dir" then hitting Enter (Figure 6.30).

```
C:\WINDOWS\system32\CMD.exe
Microsoft Windows [Version 5.2.3790]
(C) Copyright 1985-2003 Microsoft Corp.

C:\Documents and Settings\Student>cd\

C:\>cd Joes2Pros

C:\Joes2Pros>dir
 Volume in drive C is C_Drive
 Volume Serial Number is 8C5F-48AA

 Directory of C:\Joes2Pros

04/19/2009  10:42 AM    <DIR>          .
04/19/2009  10:42 AM    <DIR>          ..
04/19/2009  10:42 AM               578 CreateDBMovie.sql
               1 File(s)            578 bytes
               2 Dir(s)       6,746,112 bytes free

C:\Joes2Pros>
```

Figure 6.30 Using the command prompt to show the script exists in the C:\Joes2Pros folder.

At this point, we are going to use the command-line tool known as SQLCMD. You can use SQLCMD to connect to your machine or another SQL Server on your network. The choices you have with this tool are called switches (Fig 6.33). For example, to run on your local server, you can specify a capital S and the server name –S(local). Be mindful that the command-line is upper/lower case sensitive. If you type a lower case s for server, it will not work properly. The command to run this script from SQLCMD is seen in Figure 6.31.

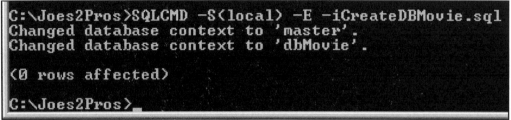

```
C:\Joes2Pros>SQLCMD -S(local) -E -iCreateDBMovie.sql
Changed database context to 'master'.
Changed database context to 'dbMovie'.

(0 rows affected)

C:\Joes2Pros>
```

Figure 6.31 SQLCMD runs input file CreateDBMovie.sql on the Local server using a Trusted Connection.

The S must be a capital -S which stands for Server. The E must be a capital -E which stands for trusted connection. The -i (must be a lower case) specifies the input file.

Now you can verify that this script has created and populated the dbMovie database. Open Management Studio and get a query window to the dbMovie database. Do a query from the tblMovie table and all your records are present (Figure 6.32).

SQLQuery7.sql ...\Student (53))*   SQLQuery6.sql ...\S

```
SELECT *
FROM tblMovie
```

m_id	m_title	m_runtime	m_Rating
1	A-List Explorers	96	PG-13
2	Bonker Bonzo	75	G
3	Chumps to Champs	75	PG-13
4	Dare or Die	110	R
5	EeeeGhads	88	G

Figure 6.32 The dbMovie database is created and populated by the SQLCMD.

152

We know –S is the Server. We've learned a few switches, but what if you forget these and want some help? To learn what a given SQLCMD code switch symbol or letter means, type "SQLCMD /?" and hit enter. The SQL Server command-line tool will appear. The /? is the universal option for getting help in command-line utilities (Figure 6.33).

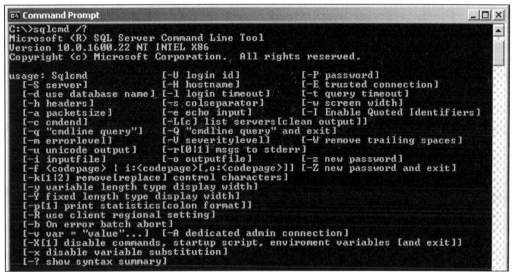

Figure 6.33 Getting the SQLCMD help by using the /? help option.

There are several ways to run scripts on SQL Server. You can open a script from Management Studio. You can invoke a script from the Windows Explorer by double-clicking it. You can use the SQLCMD to run a script from the command-line.

If you have the SQL Server Express edition then you need to know the exact name of your SQL server instance. To do this, verify your server name at the top of your Object Explorer. In Figure 6.34 you see the instance name of Reno\SQLEXPRESS.

Figure 6.34 SQL Express on the Reno server will have the instance name of Reno\SQLExpress.

To run your CreateDBMovies.sql script with SQLCMD use the correct Server switch (-S) you saw from the top of your Object Explorer. In Figure 6.35 we use the name found from Figure 6.34 for the Server name switch.

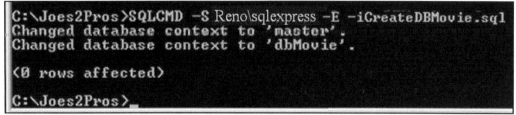

```
C:\Joes2Pros>SQLCMD -S Reno\sqlexpress -E -iCreateDBMovie.sql
Changed database context to 'master'.
Changed database context to 'dbMovie'.

(0 rows affected)

C:\Joes2Pros>_
```

Figure 6.35 The Get SQL Express to work we need to use the server name from the last Figure.

Lab 6.4: Using Scripts

Lab Prep: Before you can begin the lab you must exit out of Management Studio and have created a folder on your C: drive named Joes2Pros. From your companion CD in the Resources folder is a file named Chapter6.4SetupAll.sql. Copy this file to your C:\Joes2Pros folder.

Skill Check 1: Using SQLCMD run the C:\Joes2Pros\Chapter6.4SetupAll.sql script using SQL CMD

```
█ Command Prompt
(1 rows affected)
Changed database context to 'master'.
Changed database context to 'dbTester'.
Changed database context to 'master'.
Changed database context to 'master'.
Changed database context to 'dbMovie'.
Changed database context to 'master'.
Changed database context to 'dbMovie'.

(1 rows affected)
Changed database context to 'JProCo'.

(1 rows affected)
Changed database context to 'dbMovie'.

(1 rows affected)
Changed database context to 'JProCo'.

(2 rows affected)
Changed database context to 'dbMovie'.

(2 rows affected)
```

Figure 6.36 SQLCMD runs the script and displays the following status to the screen.

Answer Code: There is no answer code, but we recommend that you open Management Studio and check for your database and records.

Scripts - Points to Ponder

1. A SQL script is a collection of lines of SQL code saved as a file.

2. A single script can create a database, create all of that database's tables, and even populate those tables with records.

3. Scripts are useful for re-running the same code repeatedly either on your computer or other computers.

4. A script file for SQL Server has ".SQL" or ".sql" extension. File extensions are not case sensitive.

5. SQLCMD is a command-line utility that allows you to run sql scripts.

6. SQLCMD has optional runtime parameters like –E for trusted connection or –P for password.

7. SQLCMD is case-sensitive. For example, -p and –P are different parameters.

8. To find all optional runtime parameters that SQLCMD accepts, you type "SQLCMD /?" in the command prompt.

Chapter Glossary

DDL: Data Definition Language.
Delete: Removes records from a table, but does not remove the table from the database.
DML: Data Manipulation language.
Insert: This DML keyword is a statement used to add new records to tables.
Populate: The process of adding data to a table.
Row Constructors: These allow you to insert multiple records in on INSERT INTO statement.
Script: SQL code saved as a file.
Set: A SQL keyword that assigns values to variables.
SQLCMD: A command-line tool to run SQL scripts or individual SQL statements.
Unpopulated Table: A table with no records.
Update: A statement that changes – or *manipulates* – existing data without adding any new records.

Review Quiz

1.) Insert, update and delete belong to what family of language statements?

O a.   DDL
O b.   XML
O c.   DML

2.) Which is the appropriate SQL code to add records to a table?

O a.   INSERT into tblSports value(1,'Football',)
O b.   INSERT into tblSports values(1,'Football')

3.) What is a script?

O a.   Any SQL code.
O b.   SQL code saved as a file.
O c.   It's another name for a stored procedure.

4.) Which is the newest recommended command-line utility that enables running of SQL scripts?

O a.   OSQL
O b.   ISQL
O c.   SQLCMD

5.) Which of the following is not a way to run a SQL script?

O a.   Run it in a query window.
O b.   Use the script file in a command-line utility.
O c.   Open Windows Explorer and double-click the .sql file.
O d.   Double click .mdb (Microsoft Database File) file in Windows Explorer.

6.) Your Employee table holds all employees and their work locationID. Your [Grant] table contains a list of grants and the employee ID number of the person who found the grant in an EmpID field. Your Boston location only accepts grants in the exact amount of $50,000 from each donor. You have noticed incorrectly entered values in the Amount field of the [Grant] table for your Boston employees. You need to set the amount to $50,000 for all entries in the [Grant] table to correspond to employees at Location 2 (Boston). You must not change the grant amounts of the other locations. Which SQL statement should you use?

O a. UPDATE [Grant] SET Amount = 50000
      WHERE EXISTS(
      SELECT * FROM Employee E
      WHERE E.LocationID = 2)

O b. UPDATE G SET Amount = 50000
      FROM [Grant] G
      INNER JOIN Employee E
      ON G.EmpID = E.EmpID
      WHERE E.LocationID = 2

7.) Which of the following is the correct way to name a SQL script?

O a.   .jpg
O b.   .sql
O c.   .trc
O d.   .SqlPlan

Answer Key

1.) DDL (Data Definition Language), as we learned in chapter 5, is all about defining the structures to hold data with CREATE, ALTER or DROP so (a) is incorrect. XML (Extensible Markup Language) is a set of rules for encoding documents electronically and does not do anything within an RDBMS so (b) is not correct either. INSERT, UPDATE and DELETE are statements which make changes to or manipulate the data so they are part of the DML (Data Manipulation Language) making (c) the correct answer.

2.) *INSERT into tblSports value(1,'Football',)* is missing an 's' at the end of 'values' and will result in a syntax error so (a) is incorrect. *INSERT into* tblSports *values(1,'Football')* is written correctly so (b) is the correct answer.

3.) Not just 'Any SQL code' is a script; it must be saved as a file with a .sql extension so (a) is incorrect. A stored procedure (see chapter 8) is SQL code saved to SQL Server rather than its own file so (c) is also incorrect. SQL code saved as a file is a script so (b) is the correct answer.

4.) OSQL and ISQL are both command line utilities provided with SQL Server 2000 so they are not the newest recommended command-line utility that enables running of SQL scripts, making both (a) and (b) wrong answers. SQLCMD is the newest recommended command-line utility that enables running of SQL scripts making (c) the correct answer.

5.) SQL scripts can be run in a query window, with a command-line query or by double-clicking the .sql file in Windows Explorer so (a), (b) and (c) are all wrong.

Double-clicking a .mdb (Microsoft Database File) file in Windows Explorer will open Microsoft Access if it is installed so (d) is the correct answer.

6.) Using EXISTS as a predicate in the WHERE clause, will update either all or none of the records in the Grant table so (a) is incorrect. Correct use of an INNER JOIN and predicating the WHERE clause to filter on Employee records with a LocationID of 2 will ensure that only Grant records that have a related Employee record will be updated making (b) the correct answer.

7.) .jpg is for pictures so (a) is incorrect. SQL Server Profiler Stored Procedures create files using the .trc extension, making (c) an incorrect answer too. The .SqlPlan extension identifies SSMS Execution Plan files so (d) is also a wrong answer. SQL Scripts are created with the .sql extension by default, making (b) the correct answer.

Bug Catcher Game

To play the Bug Catcher game run the BugCatcher_Chapter6.pps from the BugCatcher folder of the companion files. You can obtain these files from the www.Joes2Pros.com web site.

Chapter 7. Maintaining Tables

Tables get lots of attention. After all, they hold all of the data. You need to add or remove data constantly. Designing the table correctly with the right number of fields is part of good planning. You may also need to re-design tables that already have data in them. This chapter is all about the choices you have for setting up and maintaining tables.

READER NOTE: *Please run the script Chapter7.0SetupAll.sql in order to follow along with the examples in the first section of this chapter. The setup scripts for this book are posted at Joes2Pros.com.*

DELETE vs. DROP

In previous chapters we encountered the DELETE command (i.e., a DML statement that eliminates some records from an existing table) and the DROP command (i.e., a DDL statement eliminating a database or table). While intuitively they both have the effect of eliminating items, it's vital to be clear on the distinct usage of each command with tables.

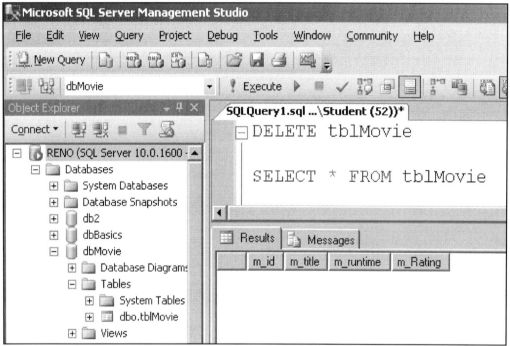

Figure 7.1 A DELETE statement with no criteria tells SQL to delete all records from a table.

As we saw in Chapter 6, the DELETE command removes entire records, so it's one we want to be especially careful with. In most instances, you use filter criteria to remove only one record or a specific subset of records. Recall when we specified the m_id field? SQL deleted just that record with the query

DELETE tblMovie WHERE m_id = 1.

Later when we accidentally changed all the movie names to "A-List Explorers" we had to take the more drastic step of using DELETE without criteria (DELETE tblMovie) to get rid of **all** records in the tblMovie. Any future queries on a table you delete returns **zero records** to your result set.

DROP is an even more drastic step. It's the most drastic thing you can do to a table. *Besides getting rid of all your records, the drop command goes a step further and removes the entire table and its design!* In other words, all the DDL and DML statements you used to build the structure of your table and populate it with data will be wiped out by a drop statement. Following is the syntax to drop a table:

```
DROP TABLE tblMovie
```

When you query the table that you have dropped, you can see no such table exists. Trying to query the table gives you an error (Figure 7.2).

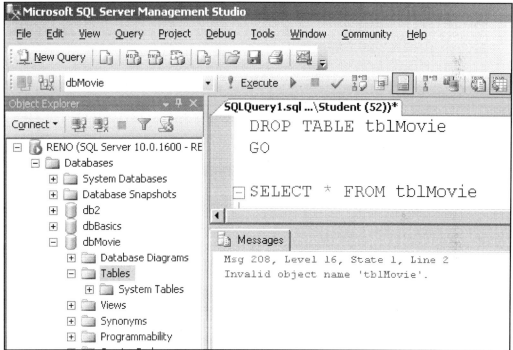

Figure 7.2 The drop statement removes the entire table and its contents from your database.

Drop does not accept criteria since DROP is a DDL statement. You dropped this table so there is no tblMovie table to query. Go to the Object Explorer window and use Refresh to confirm that the table is gone (Figure 7.2). That is why SQL returns an error when you try to query the table.

The next section titled "Altering Table Design" uses tblMovie. In preparation, please run the following code and save as a script to create and populate the tblMovie table:

```
USE master
GO


IF EXISTS(SELECT * FROM sys.sysdatabases
        WHERE [name] = 'dbMovie')
DROP DATABASE dbMovie
GO


CREATE DATABASE dbMovie
GO


USE dbMovie
GO


create table tblMovie
(m_id int primary key,
m_Title varchar(30) not null,
m_Runtime int,
m_Rating varchar(10))

INSERT INTO tblMovie
VALUES (1,'A-List Explorers',96,'PG-13')

INSERT INTO tblMovie
VALUES (2,'Bonker Bonzo',75,'G')

INSERT INTO tblMovie
VALUES (3,'Chumps to Champs',75,'PG-13')
INSERT INTO tblMovie
VALUES (4,'Dare or Die',110,'R')

INSERT INTO tblMovie
VALUES (5,'EeeeGhads',88,'G')
```

Altering Table Design

We have a populated table and just learned we must add a new field called m_Description. Every new movie will now have a marketing description. One option is to drop and rebuild the table from scratch. We saved our code as a script, so we could modify the code to include the new field and add description values for those five existing records to the script. However, we haven't yet received descriptions for the five records and the manager wants this field added ASAP before anyone adds more movies into the database.

A better way to succeed in this scenario is to simply use an ALTER TABLE statement to add the new field. If records already exist and you want to populate them later, it's a good idea to have the field accept null data types. While you might consider rebuilding a five-record table that has just a few columns, you wouldn't want to rebuild a table that contained hundreds of records. Run the following code to add the m_Description field:

```
ALTER TABLE tblMovie
ADD m_Description Varchar(100) NULL
```

A quick look at our table with a select query will show us several things. We now have a field called m_Description. We also haven't yet specified a value for any of the old records. The unknown value is currently set as NULL (Figure 7.3).

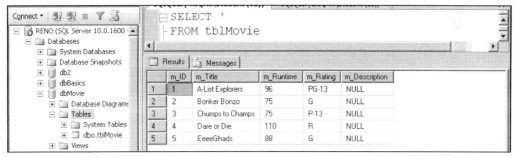

Figure 7.3 All five existing records are NULL for the new m_Description field until you add data.

Adding fields after you've already designed a database and its tables can be tricky. For example, you allowed this field to be nullable only because you already had records. You now risk someone entering more null records to the table using the following code:

```
INSERT INTO tblMovie
VALUES (6,'Fire Shaft',75,'R',NULL)
```

You know the manager doesn't want new movies entered without a description. You can't change the field to "Not Null" because your five existing records would violate this rule. Fortunately, there are ways to restrict future records from allowing nulls while giving you some freedom on the existing records. First off, let's drop the existing field with the following code:

```
ALTER TABLE tblMovie
DROP COLUMN m_Description
```

In order to add a new, non-nullable field to tblMovie, we need to think about what description the existing records should get. We can assign a default value at the time the field is created. The first five movies should have a description that reads "Description Coming Soon." The following code creates the non-nullable m_Description field with our default value:

```
ALTER TABLE tblMovie
ADD m_Description Varchar(100) NOT NULL
DEFAULT 'Description Coming Soon'
```

Now we have the new field in place and our existing records show the default description (Figure 7.4). This also means future movies entered must have some value for the description since m_Description will not accept nulls (Figure 7.4). To insert new records with a default value just use the **Default** keyword in the insert statement:

```
--Example of how to insert default values
INSERT INTO tblMovie
VALUES (6,'Fire Shaft',75,'R',Default)
```

m_id	m_title	m_runtime	m_Rating	m_Description
1	A-List Explorers	96	PG-13	Description Coming Soon
2	Bonker Bonzo	75	G	Description Coming Soon
3	Chumps to Champs	75	PG-13	Description Coming Soon
4	Dare or Die	110	R	Description Coming Soon
5	EeeeGhads	88	G	Description Coming Soon
6	Fire Shaft	75	R	Description Coming Soon

Figure 7.4 The existing records get the default value of "Description Coming Soon" for the new field.

In addition to adding new fields to existing tables, you can also rename fields. To change the title of m_Description to m_Teaser, you would run the following code:

```
sp_rename 'tblMovie.m_Description', 'm_Teaser'
```

A query from the tblMovie table confirms this change (Figure 7.5).

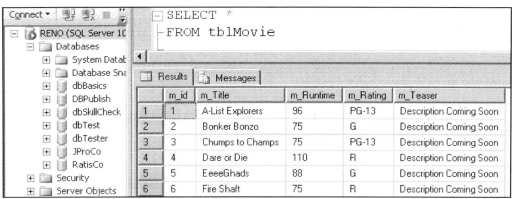

Figure 7.5 The last field in this query has been renamed to m_Teaser.

Changing a name that has been in use is considered risky. Many users and calling applications may be expecting a field name that is no longer there. This can cause a dependent process to break. Therefore, expect the following error message when you rename a field:

"Caution: Changing any part of an object name could break scripts and stored procedures."

With sp_rename we have wandered outside the SQL language and into a Microsoft-specific procedure. But since this is a curiosity point that frequently comes up in class, we will demo it here. Stored procedures are discussed more in the next chapter. Next, we want to change our tblMovie table to just be called Movie. This can be achieved with the following code:

```
sp_rename 'tblMovie', 'Movie'
```

Now we can query from the Movie table. Change your SELECT statement after the FROM clause. Use the name Movie and you see all the same records and fields as before.

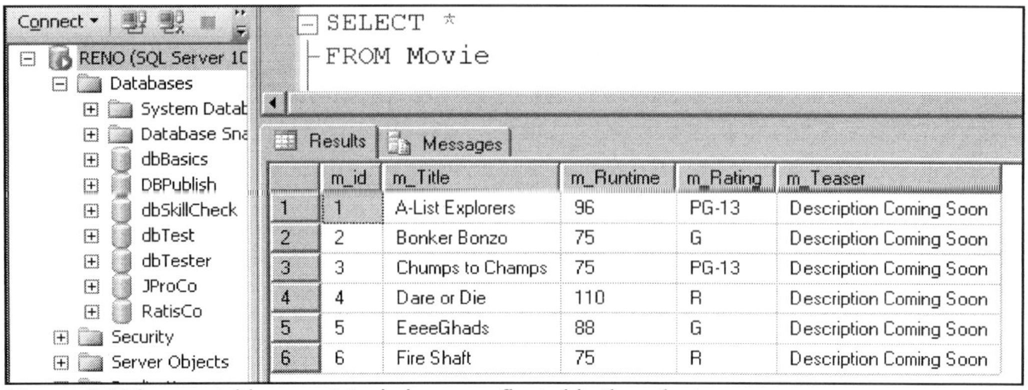

Figure 7.6 The new table name Movie is now reflected in the select query.

The table below helps to summarize our table altering actions.

Table 7.1 A summary of SQL code for table definitions.

Task	Explanation and code sample
Dropping a table	In the following, we remove the entire tblMovie table. DROP TABLE tblMovie
Adding a nullable field to an existing table	In the following, we add a new field to the tblMovie table that allows nulls. ALTER TABLE tblMovie ADD m_Description Varchar(100) NULL
Adding a non-nullable field to an existing table	In the following, we add a new non-nullable field to tblMovie with a default value. ALTER TABLE tblMovie ADD m_Description Varchar(100) NOT NULL DEFAULT 'Description Coming Soon'
Dropping a column from a table	In the following, we remove the m_Description field from the tblMovie table. ALTER TABLE tblMovie DROP COLUMN m_Description
Rename a Table	In the following, we rename the Location table to Locations. sp_rename 'Location' ,'Locations'
Rename a Column in a Table	In the following, we rename the Street field in the Location table to Address. sp_rename 'Location.Street' , 'Location.Address'

Lab 7.1: Altering Tables

Lab Prep: Before you can begin the lab you must have SQL Server installed and run the Chapter7.1SetupAll.sql script. It is recommended that you have completed the steps in the chapter that have lead up to this lab.

Skill Check 1: Add a new non-nullable integer field called m_Release to the Movie table. The default value for your new field should be 2000. When you are done, your screen should resemble Figure 7.7 below.

```
SELECT *
FROM Movie
```

	m_ID	m_Title	m_Runtime	m_Rating	m_Teaser	m_Release
1	1	A-List Explorers	96	PG-13	Description Coming Soon	2000
2	2	Bonker Bonzo	75	G	Description Coming Soon	2000
3	3	Chumps to Champs	75	P-13	Description Coming Soon	2000
4	4	Dare or Die	110	R	Description Coming Soon	2000
5	5	EeeeGhads	88	G	Description Coming Soon	2000

Figure 7.7 Skill Check 1.

Answer Code: The SQL code to this lab can be found from the downloadable files named Lab7.1_AlteringTables.sql.

Altering Tables - Points to Ponder

1. DROP removes the entire table from the database. Statements starting with DROP are DDL statements.

2. You can add more fields to a table even after you have initially created the table.

3. You can add new columns to a table by using the ALTER TABLE statement:
   o **ALTER TABLE tblMovie ADD m_Description varchar(300) NULL**

4. You can remove table columns by using the following code:
   o **ALTER TABLE Employee DROP column m_Runtime**

5. ALTER TABLE statements are DDL statements. DDL statements never use filtering criteria.

Bulk Copy Program (BCP)

There are many ways to get data into your SQL server database. We have discussed scripts extensively and have also seen many ways to run these scripts. Most of the time, the source of your data will be plain, raw data. Raw data often comes to me as a block of values separated by commas with no SQL code whatsoever. In your SQL career, you no doubt will receive inputs in the form of spreadsheets, Microsoft Access databases or another company's database.

There are utilities that understand data, and SQL Server can manage the inserting of data for you. Some programs like *SQL Server Integration Services* (SSIS) can take just about any source of data and pump it into or out of SQL Server. In this chapter, we explore how to use the *Bulk Copy Program* (BCP), which was designed for the flow of data between SQL and text files. It's a simple utility that does one of the most common types of bulk copying.

Importing Data

If you have data in a text file and you need to move it into a SQL table, you're ready to import that file into SQL Server using BCP. A quick visual comparison of the data in the input file and the destination table will really help. We need to confirm that the text data can supply enough data to populate each field for each record in the destination table.

Let's start off by looking at the destination where you intend to import this new data. Usually this will be an existing table. In this example let's look at the Movie table of the dbMovie database (Figure 7.8).

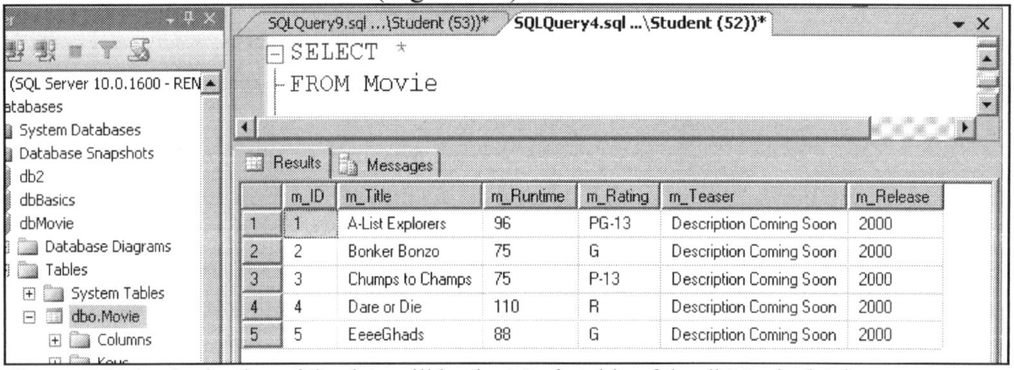

Figure 7.8 The destination of the data will be the Movie table of the dbMovie database.

We currently have six fields. It can also be said that we need six values for each record in this table.

We have five records in our Movie table and two records in the file called Ch7MovieFeed.txt (Figure 7.9). Our goal is to import movies 6 and 7 into the Movie table.

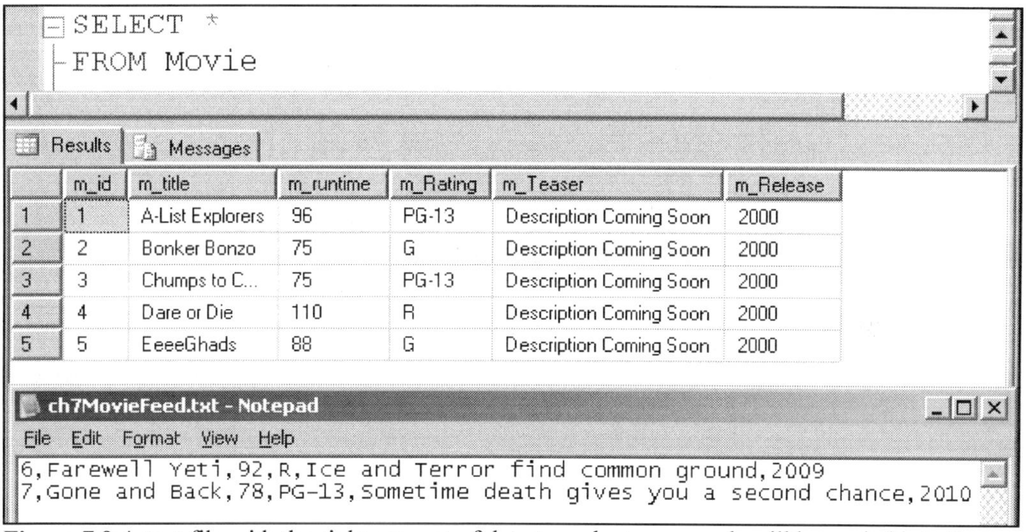

Figure 7.9 A text file with the right amount of data to make two records will be copied into the Movie table.

Locate the file Ch7MovieFeed.txt in the Resources folder of your companion CD. Copy this file into your C:\Joes2Pros folder.

The first record of the text file is m_id 6. Note the value 6 is terminated with a comma to separate it from the second field value of "Farewell Yeti." After the next separating comma is the third field, which shows a runtime of 92 minutes. The pattern repeats until the final field in each record is reached. At that point, a return (a carriage return or hitting the Enter key) signals the end of the record. Just remember that *commas separate fields*, and after each line the *return separates records*.

OK, we've confirmed the data in the source file and now are confident the data conforms to the destination format (the Movie table). BCP should run without a problem. We first need to provide a few logistical items to BCP: the filepath of the source file, which table we want the data copied into, and some other basics, such as the designation of commas as *field terminators*. Close out of the Movie database. From your desktop click Start > Run. Type in the letters CMD in the Run box and hit OK (Figure 7.10).

Run
Type the name of a program, folder, document, or Internet resource, and Windows will open it for you.
Open:
OK
Cancel
Browse...
Start

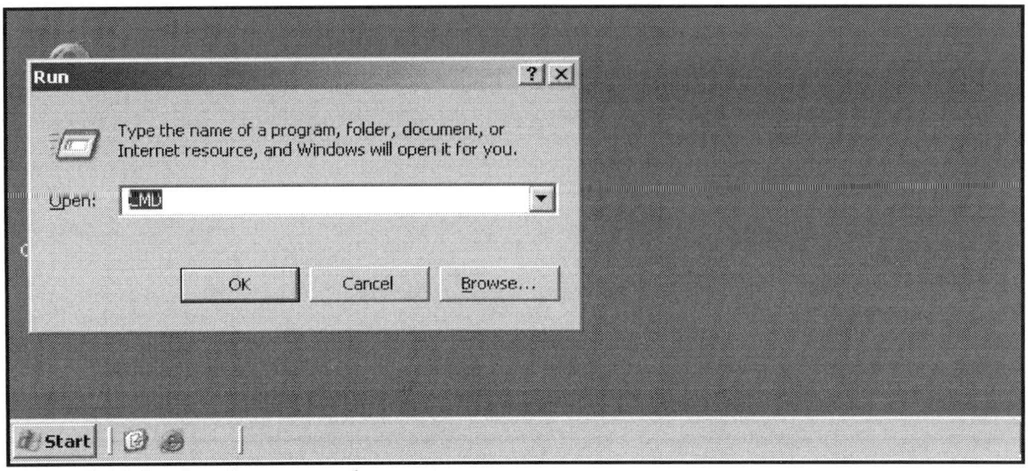

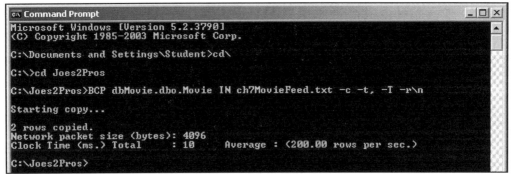

Figure 7.10 Starting the command prompt.

With the command prompt open (see Figure 7.11), we can go to the root of the C: drive with a "cd\" command and hit Enter. Go into the folder with a "cd Joes2Pros" command. While in the folder, a good practice is to make sure the Ch7MovieFeed.txt is in the directory. You can type "dir" to see this listing. Once you know it's there, you can proceed to invoke BCP.

We want to tell BCP to expect character data (-c) with fields terminated by commas (-t,). Windows has already authenticated our password. SQL trusts Windows. Since we are logged on as a user with permissions, we don't want to re-type our password. Use the Trusted connection with an upper case (-T). Lastly, we have multiple records in the text file. Each record is separated by a new line (\n) or (r\n carriage return\newline) in your text file. Put all these command switches together as you see in Figure 7.11. *Note*: If you are using SQL Express, you will have to use the –S switch, similar to what you saw in Figure 6.35.

Command Prompt
Microsoft Windows [Version 5.2.3790]
(C) Copyright 1985-2003 Microsoft Corp.
C:\Documents and Settings\Student>cd\
C:\>cd Joes2Pros
C:\Joes2Pros>BCP dbMovie.dbo.Movie IN ch7MovieFeed.txt -c -t, -T -r\n
Starting copy...
2 rows copied.
Network packet size (bytes): 4096
Clock Time (ms.) Total : 10 Average : (200.00 rows per sec.)
C:\Joes2Pros>

Figure 7.11 After directing your way into the C:\Joes2Pros folder, you can run BCP to pump two new records into the Movie table.

Query your Movie table and you will notice two new records for a total of seven. The m_id 6 and 7 were successfully added by BCP.

```
SELECT *
FROM Movie
```

	m_ID	m_Title	m_Runtime	m_Rating	m_Teaser	m_Release
1	1	A-List Explorers	96	PG-13	Description Coming Soon	2000
2	2	Bonker Bonzo	75	G	Description Coming Soon	2000
3	3	Chumps to Champs	75	P-13	Description Coming Soon	2000
4	4	Dare or Die	110	R	Description Coming Soon	2000
5	5	EeeeGhads	88	G	Description Coming Soon	2000
6	6	Farewell Yeti	92	R	Ice and Terror find common ground	2009
7	7	Gone and Back	78	PG-13	Sometime death gives you a second chance	2010

Figure 7.12 The result set after running BCP shows there are now seven movie records.

Exporting Data

Now you are required to share this information with a parent company. That company needs all seven records from your Movie table. Since they do not have permissions to your SQL Server, they have requested that you send them the data in a text file delimited by hash # marks.

Essentially you will now reverse the import process to BCP data from your table in SQL Server and save it as a text file. Start your command prompts and specify the Movie table going out to the Ch7PartnerFeed.txt using character data terminated by hash marks (Figure 7.13).

```
Command Prompt

Microsoft Windows [Version 5.2.3790]
(C) Copyright 1985-2003 Microsoft Corp.

C:\Documents and Settings\Student>cd\

C:\>cd Joes2Pros

C:\Joes2Pros>BCP dbMovie.dbo.Movie OUT ch7PartnerFeed.txt -c -t# -T -r\n

Starting copy...

7 rows copied.
Network packet size (bytes): 4096
Clock Time (ms.) Total      : 10      Average : (700.00 rows per sec.)

C:\Joes2Pros>_
```

Figure 7.13 The BCP process is saving all seven files as a text file.

Now we can open the file C:\Joes2Pros\Ch7PartnerFeed.txt and examine its contents. This file uses hash marks as field terminators and has seven records in total (Figure 7.14).

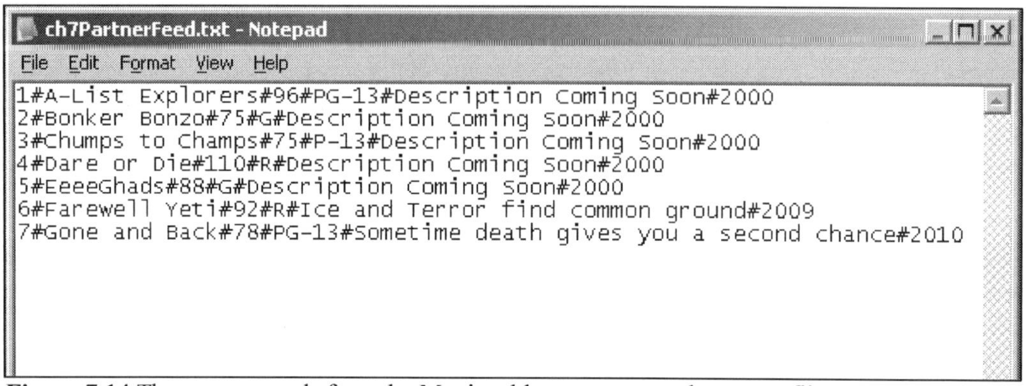

Figure 7.14 The seven records from the Movie table were exported to a text file.

There are many options to tell BCP how to run. Different file types and security settings are among the choices. See the list of all command line switches for BCP as shown in Figure 7.15 by typing "BCP/?" at the command prompt.

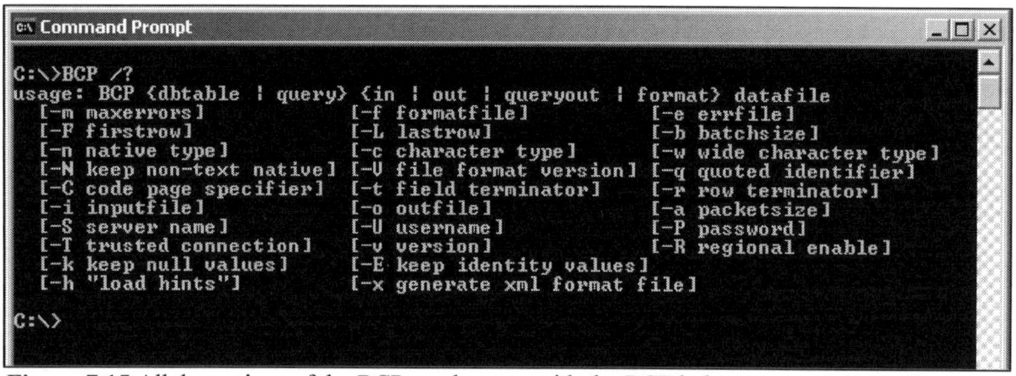

Figure 7.15 All the options of the BCP can be seen with the BCP help command (BCP /?).

In order for BCP to communicate with SQL Server, it needs the right password or credential. This means you must either supply it with a trusted connection or password. It's also a best practice to specify a terminator otherwise BCP will pick one for you.

If you didn't specify a terminator in the previous example (see Figure 7.13), your code would appear as follows:

```
BCP dbMovie.dbo.Movie OUT Ch7TabFeed.txt -c -T -r\n
```

If a field terminator is not specified, a tab-delimited text file is created by default. As shown in Figure 7.16, it can be hard to see where fields of varying lengths end since columns don't line up uniformly. In this case, a comma-delimited text file would be easier to quickly scan and verify visually.

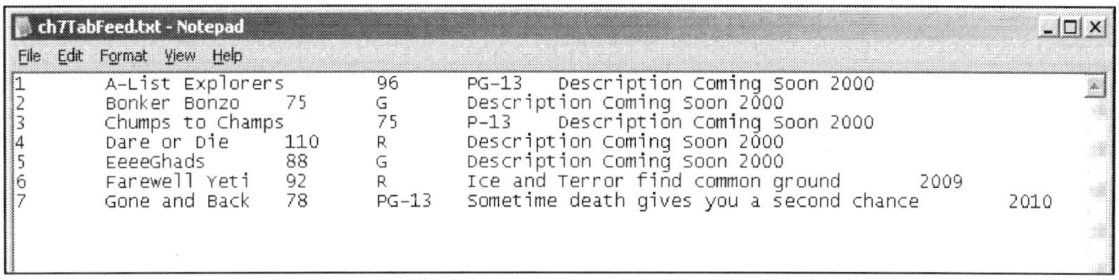
ch7TabFeed.txt - Notepad

File Edit Format View Help

```
1	A-List Explorers	96	PG-13	Description Coming Soon 2000
2	Bonker Bonzo	75	G	Description Coming Soon 2000
3	Chumps to Champs	75	P-13	Description Coming Soon 2000
4	Dare or Die	110	R	Description Coming Soon 2000
5	EeeeGhads	88	G	Description Coming Soon 2000
6	Farewell Yeti	92	R	Ice and Terror find common ground	2009
7	Gone and Back	78	PG-13	Sometime death gives you a second chance	2010
```

Figure 7.16 The tab-delimited text file is the default for BCP when you don't specify a terminator type.

Lab 7.2: Using BCP

Lab Prep: Before you can begin the lab you must have SQL Server installed and run the Chapter7.2SetupAll.sql script.

Skill Check 1: Your Customer table of JProCo has five test records inside. The Lab72CustomerFeed.txt in the downloadable files has 775 verified records. Make sure the Lab72CustomerFeed.txt is located in C:\Joes2Pros folder.

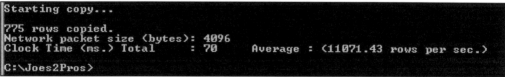

```
  SELECT *
  FROM Customer
```

Results | Messages

	CustomerID	CustomerType	FirstName	LastName	CompanyName
1	1	Consumer	Mark	Williams	NULL
2	2	Consumer	Lee	Young	NULL
3	3	Consumer	Patricia	Martin	NULL
4	4	Consumer	Mary	Lopez	NULL
5	5	Consumer	NULL	NULL	MoreTechnology.com

Lab72CustomerFeed.txt - Notepad

File Edit Format View Help

```
1,Consumer,Mark,Williams,
2,Consumer,Lee,Young,
3,Consumer,Patricia,Martin,
4,Consumer,Mary,Lopez,
5,Business,,,MoreTechnology.com
6,Consumer,Ruth,Clark,
7,Consumer,Tessa,Wright,
8,Consumer,Jennifer,Garcia,
9,Consumer,Linda,Adams,
10,Consumer,ÿRobert,Wilson,
11,Consumer,Kimberly,Taylor,
12,Consumer,Helen,Hernandez,
13,Consumer,Linda,Hernandez,
```

Figure 7.17 The Lab72CustomerFeed.txt is a comma-delimited file which can be imported in the Customer table of JProCo.

You need to delete all five test records from your Customer table and import the 775 comma-delimited data from your Lab72CustomerFeed.txt file. Your BCP screen will look like Figure 7.18 when you are done.

```
Starting copy...

775 rows copied.
Network packet size (bytes): 4096
Clock Time (ms.) Total      : 70      Average : (11071.43 rows per sec.)

C:\Joes2Pros>
```

Figure 7.18 BCP is showing 775 records have been inserted.

Answer Code: There is no answer code for the BCP process.

Using BCP - Points to Ponder

1. BCP stands for Bulk Copy Program.

2. BCP lets you perform data imports and exports using a command-line utility.

3. In BCP, the –t switch is used to specify how your fields are terminated. For example, if you use commas between each field, use **–t,** and if you use ampersands between them, use **–t&** for the switch.

4. To see all the available switches for BCP run the following command: BCP /?

5. A script is one or many lines of working SQL statements stored in a file.

6. Upper and lower case switches have different meanings in BCP and all Command Prompt utilities.

Chapter Glossary

ALTER: A DDL statement that changes the design or properties of a database or database object.

BCP: Bulk Copy Program is a command-line utility for importing or exporting data from a delimited text file.

DROP: A DDL statement that removes a database or database object.

EXPORT: A process take data from a table and save it as another type of data storage.

IMPORT: A process to bring data into a SQL table.

TAB-DELIMITED TEXT FILE: A text file where each field is separate by a tab character.

TERMINATOR: The type of marker the designates the ending of a column or a row.

Review Quiz

1.) Which code would correctly add a new field called Status to the Location table?

O a.   ALTER TABLE Location ADD Status varchar(300) NULL
O b.   CREATE TABLE Location ALTER Status varchar(300) NULL
O c.   CREATE FIELD Location ADD Status varchar(300) NULL
O d.   ALTER FIELD Location ADD Status varchar(300) NULL

2.) What is the correct way to insert the default value in the third field of the Activity table ?

O a.   INSERT INTO Activity VALUES (1,100, NULL)
O b.   INSERT INTO Activity VALUES (1, 100, Default)
O c.   INSERT INTO Activity VALUES (1,100, 'NULL')
O d.   INSERT INTO Activity VALUES (1,100, 'Default'')

3.) BCP is a command-line utility that does what?

O a.   It runs SQL scripts.
O b.   It installs SQL Server.
O c.   It imports data from any type of file.
O d.   It imports data from a text file.

4.) What does the –t switch in BCP do?

O a.   It specifies a trusted connection.
O b.   It specifies a row terminator.
O c.   It specifies a field terminator.
O d.   It specifies the time out in seconds.
O e.   It specifies the terminal connection.

5.) If you do not specify a way to delimit your fields what does BCP do?

O a.   You get an error message.
O b.   It picks the most recently used delimiting option.
O c.   You don't get any delimited file.
O d.   You get a comma delimited file.
O e.   You get a tab delimited file.

6.) You receive text files with updated movie data from across the country. Columns are separated by # signs. You need to import them into your database. *What do you do?*

O a.   Re-create the text file in a custom format.
O b.   Import them with BCP and specify the # as the field terminator.
O c.   Import them with BCP and don't specify a terminator. It will be picked automatically.

7.) You receive text files with updated movie data from across the country. Columns are separated by tab characters. You need to import them into your database. *What do you do?*

O a.   Re-create the text file in a custom format.
O b.   Use BCP and specify the # as the field terminator.
O c.   Use BCP and don't specify a terminator. It will be picked automatically.
O d.   Re-create the text file as an Excel spreadsheet.

8.) Which statement describes the difference between the DROP and DELETE clauses for tables?

O a.   They do exactly the same thing.
O b.   DROP leaves you with an empty table and DELETE removes the table.
O c.   DELETE empties the table and DROP eliminates the table.

9.) You are modifying a table named [Product] in a SQL Server 2008 database. You want to add a new column named Friendlyname to the product table. A friendly name for each product will be stored in this column. The table currently contains data. The sales department has not yet created a friendly name for each product. Friendly names are a required value for each product. You want to add this new column by using the least amount of effort. *What should you do?*

O a.   Define the new column as NOT NULL with a default value of Undefined.

O b.   Define the new column as NULL with a default value of Undefined.

O c.   Define the new column as NULL and update the records later.

O d.   Define the new column as NOT NULL with no default.

Answer Key

1.) Since the CREATE statement is used to initially define a new object both (b) and (c) are incorrect. The ALTER statement is used on existing tables not fields so (d) is also wrong. The correct answer is (a) because the ALTER statement is altering the table to add a new field.

2.) Inserting a NULL is not the same as inserting the declared default value so (a) is wrong. Both (c) and (d) are attempting to insert a string contained within quotes rather than the declared default values so they are also incorrect. To insert the default value, use the word default without quotes as in (b), which is the correct answer.

3.) SQL Server runs SQL scripts so (a) is incorrect. Installation discs are used for installing SQL Server so (b) is wrong too. Programs like SQL Server Integration Services (SSIS) can import data from most types of files so (c) is also wrong. The correct answer is (d) because BCP (Bulk Copy Program) imports data from text files.

4.) The –T switch specifies a trusted connection and the –r switch specifies the row terminator making (a) and (b) incorrect answers. The BCP utility doesn't have switches for specifying the time out or the terminal connection so (d) and (e) are also both wrong. The correct answer is (c) because the –t switch specifies a field terminator.

5.) Since, by default, you get a tab delimited file when you do not specify a way to delimit your fields using the –t switch then (a), (b), (c), and (d) are all wrong. BCP will create a tab delimited file if the –t switch is not used making (e) the correct answer.

6.) Re-creating the text file in a custom format is a waste of your valuable time by creating unnecessary work so (a) is incorrect. The default field terminator is a tab character so (c) will not work in this case. If the columns in the text file are separated by # signs then you must specify the # as the field terminator therefore (b) is correct.

7.) Re-creating the text file in a custom format is a waste of your valuable time by creating unnecessary work so (a) is incorrect. If the columns in the text file are separated by a something other than the tab character then the field terminator must be specified, therefore (b) is also incorrect. The default field terminator is a tab character so (c) will work in this case.

8.) Because DROP removes the table from the database while DELETE removes records from the table (a) and (b) are both incorrect. The correct answer is (c) because DROP eliminates the table and DELETE empties the table.

178

9.) Defining the new column as NULL will not satisfy the requirement that each product have a friendly name so (b) and (c) will not work here. Not assigning a default value when adding the field will cause an error because of the records that already exist so (d) will not work either. The correct answer is (a) because it will require each record to have a friendly name and assign the existing records something that could be changed later with little effort.

Bug Catcher Game

To play the Bug Catcher game run the BugCatcher_Chapter7.pps from the BugCatcher folder of the companion files. You can obtain these files from the www.Joes2Pros.com web site.

Chapter 8. Stored Procedures

One of my fondest childhood memories is that of my father building a tree house with me. That was my first true practice with real tools. Using an actual hammer and nails was far superior to just grabbing the nearest rock. My aim and efficiency got better with each use as I figured out my swing. Soon I was able to brag about getting a nail to go flush into the wood using four or fewer swings – AND with no misses or bent nails!

Compare the first swing of your hammer with the first run of a brand new SQL Server query. Behind the scenes, SQL Server evaluates the new query and attempts to guess the fastest way to accomplish it. Each time it runs, it gets faster. Code simply saved as a script won't retain the execution history and optimization. However, if you save your code as a *stored procedure* instead of a script, the preserved execution history and optimization are quite beneficial. This chapter explores the value of saving your code as a stored procedure.

READER NOTE: *Please run the script Chapter8.0SetupAll.sql in order to follow along with the examples in the first section of this chapter. The setup scripts for this book are posted at Joes2Pros.com.*

Creating Stored Procedures

Creating our first stored procedure will be simply creating a query and then giving it a name. Oftentimes this will be a query you intend to reuse. Using the following query, we can find all JProCo employees who work in Washington:

```
SELECT E.FirstName, E.LastName,
L.City, L.[State]
FROM Employee E
INNER JOIN Location L
ON E.LocationID = L.LocationID
WHERE L.[State] = 'WA'
```

This query gets all Washington employees. Knowing what it does helps you to come up with an intuitive name. Let's create a stored procedure called GetWashingtonEmployees that is built around this query.

Put the CREATE PROCEDURE statement before the name you wish to give it and follow with the keyword AS right before the query begins. Just use the code you see in Figure 8.1 and run the code to create the new procedure.

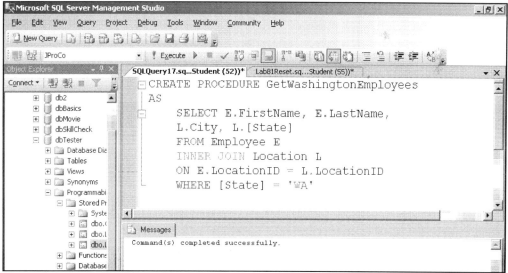

Figure 8.1 The GetWashingtonEmployees stored procedure is created, but not yet executed.

Executing Stored Procedures

The stored procedure was successfully created. Now it's ready for use and reuse. To execute a stored procedure, use the EXEC statement followed by the stored procedure's name (Figure 8.2).

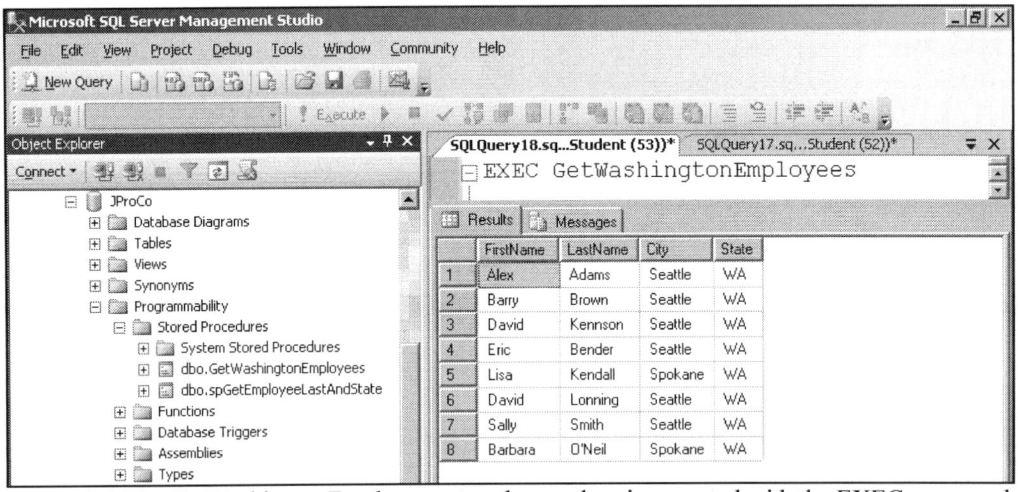

Figure 8.2 The GetWashingtonEmployees stored procedure is executed with the EXEC command.

Let's try that again with slightly different code that will get employees *not* working in Washington. We create GetNonWashingtonEmployees by using the following code:

```
CREATE PROCEDURE GetNONWashingtonEmployees
AS
    SELECT E.FirstName, E.LastName,
    L.City, L.[State]
    FROM Employee E
    INNER JOIN Location L
    ON E.LocationID = L.LocationID
    WHERE L.[State] != 'WA'
```

The word *procedure* is a long one to type repeatedly, so you have the option of shortening your first line to use the following code:

```
CREATE PROC GetNONWashingtonEmployees
```

To call this procedure, use the EXEC command (Figure 8.3).

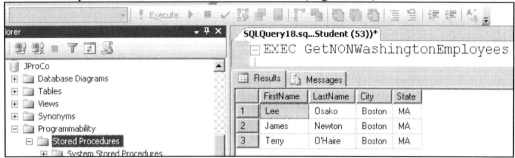

Figure 8.3 The GetNONWashingtonEmployees stored procedure is executed with the EXEC command.

Lab 8.1 Stored Procedures

Lab Prep: Before you can begin the lab you must have SQL Server installed and have run the Chapter8.1SetupAll.sql script.

Skill Check 1: Create a stored procedure in JProCo called GetOvernightProducts that shows all the Overnight-Stay records from the CurrentProducts table. Your screen should resemble Figure 8.4 when you're done.

ProductID	ProductName	RetailPrice	OriginationDate	ToBeDeleted	Category
2	Underwater Tour 2 Days West Coast	110.6694	2007-10-03 23:43:22.813	0	Overnight-Stay
8	Underwater Tour 2 Days East Coast	145.5462	2005-06-11 09:52:12.910	0	Overnight-Stay
14	Underwater Tour 2 Days Mexico	189.1062	2008-02-22 23:42:31.903	0	Overnight-Stay
20	Underwater Tour 2 Days Canada	154.053	2006-10-30 10:10:51.630	0	Overnight-Stay
26	Underwater Tour 2 Days Scandinavia	209.0124	2005-05-26 10:01:01.373	0	Overnight-Stay
38	History Tour 2 Days East Coast	192.8862	2005-07-05 06:15:19.480	0	Overnight-Stay
50	History Tour 2 Days Canada	203.9166	2006-06-13 01:47:12.853	0	Overnight-Stay
56	History Tour 2 Days Scandinavia	201.123	2004-02-22 07:37:52.607	0	Overnight-Stay
62	Ocean Cruise Tour 2 Days West Coast	220.3938	2006-11-19 13:56:26.517	0	Overnight-Stay
68	Ocean Cruise Tour 2 Days East Coast	111.348	2008-09-21 21:07:09.723	0	Overnight-Stay
74	Ocean Cruise Tour 2 Days Mexico	58.6818	2006-01-19 03:10:17.813	0	Overnight-Stay
80	Ocean Cruise Tour 2 Days Canada	112.5792	2006-01-15 10:39:59.820	0	Overnight-Stay
86	Ocean Cruise Tour 2 Days Scandinavia	192.915	2002-09-03 13:09:51.850	0	Overnight-Stay
92	Fruit Tasting Tour 2 Days West Coast	154.6794	2004-10-09 01:24:45.163	0	Overnight-Stay
98	Fruit Tasting Tour 2 Days East Coast	125.9856	2005-08-27 01:17:03.407	0	Overnight-Stay
104	Fruit Tasting Tour 2 Days Mexico	143.2746	2007-05-10 08:21:49.353	0	Overnight-Stay
110	Fruit Tasting Tour 2 Days Canada	86.0274	2006-07-14 13:13:34.560	0	Overnight-Stay
116	Fruit Tasting Tour 2 Days Scandinavia	196.8876	2003-11-01 07:22:49.733	0	Overnight-Stay
122	Mountain Lodge 2 Days West Coast	161.1018	2001-09-03 15:07:17.133	0	Overnight-Stay
128	Mountain Lodge 2 Days East Coast	94.8258	2006-09-03 14:58:46.753	0	Overnight-Stay
134	Mountain Lodge 2 Days Mexico	157.3848	2007-04-16 22:30:39.013	0	Overnight-Stay

Figure 8.4 Executing the GetOvernightProducts stored procedure.

Skill Check 2: Create two more stored procedures called GetMediumProducts and GetLongTermProducts. The GetMediumProducts stored procedure should get all products categorized as Medium-Stay from the CurrentProducts table. The GetLongTermProducts should get all products categorized as LongTerm-Stay from the CurrentProducts table.

Answer Code: The SQL code to this lab can be found from the downloadable files named Lab8.1_StoredProcedures.sql.

Stored Procedures - Points to Ponder

1. A script is a file that consists of a series of SQL code with the .sql extension.

2. Stored procedures are also saved SQL statements, but they are saved to SQL Server rather than to their own file.

3. A stored procedure makes it possible for you to save SQL code to your database and give it an easy-to-reference name.

4. The CREATE PROCEDURE statement can be shortened to CREATE PROC.

5. To call a stored procedure, you can use the EXEC *proc-name* statement.

Introducing Variables

Many computer concepts are borrowed from the everyday non-computer world. Perhaps the biggest one we have not yet put a name to is *variables*. Think back to grade school when the teacher handed you a test. In the upper-right corner of the paper was an empty box for a student's name. The teacher did not pre-fill or order the tests with your name on it. The empty box held the space for a variable, and every student would complete that variable by filling the box with his or her own name.

A job application is just a big sheet full of declared empty variables for each individual applicant to set. The employer has declared the variables it wants to see in order to consider you for hire. When you fill out the application, you are setting values to the variables.

This relates in computer terms as well. Since different people want to see their own items based on whom or where they are, we use variables. This section shows you how to pick a variable, set the value, and have the query show records related to what you picked. You have done something similar to this in the first three chapters. At first, people see the use of variables as taking extra steps in writing their queries, but it is worth the work because we can make the same query work for different people without re-coding every query.

Before we use a variable with queries, we need to see how they work on their own. If you wanted to capture someone's first and last names, you will be setting two values. We would likely name these variables after what we want to capture. When you decide what type of information you are going to store, it's time to declare the data type and the name. All variables in SQL begin with the @ or "at symbol."

To declare the @Firstname and @LastName variable to hold variable length characters, use the following code:

```
DECLARE @Firstname varchar
DECLARE @LastName varchar
```

We will use the name John Smith for the above variables. By setting the @Firstname to John and the @LastName to Smith these variables now hold values. Once set, those values can be used in queries or other SQL statements (Figure 8.5).

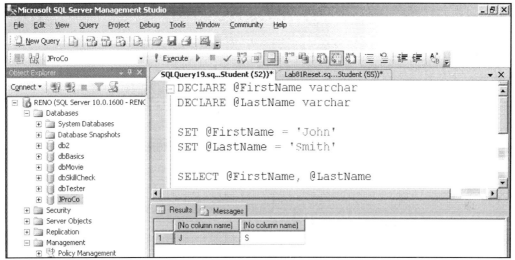

Figure 8.5 The variables have been declared and set. Since varchar size was not specified, it only holds the first character from the SET statement.

This works pretty well except for the size of the variable length characters (varchar). We want to specify that first names hold up to 20 characters and last names up to 30 characters (Figure 8.6).

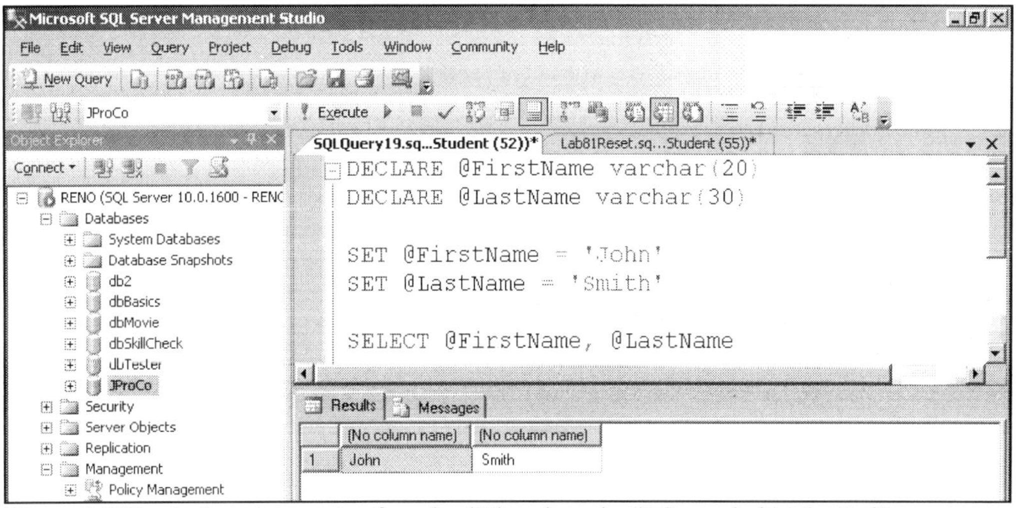

Figure 8.6 The declare statements of varchar(20) and varchar(30) now hold John Smith.

Variables most frequently come in the form of numbers. Let's say you are planning a vacation and the travel company asks for your maximum price limit. Perhaps you are willing to pay no more than $1,000 for your trip. They asked for a @MaxPrice variable and you set it at 1,000 in response. The code for that example can be seen in Figure 8.7.

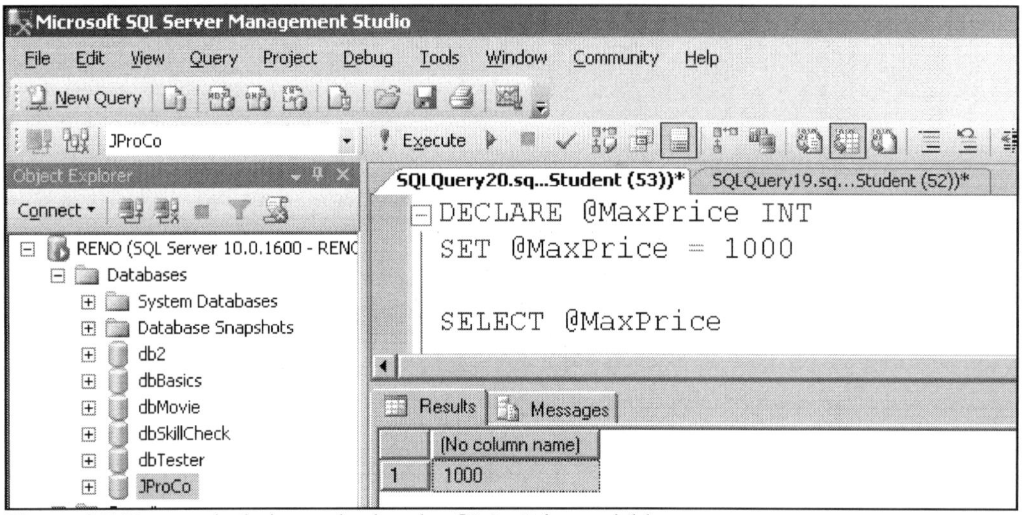

Figure 8.7 You are declaring and using the @MaxPrice variable.

Later they would use this number to help identify good trips for you. The next customer might come in and set $500 as their maximum price. The same variable with a different set of values can change how a company responds. In SQL Server, we use variables the same way we use them in everyday life.

Using Variables with Queries

We know how to write queries and we know how to use variables. Knowing how to use them both to make robust code is an essential skill in the workplace. Why? You can get millions of different requests from customers that are all a bit different. If you would rather write one query with variables versus a million rigid ones (i.e., hard-coded), then this is your answer.

If a customer came in to see all your high-end products, you would want to oblige. What is defined as high-end to this customer is a useful piece of information. They ask to see all products costing more than $1,000 dollars. To pull up this list, you run a query for the RetailPrice to be greater than 1,000 (Figure 8.8).

The next person might want to see all products over $800. To do this, you must re-write part of your query. You would change the WHERE clause as seen in the code below:

```
SELECT *
FROM  CurrentProducts
WHERE RetailPrice > 800
```

The goal is to change your critera without touching any code after the SELECT keyword.

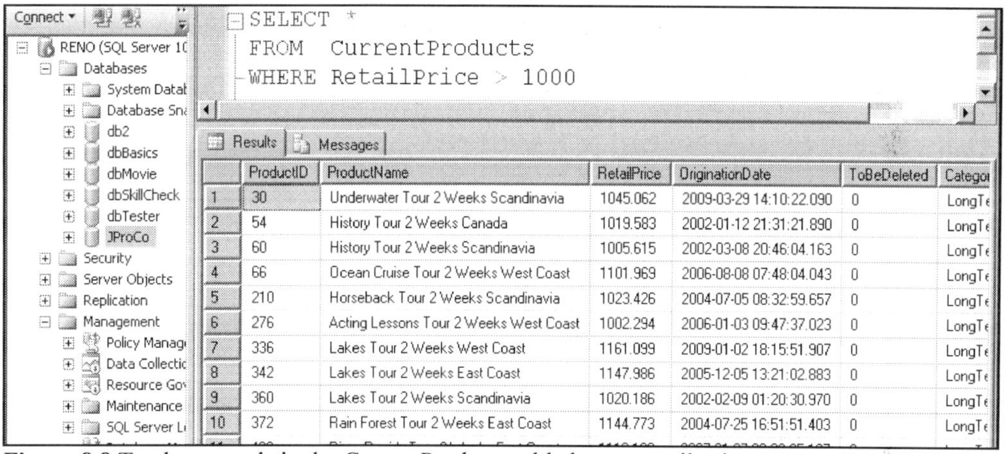

Figure 8.8 Twelve records in the CurrentProducts table have a retail price greater than $1,000.

The solution is to use a variable in your query and set the variable before the SELECT keyword.

The next customer wants to see everything above the $800 minimum. Without changing the actual query itself, you can use a variable to change it to run correctly for the next customer. You would use the following code:

```
DECLARE @MinPrice INT
SET @MinPrice = 800

SELECT *
FROM  CurrentProducts
WHERE RetailPrice > @MinPrice
```

You still had to make a change so this may seem like only a slight improvement. What if it's not you making the change? If the value is passed through an automated web process, this query would work for any e-commerce customer who wanted to see minimum price amounts.

You can use as many variables in your query as you like. For example, consider the following query:

```
SELECT *
FROM  CurrentProducts
WHERE RetailPrice BETWEEN 900 AND 1000
```

This uses two numbers and could easily use two variables. We can say 900 is the minimum price and 1,000 is the maximum price. By declaring the @MinPrice and the @MaxPrice above the query, we can use the variable in the query (Figure 8.9).

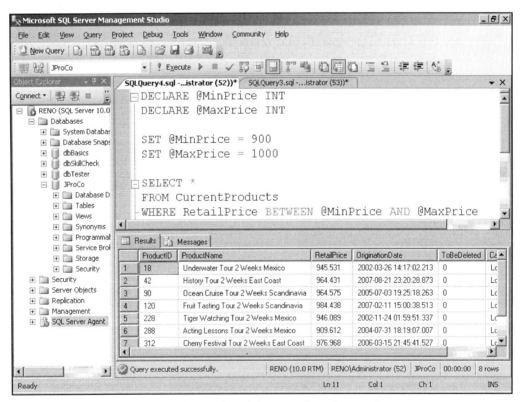

Figure 8.9 Two variables are used to set the minimum and maximum price range.

Variables allow the user to customize the same query for different calling processes. It does this because the criteria can change without having to make any code changes to the query. It may appear a little messy at the top, but with the use of stored procedure parameters we can clean this up significantly.

Variables in SQL 2008

In all the versions of SQL before 2008 you needed to declare the variable on one line and set the value on another. A good example of this is the code below:

```
DECLARE @MinPrice INT
SET @MinPrice = 800

SELECT *
FROM   CurrentProducts
WHERE RetailPrice > @MinPrice
```

New to SQL 2008 you can declare and set the value on the same line as you see in the code example here:

```
DECLARE @MinPrice INT = 800

SELECT *
FROM   CurrentProducts
WHERE RetailPrice > @MinPrice
```

Lab 8.2: Using Variables

Lab Prep: Before you can begin the lab you must have SQL Server installed and run the Chapter8.2SetupAll.sql script.

Skill Check 1: Go to the JProCo database and declare two integers called @MinGrant and @MaxGrant. Set these integers to 20,000 and 40,000, respectively. Use both variables in your criteria to find all grants in the range of 20,000 to 40,000. When you are done, your screen should resemble the Figure 8.10.

```
SELECT *
FROM [Grant]
WHERE Amount BETWEEN @MinGrant AND @MaxGrant
```

	GrantID	GrantName	EmpID	Amount
1	004	Norman's Outreach	NULL	21000.00
2	005	BIG 6's Foundation%	4	21000.00
3	006	TALTA_Kishan International	3	20000.00
4	007	Ben@MoreTechnology.com	10	20000.00
5	008	@Last-U-Can-Help	7	25000.00
6	009	Thank you @.com	11	21500.00

Figure 8.10 Skill Check 1 uses the results of using two integer variables to filter the result set.

Answer Code: The SQL code to this lab can be found from the downloadable files named Lab8.2_UsingVariables.sql.

Using Variables - Points to Ponder

1. Variables are named placeholders for values.

2. Local variables begin with a single @ symbol.

3. You can change the values and results of your query without changing any code inside the query itself by passing it variable(s) and having it do calculations against those variables.

4. You must specify a data type when you declare a variable.

5. You must declare a variable before you set the value.

6. Variables can change like the integer @CurrentTemperature would change throughout the day.

7. Declaring allocates the use of computer memory that will be used when the value is set.

8. Think of DECLARE as reserving your seat ahead of time in a nice restaurant. Think of SET as when you actually sit at the table.

9. The identifier for the variable in the code below is called @MinGrant:

   o **DECLARE @MinGrant int**

10. Reserved words like OUTER can never be used as object identifiers. Keywords like GRANT can be used as object identifiers if they are enclosed in square brackets. However, variables starting with @ can use any reserved word or keyword in combination with the @ symbol.

Parameterized Stored Procedures

When you execute a stored procedure ("SP" or "proc") the code you specify in its definition is run. For example, look at the code below which will create the proc GetEmployeesFromSeattle:

```
CREATE PROC GetEmployeesFromSeattle
AS
    SELECT E.FirstName, E.LastName,
    L.City, L.[State]
    FROM Employee AS E
    INNER JOIN Location AS L
    ON E.LocationID = L.LocationID
    WHERE L.City = 'Seattle'
```

You run – or *invoke* – a stored procedure like this by using EXEC followed by the sproc name (Figure 8.11).

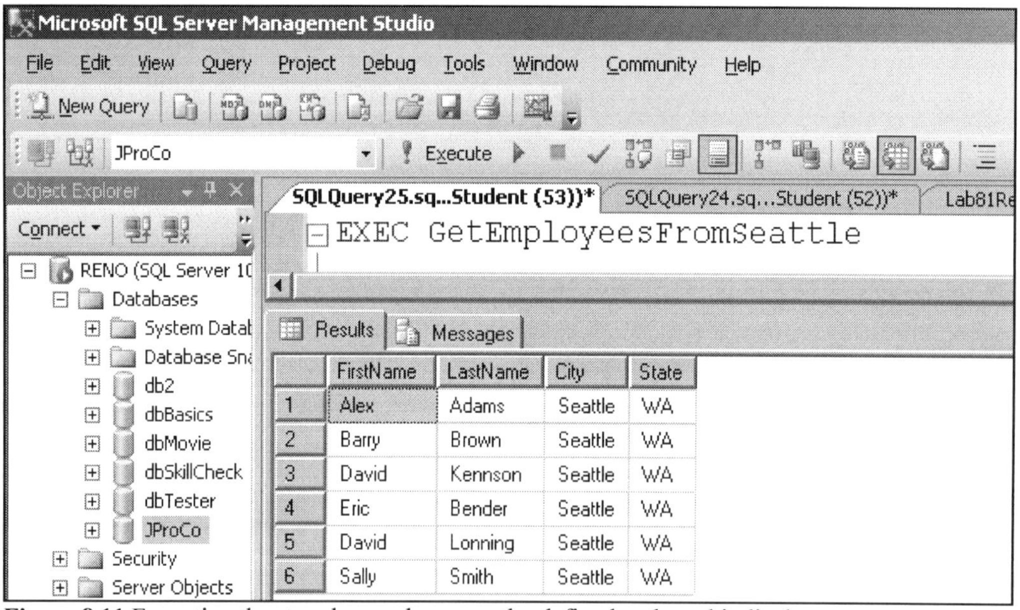

Figure 8.11 Executing the stored procedure runs the defined code and it displays to your screen.

If you wanted to create a stored procedure for each city in the Location table, you are free to do so. Alternatively, we can get one stored procedure to work for each city by using variables. When you define variables in stored procedures they are called *parameters*.

194

Let's pick a descriptive name for a new stored procedure. Its name should imply that we will get the results by city and for each employee in that city. The stored procedure should be ready to accept a variable length of characters up to the longest city name you could expect. To create the GetEmployeesByCity stored procedure, which will accept up to 50 characters, use the following code:

```
CREATE PROC GetEmployeesByCity @City
VARCHAR(50)
AS
    SELECT E.FirstName, E.LastName,
    L.City, L.[State]
    FROM Employee AS E
    INNER JOIN Location AS L
    ON E.LocationID = L.LocationID
    WHERE L.City = @City
```

To call this stored procedure, SQL Server expects you to pass a varchar parameter. Simply put the word 'Boston' in single quotes after the stored procedure name (Figure 8.12).

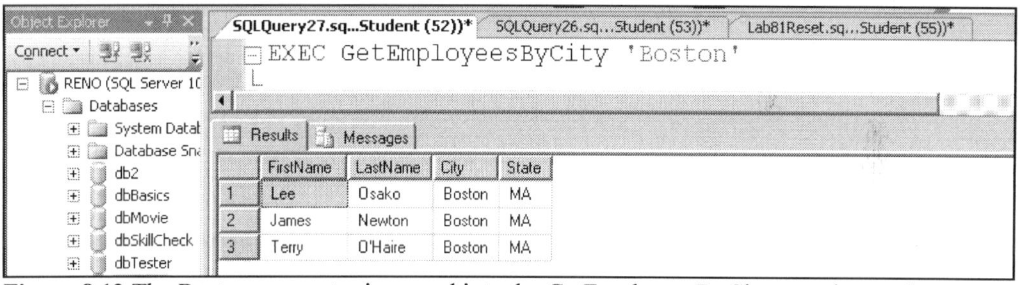

Figure 8.12 The Boston parameter is passed into the GetEmployeesByCity stored procedure to get the Boston employees.

This same stored procedure can be used for all cities. By changing the parameter to 'Spokane' you get the two resulting employees from Spokane.

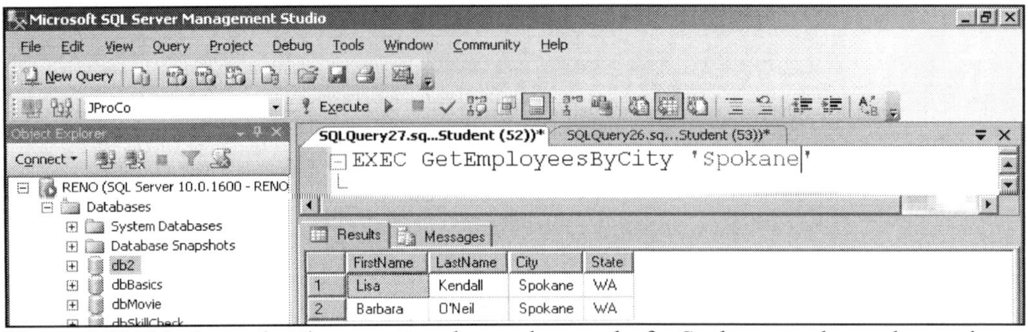

![Microsoft SQL Server Management Studio showing EXEC GetEmployeesByCity 'Spokane' with results for Lisa Kendall and Barbara O'Neil, both in Spokane, WA]

Figure 8.13 This shows that the same stored procedure works for Spokane employees by passing the 'Spokane' parameter.

If you choose a city that does not exist in your database, such as Tampa, then you get no employees (Figure 8.14). This is not an error since you passed a valid varchar. The query critera just found no records as a result.

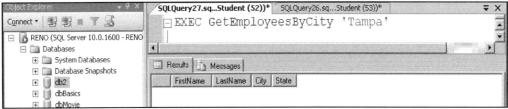

Figure 8.14 Passing a valid parameter with no matching records gives back an empty record set.

If a stored procedure requires a parameter, you must supply it with one. By calling this stored procedure without a parameter, you get an error message (Figure 8.15).

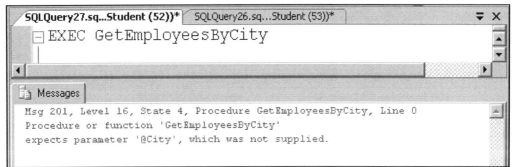

Figure 8.15 The GetEmployeesByCity will not run if you forget to supply the parameter.

Default Parameter Values

You created the GetEmployeesByCity stored procedure weeks ago and want to make a change. To view the code that created the stored procedure, use the sp_helptext with the procedure name (Figure 8.16).

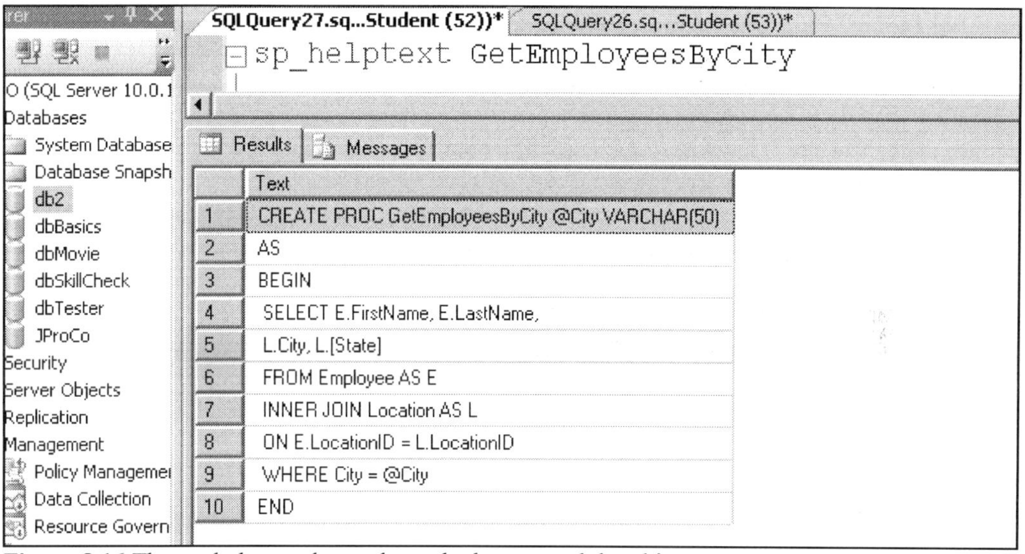

Figure 8.16 The sp_helptext shows the code that created the object.

By copying and pasting these lines into a new query window, you can see the original code that created the stored procedure.

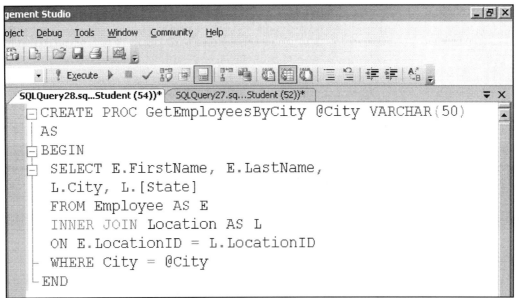

Figure 8.17 The code that created the GetEmployeesByCity stored procedure is displayed after cutting and pasting from the sp_helptext statement.

If you try to create the stored procedure you will get an error. To re-create it, use the following code:

```
DROP PROC GetEmployeesByCity
GO

CREATE PROC GetEmployeesByCity @City
VARCHAR(50)
AS
  SELECT E.FirstName, E.LastName,
  L.City, L.[State]
  FROM Employee AS E
  INNER JOIN Location AS L
  ON E.LocationID = L.LocationID
  WHERE City = @City
```

We want to make one change. If the caller of the stored procedure does not specify a city, then the city value should default to Seattle. Simply set the Seattle value with the following code:

```
DROP PROC GetEmployeesByCity
GO

CREATE PROC GetEmployeesByCity @City
VARCHAR(50)='Seattle'
AS
 SELECT E.FirstName, E.LastName,
 L.City, L.[State]
 FROM Employee AS E
 INNER JOIN Location AS L
 ON E.LocationID = L.LocationID
 WHERE City = @City
```

This tells the stored procedure to use Seattle unless the caller of the stored procedure uses another value. Test this stored procedure by omitting the parameter (Figure 8.18).

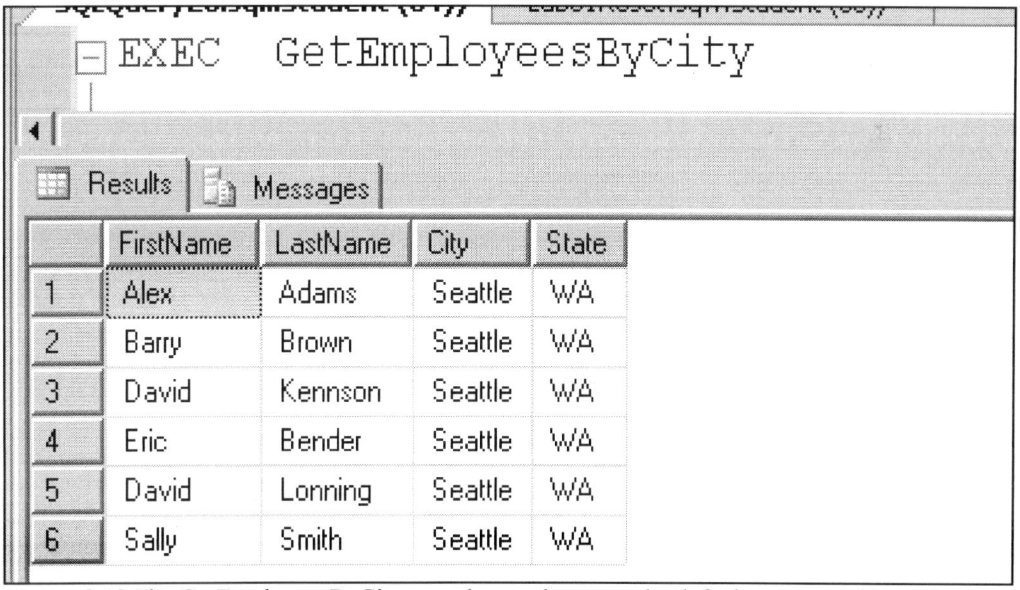

	FirstName	LastName	City	State
1	Alex	Adams	Seattle	WA
2	Barry	Brown	Seattle	WA
3	David	Kennson	Seattle	WA
4	Eric	Bender	Seattle	WA
5	David	Lonning	Seattle	WA
6	Sally	Smith	Seattle	WA

Figure 8.18 The GetEmployeesByCity stored procedure uses the default parameter if you don't supply one.

Notice it still uses a city parameter of Seattle that was self-supplied. If a stored procedure is most often run with the same parameter, you can save the calling code some work. Seattle can now be called on by either of the code choices below:

```
EXEC GetEmployeesByCity
EXEC GetEmployeesByCity 'Seattle'
```

Lab 8.3: Stored Procedure Parameters

Lab Prep: Before you can begin the lab you must have SQL Server installed and run the Chapter8.3SetupAll.sql script.

Skill Check 1: Create a stored procedure in JProCo called GetProductListByCategory that expects a varchar(50) parameter called @Category and returns the ProductID, ProductName and RetailPrice for all products in the category specified. Run and test your code and call on this stored procedure by passing it 'No-Stay' and expect 80 records. Your screen should resemble Figure 8.19.

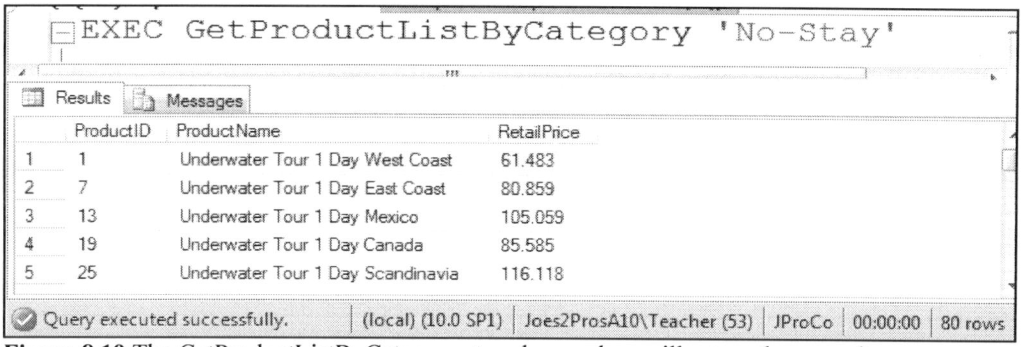

```
EXEC GetProductListByCategory 'No-Stay'
```

	ProductID	ProductName	RetailPrice
1	1	Underwater Tour 1 Day West Coast	61.483
2	7	Underwater Tour 1 Day East Coast	80.859
3	13	Underwater Tour 1 Day Mexico	105.059
4	19	Underwater Tour 1 Day Canada	85.585
5	25	Underwater Tour 1 Day Scandinavia	116.118

Query executed successfully. (local) (10.0 SP1) | Joes2ProsA10\Teacher (53) | JProCo | 00:00:00 | 80 rows

Figure 8.19 The GetProductListByCategory stored procedure will return these results.

Skill Check 2: Create a stored procedure in JProCo called GetGrantsByEmployee that expects a varchar(50) parameter called @LastName and returns the GrantName, Amount, EmpID, FirstName and LastName for all grants found by that employee. The GrantName and Amount will come from the [Grant] table. The EmpID, Firstname and LastName fields will come from the Employee table. Run and test your code by using 'Lonning' as your parameter. Your screen should resemble Figure 8.20.

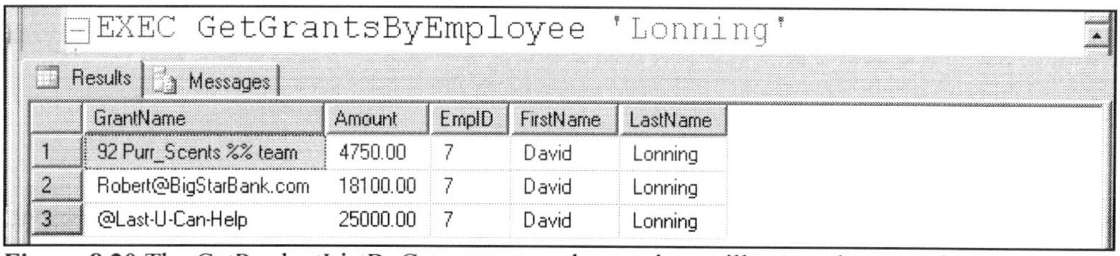

```
EXEC GetGrantsByEmployee 'Lonning'
```

	GrantName	Amount	EmpID	FirstName	LastName
1	92 Purr_Scents %% team	4750.00	7	David	Lonning
2	Robert@BigStarBank.com	18100.00	7	David	Lonning
3	@Last-U-Can-Help	25000.00	7	David	Lonning

Figure 8.20 The GetProductListByCategory stored procedure will return these results.

Answer Code: The SQL code to this lab can be found from the downloadable files named Lab8.3_StoredProcedureParameters.sql.

Stored Procedure Parameters - Points to Ponder

1.   Stored procedures can take parameters.

2.   The code within a stored procedure treats the parameter as a variable.

3.   The declaration of a parameter in a stored procedure is implicit. This means you do not need to use the DECLARE statement.

4.   Once a stored procedure is designed to use a parameter, it must use an explicit or default parameter during execution.

5.   To set stored procedures to have default parameter values, you use the = sign and the value after the parameter declaration.

Chapter Glossary

Datatype: A safety mechanism on a field that allows only the correct type of data to be entered. For example, an integer data type will not let you enter your name. You may enter only numbers with no decimals.

Declare: Alocates the use of computer memory that will be used when the value is set.

Default Parameter: A value chosen if one is not explicitly specified.

EXECUTE or EXEC: Command used to execute a stored procedure.

Parameter: When you define variables in that are passed into stored procedures they are called *parameters*.

Stored Procedure: A set of defined, precompiled SQL statements stored on a SQL Server.

Variables: Named placeholders for re-use in code.

Review Quiz

1.) A variable in SQL begins with which character?

O a.   %
O b.   *
O c.   @
O d.   #

2.) What is the proper way to declare an integer variable named Minimum?

O a.   DECLARE *Minimum INT
O b.   DECLARE @Minimum INT
O c.   DECLARE INT *Minimum
O d.   DECLARE INT @Minimum

3.) How is a script different from a stored procedure?

O a.   Stored Procedures are saved code. Scripts have no code inside them.
O b.   Scripts are saved code. Stored Procedures have no code inside them.
O c.   Scripts are saved to a file, stored procedures as saved to the SQL datafile.
O d.   Stored Procedures are saved to a file, scripts as saved to the SQL datafile.

4.) How do you execute a stored procedure?

O a.   Double-click the stored procedure's name.
O b.   Run the SQL statement EXEC *StoredProcedureName.*
O c.   Use the SQL setup.exe file.

5.) What family of language statements do you use to create a stored procedure?

O a.   DDL
O b.   DML
O c.   DCL

6.) You want to create a stored procedure called GetWagesByManager that takes a parameter called EmpID. What would be the first line of your statement?

O a.   CREATE PROC GetWagesByManager @EmpID INT
O b.   CREATE PROC @EmpID INT AS GetWagesByManager
O c.   CREATE PROC GetWagesByManager WHERE @EmpID = EmpID INT

Answer Key

1.) Since variables in SQL begin with the @ character (a), (b) and (d) are incorrect. The correct answer is (c) because all variable in SQL begin with the @ character.

2.) The proper syntax is DECLARE @*variablename datatype* so (a), (c), and (d) are all incorrect. The statement in (b) is using the correct syntax.

3.) Both stored procedures and scripts are saved SQL code so (a) and (b) are incorrect. The difference between the two is that stored procedures are saved to the SQL data file while scripts are saved to a file system file making (d) incorrect too. Scripts are saved to a file while stored procedures are saved the SQL data file so (c) is the correct answer.

4.) Double-clicking the stored procedure's name will only expand that node so (a) is incorrect. The SQL setup.exe file is used to install SQL Server components so (c) is also wrong. Since running the SQL statement EXEC *StoredProcedureName* will execute a stored procedure (b) is the correct answer.

5.) The CREATE statement is a member of the Data Definition Language (DDL) of SQL so both (b) and (c) are incorrect. Because the CREATE statement is used to define new objects, it belongs to the Data Definition Language making (a) the correct answer.

6.) The correct syntax for creating stored procedure is CREATE PROC *StoredProcedureName @VariableName datatype* making (b) and (c) both wrong. Since the correct syntax for creating a stored procedure is CREATE PROC *StoredProcedureName @VariableName datatype* (a) is correct.

Bug Catcher Game

To play the Bug Catcher game run the BugCatcher_Chapter8.pps from the BugCatcher folder of the companion files. You can obtain these files from the www.Joes2Pros.com web site.

Chapter 9. Transaction Control Language (TCL)

There are several rules that systems like SQL Server must measure up to before they can be called a Relational Database Management System (RDBMS). The *Rule of Durability* means the database needs to safely be on a permanent storage location, such as a hard disk. That way, a reboot (or system or power failure) does not cause the database to lose data. To take it one step further, anytime SQL Server says "Row(s) affected" after a DML statement executes, it confirms the data was accepted and stored. The process to go from a request to a completion is known as a *transaction*. You have some options to control transactions through the use of Transaction Control language or TCL.

READER NOTE: *Please run the script Chapter9.0SetupAll.sql in order to follow along with the examples in the first section of this chapter. The setup scripts for this book are posted at Joes2Pros.com.*

The Transaction Process

First of all, only DML statements run transactions. DDL statements run in batches separated with GO. Notice we don't need to separate transactions with GO.

The simplest way to describe the steps of a transaction is to use an example of updating an existing record into a table. When the insert runs, SQL Server gets the data from storage, such as a hard drive, and loads it into memory and your CPU. The data in memory is changed and then saved to the storage device. Finally, a message is sent confirming the rows that were affected.

This is an oversimplification of the real checks and steps that happen under the hood, but that is the basic principle. Until the change is stored or saved, the transaction is considered incomplete. During the time the record has been changed in memory, but not yet committed to storage, it is known as a "dirty" record. While you are making a change to a record, no other process can access that record until the change is committed to storage. For example, the following two statements will not run at the same time:

```
UPDATE Location SET Street = '123 First Ave'
WHERE LocationID = 1

UPDATE Location SET Street = '199 First Blvd'
WHERE LocationID = 1
```

The first statement locks the record and the second update waits for the lock to finish. This usually takes just a fraction of a second. Each of the statements above is its own auto committed transaction. By default each DML statement is a transaction.

Explicit Transactions

Explicit transactions are something you do every day. When you're at a cashier paying to fill up your car with fuel, you're completing an explicit transaction. The process involves two main steps: You pay for the fuel *and* you fill your tank with fuel. Both steps must be completed for an explicit transaction to occur.

An explicit transaction is one where all events of the transaction either happen together or they don't take place at all. If you don't pay money, you won't receive fuel. If your credit card is approved, you get fuel.

When you transfer money from savings to checking, you are doing another explicit transaction. A transfer from savings to checking is actually two separate events. If you transfer $500 to checking, you expect to see a $500 withdrawal from savings and a $500 deposit to checking. Your bank would not call you the next day to say they successfully withdrew $500 from savings, but did not credit your checking account.

Would you say one out of two is not bad? No, because either the money was transferred or not. The code below is vulnerable to failure during a transfer from savings to checking:

```
UPDATE SavAccount SET Balance = Balance - 500
WHERE CustomerID = 18568

UPDATE CkAccount SET Balance = Balance + 500
WHERE CustomerID = 18568
```

If the SQL Server fails after the first update, but before the second one, you would have data loss. You need to specify that both statements above either succeeded or failed as one unit. The problem is that each update statement is usually its own transaction.

The above is a very simplified example of a transaction. Naturally a bank would have more code in place than just what is seen here. For example they might have a condition to check for a negative balance and purposefully abort the transaction if there are any negative numbers. This type of logic can be found in the SQL Programming Joes 2 Pros book. You can put many DML statements into one transaction if they need to run together. To make sure the two statements above run as an explicit transaction, use the following code:

```
BEGIN TRAN

UPDATE SavAccount SET Balance = Balance - 500
WHERE CustomerID = 18568
UPDATE CkAccount SET Balance = Balance + 500
WHERE CustomerID = 18568

COMMIT TRAN
```

A failure taking place before the COMMIT TRAN can mean the records never get committed to permanent storage. The TRAN keyword is short for transaction.

Lab 9.1: Explicit Transactions

Lab Prep: Before you can begin the lab you must have SQL Server installed and run the Chapter9.1SetupAll.sql script.

Skill Check 1: An agreement between charity conglomerate foundations Norman's Outreach and new donor Seasons Outreach means they never give to the same organization. Seasons Outreach has approached you about a grant contribution of $85,000. They noticed you already have one from Norman's Outreach and thus can't donate. Both foundations have agreed that if you delete the Norman's Outreach record, you may enter the following values for a new grant:

- GrantID: 011
- GrantName: Seasons Outreach
- EmployeeID: NULL
- Amount: 85,000.00

Create two DML statements. One is to delete Norman's Outreach and another is to create Seasons Outreach. Make sure the insert and delete statements succeed or fail as one unit. Use an explicit transaction. When you are done, run a query on the [Grant] table. Your query window should look like Figure 9.1.

```
SELECT * FROM [Grant]
```

	GrantID	GrantName	EmpID	Amount
1	001	92 Purr_Scents %% team	7	4750.00
2	002	K_Land fund trust	2	15750.00
3	003	Robert@BigStarBank.com	7	18100.00
4	011	Seasons Outreach	NULL	85000.00
5	005	BIG 6's Foundation%	4	21000.00
6	006	TALTA_Kishan International	3	20000.00
7	007	Ben@MoreTechnology.com	10	20000.00
8	008	@Last-U-Can-Help	7	25000.00
9	009	Thank you @.com	11	21500.00
10	010	Call Mom @Com	5	7500.00

Figure 9.1 Seasons Outreach has replaced Norman's in a transaction.

Answer Code: The SQL code to this lab can be found from the downloadable files named Lab9.1_ExplicitTransactions.sql.

Explicit Transactions - Points to Ponder

1. A transaction is a group of SQL statements treated as a single unit. Transactions ensure data integrity.

2. Transaction statements either all execute together or they don't at all.

3. If one statement can't run then the transaction is not committed.

4. A failed statement in a transaction means all data in the intermediate state gets discarded and none of the records will be committed.

5.   The BEGIN TRANSACTION statement marks the beginning of a group of SQL statements in a transaction.

6.   The COMMIT TRANSACTION marks the end of the transaction and saves all the changes to SQL's permanent storage.

Using Commit and Rollback

By putting a series of DML statements between the BEGIN TRAN and COMMIT TRAN you ensure all statements succeed or fail as a single unit. Any failure means the final commit is never reached because the transaction is aborted. The records are never saved for storage in a database.

Encountering an error is one way to cause a running transaction to discard all of its changes. When the transaction does this, it is called *rolling back the transaction*. Sometimes you will intentionally rollback a transaction through code logic. The code below does a rollback partway through an explicit transaction:

```
BEGIN TRAN

UPDATE SavAccount SET Balance = Balance - 500
WHERE CustomerID = 1856

IF( (SELECT Balance FROM SavAccount WHERE
CustomerID = 1856) < 0)
ROLLBACK TRAN

UPDATE CkAccount SET Balance = Balance + 500
WHERE CustomerID = 1856

COMMIT TRAN
```

In the example above, we deducted $500 from savings. If the customer only had $400 in savings, then they would be overdrawn. The IF statement checks for a negative number before crediting the full $500 to checking. The transaction is rolled back and neither of the updates is committed to the database.

The first update takes the data and puts it into an intermediate state, not a permanent state. The second update is never called upon if a negative balance occurs.

Transaction Locking

While a DML statement is changing data, no other process can access that data. This is because the data has a lock until it is completed. The waiting process is usually a few milliseconds at most.

We can slow down a simple transaction to update the price of ProductID 1 to $75.95. Normally this would take about 10 milliseconds. Now it can take up a full two minutes, 30 seconds with the following code:

```
BEGIN TRAN

UPDATE CurrentProducts SET RetailPrice = 75.95
WHERE ProductID = 1

WAITFOR DELAY '00:02:30'

COMMIT TRAN
```

The two statements above will take a combined two minutes, 30 seconds to complete. No other process will be able to use ProductID 1. Run the code above and then open another query window using the code below:

```
SELECT * FROM CurrentProducts WHERE ProductID = 1
```

Notice this very simple query appears to be running. In reality, it is waiting for the lock on ProductID 1 to be released. It does not know if the price is $65 or $75. The query does not want to give you an answer until it either commits or fails.

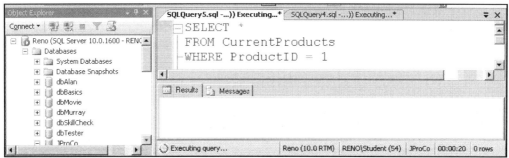

Figure 9.2 The select statement is waiting for the update statement to release the lock.

Table Hints (locking method)

For every data change to a table there is a brief moment where the change is made in the intermediate state, but is not committed. During this time, any other DML statement needing that data waits until the lock is released. This is a safety feature so that SQL Server evaluates only official data.

Some transactions take time and then rollback. In other words, the changes never become official data and in essence never took place. The example below shows a transaction that takes 15 seconds and then rolls back:

```
BEGIN TRAN

  UPDATE dbo.Employee
  SET HireDate = '1/1/1992'
  WHERE EmployeeID = 1


  WAITFOR DELAY '00:00:15'


ROLLBACK TRAN
```

If employee #1 was really hired in 1989 and you run the above code, you have incorrect data for fifteen seconds in the intermediate state. During those fifteen seconds, if a 401K vesting program ran an evaluation on all employees hired before 1990, the process would wrongfully overlook employee #1. The safety catch is the 401K process would wait until this transaction is done in order to get the official data.

A great deal of data can be changed in the intermediate state, but never get committed. *Locking* prevents other processes from making decisions on dirty data. The result is that only committed data is used to isolate transactions. The drawback is that some processes that could run instantly now have to wait. Locking lowers the level of *concurrency*, which is the ability to allow software to run many processes at the same time.

A Select query can now pull out any record being changed in the intermediate state. You could say that a query will not show any dirty records because all transactions are isolated from each other. By changing one record in your

CurrentProducts table, a query looking for records from that table will have to wait (Figure 9.3).

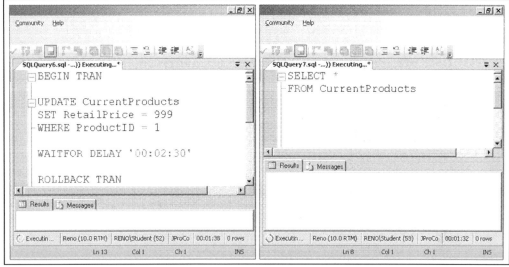

Figure 9.3 The update statement was executed first and puts data into an intermediate state. The query on the right waits for the transaction to be committed.

In Figure 9.3 we see the update statement has been running for one minute, 38 seconds and the query was started six seconds later. The committed RetailPrice is $75 and the price in the intermediate state is $999 for the next two and a half minutes. Upon completion, the price never changed. The query on the right waits until the data becomes official. The downside is the select query takes much longer to run.

If you don't want the query on the right to wait, you have some choices. If you are fine with the query on the right accessing dirty data, you can issue a locking hint for the query. The following code tells the query to run without waiting:

```
SELECT *
FROM CurrentProducts (READUNCOMMITTED)
```

In the code example from Figure 9.4, the query would run without waiting. The result is the query would show the RetailPrice value of $999.00 (Figure 9.4).

The query shows ProductID 1 to have a value in the RetailPrice field of $999.00 in the result set. The $999.00 was never a committed value in the database. Any evaluation of data running this query could give you a false report.
You run the same query three minutes later and get a different result. This is despite the fact that the table may not have really changed at all in that time.

```
SELECT *
FROM CurrentProducts (READUNCOMMITTED)
```

ProductID	ProductName	RetailPrice	OriginationDate	ToBeDeleted	Cate
1	Underwater Tour 1 Day West Coast	999.00	2006-08-11 13:33:09.957	1	No-
2	Underwater Tour 2 Days West Coast	110.6694	2007-10-03 23:43:22.813	0	Ove
3	Underwater Tour 3 Days West Coast	184.449	2009-05-09 16:07:49.900	0	Mec
4	Underwater Tour 5 Days West Coast	245.932	2006-03-04 04:59:06.600	0	Mec
5	Underwater Tour 1 Week West Co...	307.415	2001-07-18 19:20:11.400	0	Lon
6	Underwater Tour 2 Weeks West C...	553.347	2008-06-30 20:40:38.760	0	Lon
7	Underwater Tour 1 Day East Coast	80.859	2007-04-07 08:25:43.233	1	No-

Query executed successfully. | Reno (10.0 RTM) | RENO\Student (53) | JProCo | 00:00:00 | 480 rows

Figure 9.4 The query runs without waiting for committed data.

The *READUNCOMMITTED* table hint allows the query to show uncommitted (dirty) data. The advantage is the query runs much faster. This is a common solution for evaluation queries that don't need to be exact. A common example is just looking to see how many records are in a table as in the query below:

```
SELECT COUNT(*)
FROM CurrentProducts (READUNCOMMITTED)
```

You know this result changes over time and is used for general trends. In this case, SQL Server allows the query to run without waiting.

The following statements are equivalent and show a shorter way of accomplishing the same result:

```
SELECT COUNT(*) FROM CurrentProducts (READUNCOMMITTED)
SELECT COUNT(*) FROM CurrentProducts (NOLOCK)
```

Lab 9.2: Table Hints

Lab Prep: Before you can begin the lab you must have SQL installed and run the Chapter9.2SetupAll.sql script.

Skill Check 1: Write a transaction that updates all grant amount values to one dollar. Include a delay of three minutes as the second step of the transaction. End the transaction with a ROLLBACK TRAN. Open a new query window and query the Grant table for all records in the intermediate state. When you are done, your screen will look like Figure 9.5.

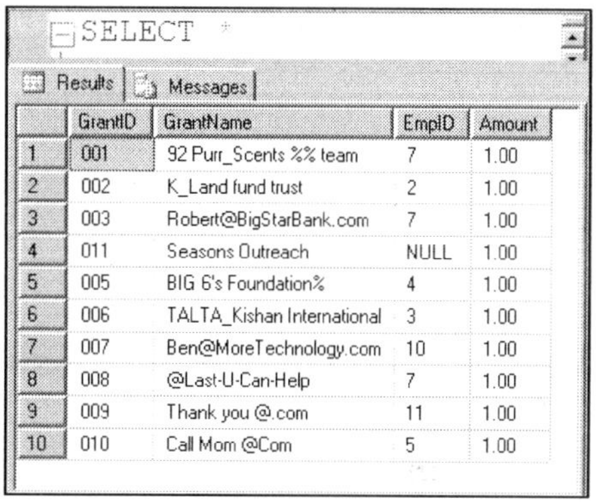

	GrantID	GrantName	EmpID	Amount
1	001	92 Purr_Scents %% team	7	1.00
2	002	K_Land fund trust	2	1.00
3	003	Robert@BigStarBank.com	7	1.00
4	011	Seasons Outreach	NULL	1.00
5	005	BIG 6's Foundation%	4	1.00
6	006	TALTA_Kishan International	3	1.00
7	007	Ben@MoreTechnology.com	10	1.00
8	008	@Last-U-Can-Help	7	1.00
9	009	Thank you @.com	11	1.00
10	010	Call Mom @Com	5	1.00

Note: If you wait three minutes and rerun the same query, you will see the original amount never changed.

Figure 9.5 A query for all grants runs instantly and gets dirty records in the intermediate state.

Answer Code: The SQL code to this lab can be found from the downloadable files named Lab9.2_TableHints.sql.

Table Hints - Points to Ponder

1. Locking is used to protect changes in your database and lets you know when it's safe to view data.

2. If you want to read dirty data, you can use the READUNCOMMITTED table hint in your query.

3. The NOLOCK and READUNCOMMITTED table hints operate identically. Since NOLOCK is easier to type, it is used more often.

4. The advantage to the NOLOCK or READUNCOMMITTED table hints is your query runs without waiting for another process to release its locks.

Chapter Glossary

Committed: A change to a record that was loaded from the database into memory was successfully saved to the datafile.

Dirty Record: A change to a record that has been loaded from the database into memory and has changed, but has not yet been saved back to the datafile.

Explicit transaction: A group of SQL statements treated where all events of the transaction occur at once or none of them takes place at all.

Intermediate State: The state a record is in after it has been loaded into memory.

Locking: Exclusive use of data in a table to ensure changes occur without conflicts or loss.

NOLOCK: A table hint that allows your query to view data in the intermediate state. NOLOCK means the same as READUNCOMMITTED.

Transaction: A group of actions treated as a single unit to ensure data integrity.

READUNCOMMITTED: A table hint that allows your query to view data in the intermediate state.

Rollback: Data in the intermediate state is discarded.

TCL: Transaction Control Language, or TCL, provides options to control transactions.

TRAN: The TRAN keyword is short for transaction.

Review Quiz

1.) Explicit transactions ensure that all their statements do what?

O a.   Succeed or fail together
O b.   Run faster
O c.   Save data one DML statement at a time

2.) What is a dirty record?

O a.   A record that can't be accepted because it violates the database constraints.
O b.   A record that replaced the original record in permanent storage.
O c.   A record that has been changed, but not yet saved to permanent storage.

3.) If you want to throw away a dirty record, which keyword do you use?

O a.   BEGIN TRAN
O b.   COMMIT TRAN
O c.   ROLLBACK TRAN
O d.   THROWBACK TRAN

4.) What happens when you try to query records in the intermediate state?

O a.   Your query waits until the data is no longer in the intermediate state.
O b.   Your query runs normally.
O c.   Your query splits the results into permanent and intermediate results.

5.) What is the shorter equivalent to the READUNCOMMITTED table hint?

O a.   LOCK
O b.   NOLOCK
O c.   UNLOCK

6.) BEGIN, COMMIT and ROLLBACK are part of which family of language statements?

O a.   DML
O b.   DDL
O c.   DCL
O d.   TCL

Answer Key

1.) Explicit transactions do not affect the speed at which the statements execute so (b) is incorrect. Since auto committed transactions save data one DML statement at a time (c) is also incorrect. Because explicit transactions ensure that all their statements succeed or fail together (a) is the correct answer.

2.) Because a dirty record does not violate any database constraints but is just not committed to permanent storage yet (a) and (b) are both incorrect. A dirty record is a record that has been changed, but not yet saved to permanent storage; therefore (c) is the right answer.

3.) BEGIN TRAN starts an explicit transaction so (a) is incorrect. COMMIT TRAN saves data to permanent storage so (b) is also incorrect. THROWBACK has no special meaning in SQL so (d) is also wrong. To throw away a dirty record use ROLLBACK TRAN making (c) the correct choice.

4.) Since the query may be waiting for data to leave the intermediate state and the results will not contain intermediate results both (b) and (c) are incorrect. Because SQL needs to ensure data integrity your query waits until the data is no longer in the intermediate state so (a) is correct.

5.) Since LOCK has no special meaning in SQL and UNLOCK applies only to SQL Server logins (a) and (c) are both incorrect. The shorter equivalent to the READUNCOMMITTED table hint is NOLOCK making (b) the correct answer.

6.) Because BEGIN, COMMIT and ROLLBACK control Transactions not Data (a), (b) and (c) are all wrong answers. BEGIN, COMMIT and ROLLBACK all control transaction processing so they belong to the TCL family of language statements thus (d) is correct.

Bug Catcher Game

To play the Bug Catcher game run the BugCatcher_Chapter9.pps from the BugCatcher folder of the companion files. You can obtain these files from the www.Joes2Pros.com web site.

Chapter 10. Data Control Language (DCL)

All the chapters up to this point have dealt with creating objects and manipulating data. DML and DDL statements, such as those you've seen in this book, comprise the lion's share of the code you are expected to know for the workplace. When it comes time to hire a new person to work with SQL Server, you need to create an account for them and understand how permissions and security work. This chapter discusses how to set the level of access to SQL Server using Data Control Language (DCL) statements.

READER NOTE: *Please run the script Chapter10.0SetupAll.sql in order to follow along with the examples in the first section of this chapter. The setup scripts for this book are posted at Joes2Pros.com.*

Introduction to Security

Security in SQL Server starts by creating types of accounts such as *logins* and *users*. Since this chapter covers the basics of security, we will focus on SQL logins. It is essential to know how to create logins and then grant or deny them the required permissions. There are different types of logins for different networks and different ways to set security. That subject in itself is an entire book! In this section, we get familiar with the most common security terms.

Securables and Permissions

When Greg logs onto his computer at work and tries to print to the network printer, several things happen. The printer checks its own list of who's who to see if Greg has permission. Most of us are familiar with the term permission. This chapter will add a few other words to your arsenal that will be a help to you in security discussions.

Greg wants access to the printer. The printer does not need access to Greg, but it does need to know who is making the request. Since Greg wants access, he is known as the *principal*. The printer is what he wishes to access, so the printer is known as the *securable*. Permissions control the level of access principals have to securables.

In reality, the Greg principal has no permission. The list of permissions resides with the securable. The printer is the securable and contains a list of principals and permissions. When a match is found, the securable allows its use.

There are many types of principals in SQL Server. The type of principal we will learn about is called a login. Logins will want access to securables such as resources, databases and tables.

Creating SQL Logins

Logins are the principals for the SQL Server security scope. To create logins, you use the CREATE keyword. The following code creates the login named Murray with the ABC password:

```
USE master
GO

CREATE LOGIN Murray
WITH PASSWORD = 'ABC'
```

The code above may or may not work depending on the operating system of your SQL Server. Beginning with SQL Server 2005 (when installed on a Windows 2003 server or higher), SQL Server likes to enforce the same level of password polices that Windows Server is running. Windows Server does not consider passwords secure if they contain only alphabetical characters. If SQL Server is enforcing password complexity, you get an error message (Figure 10.1).

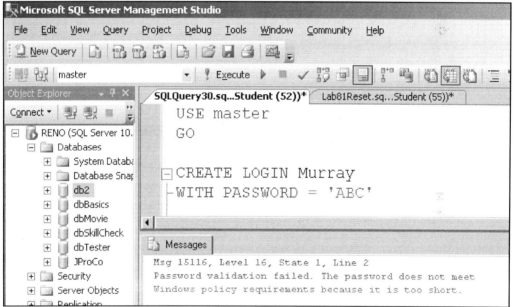

Figure 10.1 SQL will not accept simple passwords by default if installed on Windows 2003 or higher.

Most password complexity requirements call for at least seven characters with at least one numeral and one capital letter. Figure 10.2 creates the Murray login without error.

Once you create it, you can view the new Murray login. Go to your Object Explorer and expand the Security folder to look in the Logins folder. You can see the "Murray" login listed in the Logins folder in Figure 10.2.

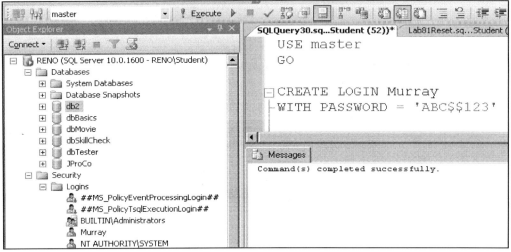

Figure 10.2 The Security node of Object Explorer shows the new Murray login located in the Logins folder.

Currently SQL Server knows about Murray and his password, but no permissions to securables have yet been granted to him. By default, new accounts get public level permissions, which means Murray can login and browse the database list. However, he would have no permissions to open, use or query databases or tables.

Authentication Modes

When you open Management Studio, SQL Server wants to know who you are. One way to do this is with a password like the one given to Murray. If you already logged into Windows with a password, SQL Server can ask Windows for your login token and not ask you again. This is Geek Speak for saying SQL Server can authenticate you or trust that Windows has done that effectively.

In the Windows Authentication mode, logging in with SQL Server passwords will not allow access. Try to log in as Murray using the ABC$$123 password using SQL Server Authentication.

Close Management Studio and get back to a blank desktop. Open Management Studio, but pause at the "Connect to Server" dialog box.

In the Authentication drop down list, choose "SQL Server Authentication" (Figure 10.3).

Figure 10.3 Change your SQL Server Authentication mode using this box.

The Login and Password text boxes are now enabled. Select "Murray" as your login and type "ABC$$123" for your password (Figure 10.4).

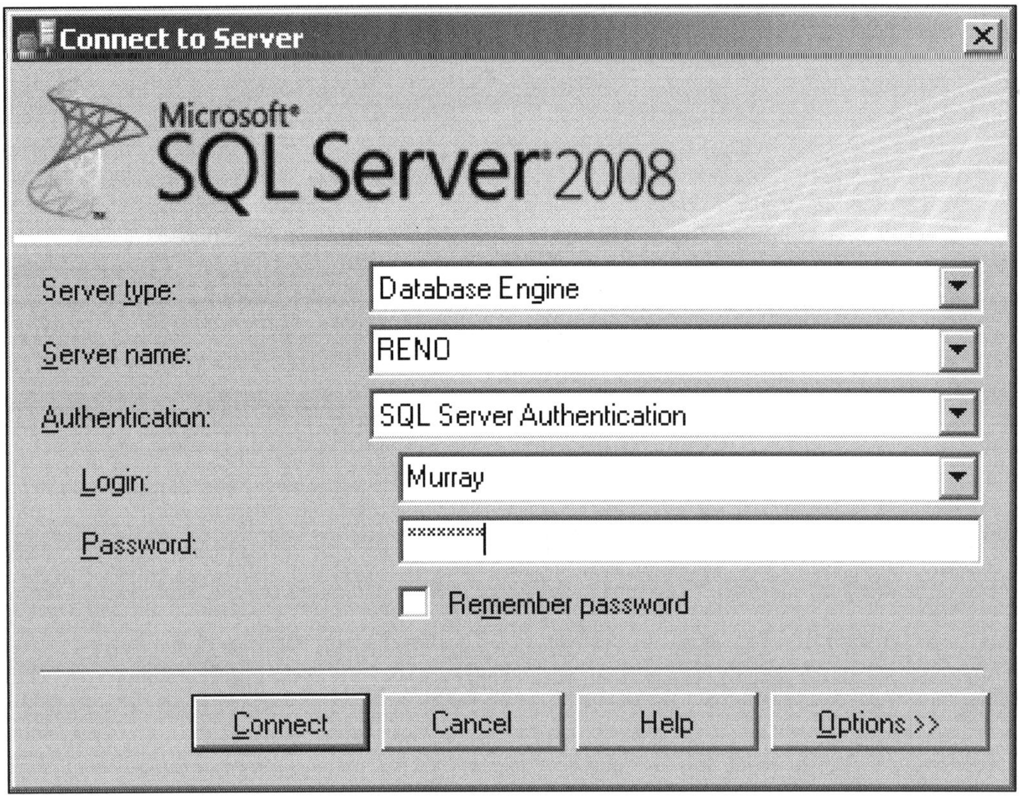

Figure 10.4 Changing to SQL Server Authentication allows you to specify the login and password.

The Login and Password boxes were not enabled previously when Windows Authentication was selected. That's because Windows relayed to SQL Server the credentials you already used when signing into Windows.

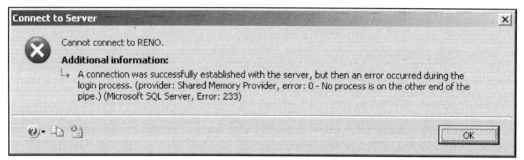

Figure 10.5 The SQL Server Authentication may not work if your SQL Server is not set up to use the right authentication mode.

Now you can hit Connect and attempt to finish your login process. Even after typing in your login and credentials correctly, you may get the error message in Figure 10.5.

Change back to Windows Authentication mode and log back into your SQL Server (Figure 10.6).

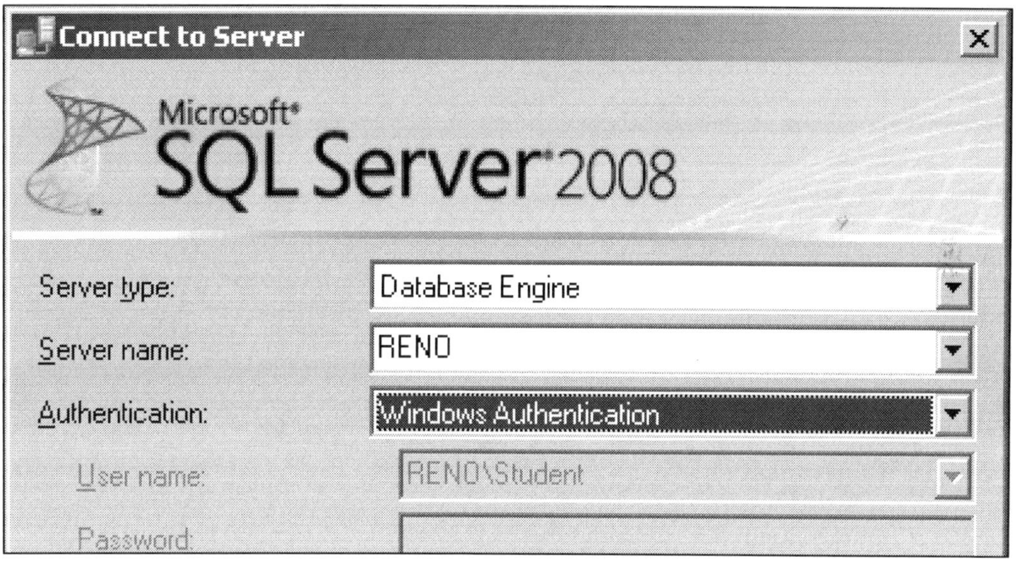

Figure 10.6 Change back to Windows Authentication and log in.

Let's use Object Explorer to access the properties of your SQL Server. Locate the yellow cylinder-shaped server icon at the top of the pane. My server is named Reno. Right-click the icon, then select "properties" at the bottom of the list. Select the Security page and the Server Properties dialog box will come up as seen in Figure 10.7.

SQL Server is often set up to let Windows do all *authentications*. SQL Server will recognize you by your Windows login. If you want SQL Server to only allow Windows to authenticate, you would set the server authentication mode to "Windows Authentication." If you want SQL Server to handle authentication for non-Windows accounts, you would use "SQL Server and Windows Authentication Mode."

The setting shown (Figure 10.7) will not allow SQL Server logins. You can create SQL logins like Murray, but they will not be able to log in where Windows Authentication is required. Now change the mode to "SQL Server and Windows Authentication mode" and click OK. You will need to restart your SQL service to get this change to take effect.

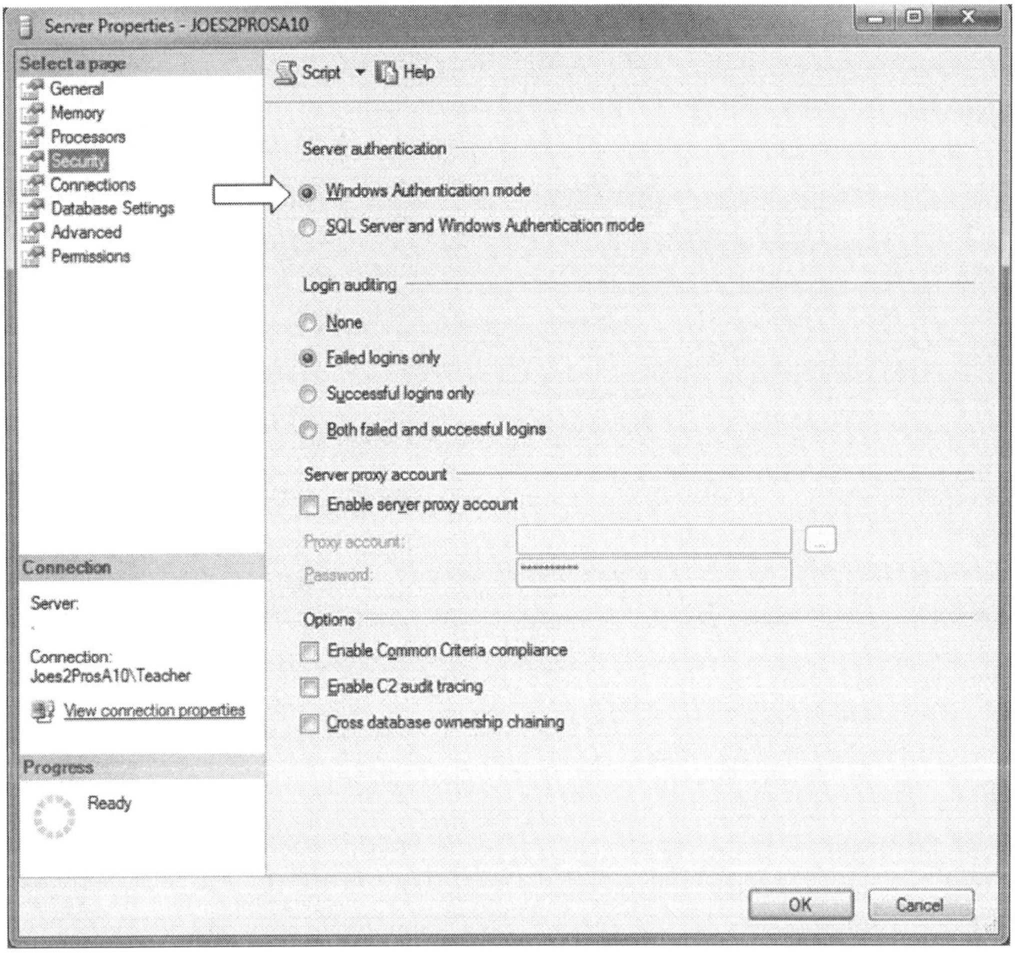

Figure 10.7 The Server Properties page shows server authentication is set to Windows Authentication Mode.

Right-click your server in the Object Explorer, then select Restart. Confirm you want to restart the SQL service by clicking the Yes button (Figure 10.8).

Close completely out of Management Studio and try to log back in as Murray. Notice he can now log into the server. The server level node of the Object Explorer shows Murray is currently logged in.

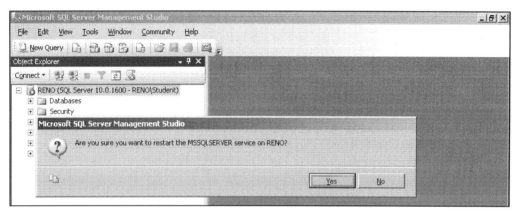

Figure 10.8. After right-clicking the server and choosing Restart, you get a confirmation box.

Murray can currently see the databases on your system, but has no permission to use them.

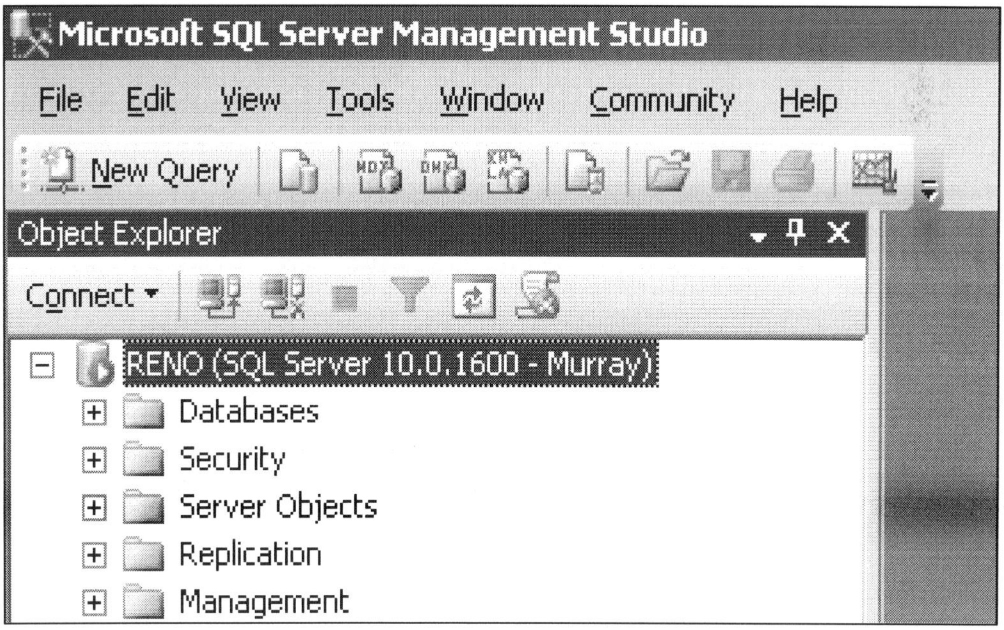

Figure 10.9 The Object Explorer shows Murray is logged into Management Studio.

Dropping SQL Logins

If you wanted to get rid of a login, all you need is the login name. Let's say you created a login named "Bernie" that was created with the following code:

```
CREATE LOGIN Bernie WITH PASSWORD = 'ABC$$123'
```

Time goes by and now Bernie no longer works for your organization, so you want to remove his access to SQL. You can drop his login. The following code would drop the Bernie login:

```
DROP LOGIN Bernie
```

Dropping a login is rare and must be done carefully. Once you drop a login, there is no way to get it back. If you made a mistake and learned that Bernie was actually still with the organization, you would need to recreate a brand new login for him. SQL Server will not allow you to reuse or reinstate the "Bernie" login. When working with logins you no longer need, it is better to disable them than to drop them altogether. To disable the Bernie login, you would use the following code:

```
ALTER LOGIN Bernie DISABLE
```

Lab 10.1: SQL Logins

Lab Prep: Before you can begin the lab you must have SQL Server installed and run the Chapter10.1SetupAll.sql script.

Skill Check 1: Create a login named "Sara" with the password ABC$$123. Open Management Studio as Sara and view all the logins on your system. Don't forget to change your SQL Server to "SQL Server and Windows Authentication," which is also known as mixed authentication. When you're done, your screen will resemble Figure 10.10.

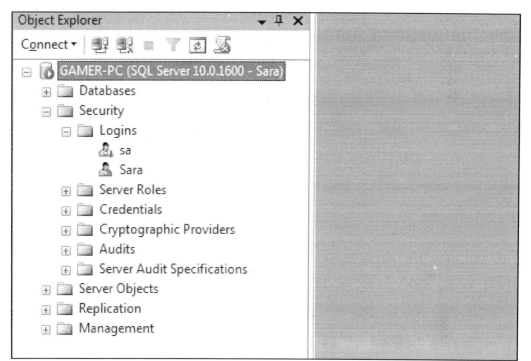

Figure 10.10 The Sara login has been created.

Answer Code: The SQL code to this lab can be found from the downloadable files named Lab10.1_SQLLogins.sql.

SQL Logins - Points to Ponder

1.　To log into SQL Server, you need to create a server-level login.

2.　To create a SQL login, use the CREATE keyword followed by the login information as seen in this example:

　　o　**CREATE LOGIN Sally WITH PASSWORD = 'ABC$$123'**

3.　There are two types of server level logins:

　　o　SQL Logins

　　o　Windows Logins

4.　SQL Server has two authentication modes:

　　o　Windows Authentication mode – Principals who have been authenticated by the Windows operating system will be the only ones able to connect to SQL Server.

　　o　SQL Server and Windows Authentication mode (mixed mode) – Principals pre-authenticated by Windows or logins with a password authenticated by SQL Server will be allowed to log into the server.

5.　SQL Server's default setup is to allow Windows logins that have proper permissions to SQL Server. Allowing SQL logins is optional and can be turned on and off.

6.　Only use "SQL Server and Windows Authentication" mode when you must allow accounts or applications who do not have Windows credentials to connect to SQL Server.

Granting Permissions

In the examples thus far, you have the Murray and Sara logins that SQL Server recognizes. They can log into SQL Server, but can do virtually nothing after that point. If you logged in as Murray and then tried to expand the JProCo database, it would not be accessible (Figure 10.11).

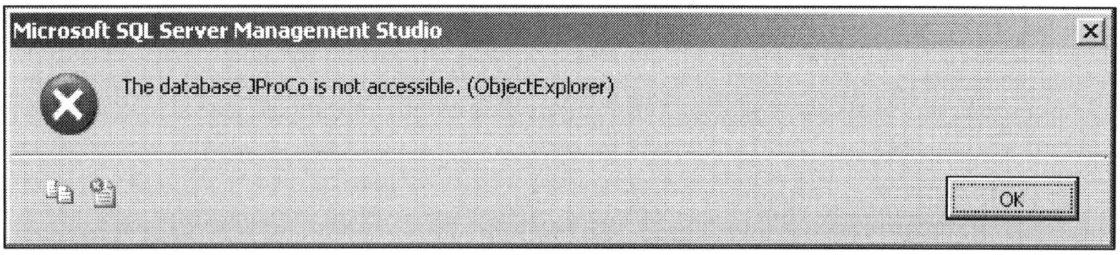

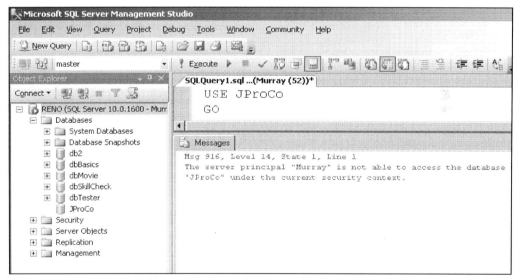

Figure 10.11 When Murray tried to expand the JProCo database in Object Explorer, it was not accessible.

You might try another way to get to JProCo through a query window. Open a new query window and set your context to the JProCo database. You will find the Murray principal does not have the necessary level of security (Figure 10.12).

Figure 10.12 The Murray principal has no access to JProCo through any means.

Murray has access to the master database, but will be unable to access any user databases until appropriate permissions are granted (Figure 10.13).

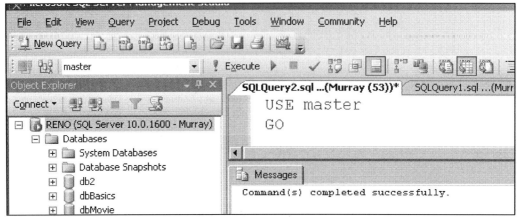

Figure 10.13 While logged in as Murray, you can access the master database.

The master database is a powerful database. From there you can drop other databases. Let's see if Murray has the power to drop the dbBasics database from the master database.

Murray may use the master database context, but not perform any DDL statements to create, alter or drop any objects (Figure 10.14).

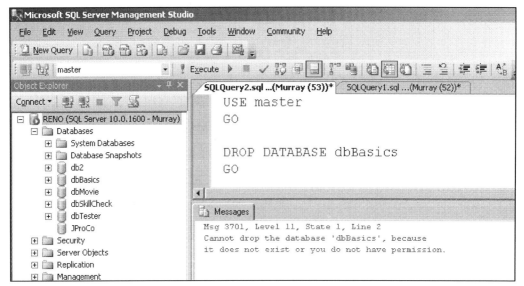

Figure 10.14 Murray does not have permission to alter or drop databases from the server.

JProCo is a securable, and the Murray principal wants some level of access to it. We can change the securable to authorize Murray by giving him permissions. The GRANT keyword adds permission listings to allow principals access to securables.

There are different levels of permissions for each securable. You might want total control for a database while another user just needs to make DDL changes. To grant the Rick login control of the entire server, you would use the following code:

```
USE Master
GO
GRANT CONTROL SERVER TO Rick
```

The principal is Rick and the securable is the server. The level of permission that the server is granting to Rick is called *control*. Control allows you to run all DML, DDL and DCL statements to any database on the server. Log back in as an administrator so you can issue Grant DCL statements.

Oftentimes the control level of permissions is higher than an employee really needs. For Murray, we want to allow him to create, alter or drop databases. Grant Murray the ability to alter any database with the following code:

```
GRANT ALTER ANY DATABASE TO Murray
```

Log back in as Murray with the ABC$$123 password. Try again to drop the dbBasics database with the following code:

```
USE master
GO

DROP DATABASE dbBasics
GO
```

Murray is now able to drop the database (Figure 10.15). All databases reside on the server. Therefore, any permission that works on all databases means it is a server-level securable.

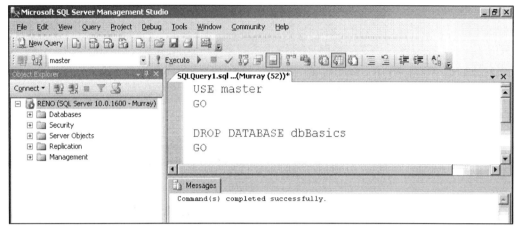

Figure 10.15 The Murray login now has permissions to drop a database.

Murray is able to run DDL statements on databases, but not on tables or other objects. When Murray attempts to access the JProCo database, the permissions still do not allow this action.

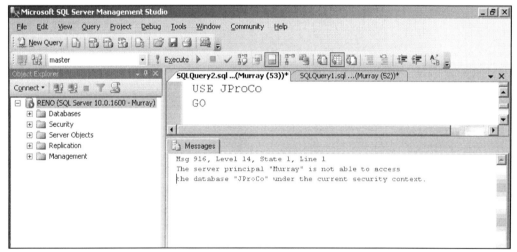

Figure 10.16 Murray can alter databases, but still can't use their context.

Murray has important work to do. Let's give Murray the ultimate server-level permission of *control*. Log back in as an administrator so you can issue some GRANT DCL statements. To grant the login Murray to control the entire server, the following code would be used:

```
USE Master
GO
GRANT CONTROL SERVER TO Murray
```

Log back in as Murray and notice he has unlimited access to all server and database resources.

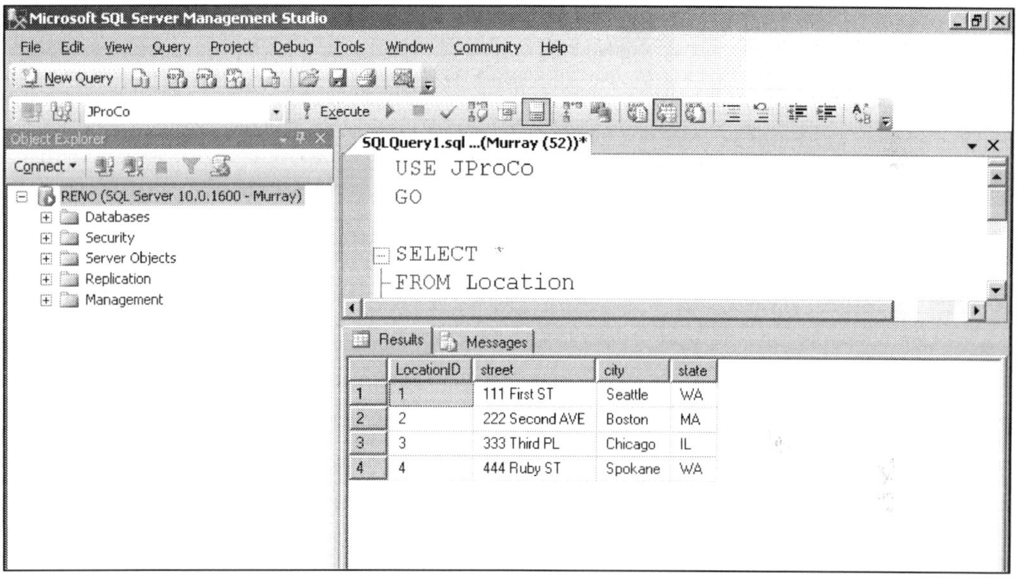

Figure 10.17 While logged in as Murray, you can run all DDL, DML and DCL statements on the server.

Lab 10.2: Granting Permissions

Lab Prep: Before you can begin the lab you must have SQL Server installed and run the Chapter10.2SetupAll.sql script.

Skill Check 1: Grant Sara the CONTROL SERVER permission. Once the permission is in place, log in as Sara and use the JProCo database to select all records from the Location table. When you are done, your screen should resemble Figure 10.18.

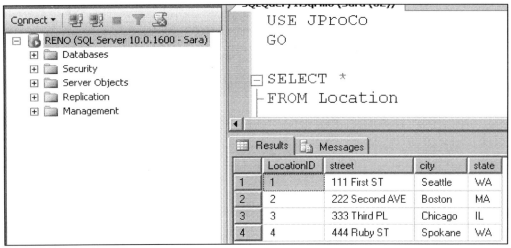

Figure 10.18 The Sara login has control permissions that allow her to query the JProCo database.

Answer Code: The SQL code to this lab can be found from the downloadable files named Lab10.2_GrantingPermissions.sql.

Granting Permissions - Points to Ponder

1. To add server permissions to a login, use the GRANT keyword.

2. GRANT is a DCL (Data Control Language) permission statement.

3. Immediately after the GRANT keyword is the permission type you want to grant. For example, if you wanted to grant CONTROL SERVER permission to Josh, use the following syntax:
   o   GRANT CONTROL SERVER TO Josh

Revoking and Denying Permissions

We learned that the GRANT keyword is a DCL statement that creates permissions on a securable and grants these permissions to a principal. OK, that is Geek Speak again, so let's use an example. With the GRANT keyword, you could tell the server (securable) to allow control (permission level) to Murray (principal).

In the steps leading up to this point, we set the following permissions (Table 10.1).

Table 10.1 Shows all permissions granted to Murray and Sara.

Principal	Permissions
Murray	Server Level : Control Server = Granted Server Level: Alter Any Database = Granted
Sara	Server Level : Control Server = Granted

We have granted two permissions from the server to Murray and one to Sara. Despite this, they have the same level of resource access. That's because CONTROL SERVER can do everything including alter databases. Sara can effectively do everything at the same level as Murray.

Let's test this by closing Management Studio. We will now open Management Studio as Sara. While logged in as Sara, we will create a database named dbSara (Figure 10.19).

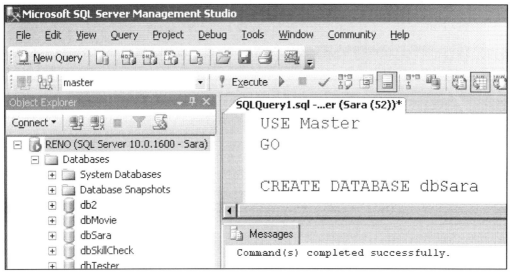

Figure 10.19 While logged in as Sara, we can create the dbSara database.

With full control over the server, Sara can also drop databases. Close the query window and open a new one. In the new query window, let's have Sara drop the dbSara database (Figure 10.20).

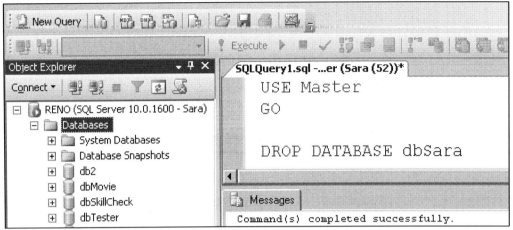

Figure 10.20 Sara is able to drop the dbSara database.

Log out and log back in as an administrator. If we wanted Sara to be able to do everything except alter any database, we can keep the control server permission in place and then deny her that one permission. To stop Sara from altering databases, you would issue the following DCL statement:

DENY ALTER ANY DATABASE TO Sara

Close Management Studio and log back in as Sara. She can still query all the databases and do pretty much the work she was able to do before (Figure 10.21).

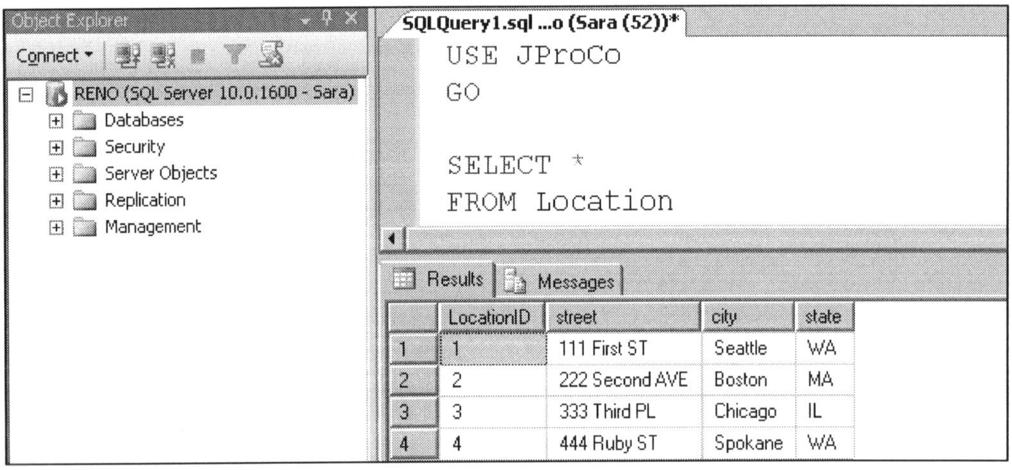

Figure 10.21 Sara has DML permissions for all the databases from Control Server permissions.

Sara has been granted control to the server, but denied permission to alter any database. This restriction causes a problem when Sara tries to create the dbSara database (Figure 10.22).

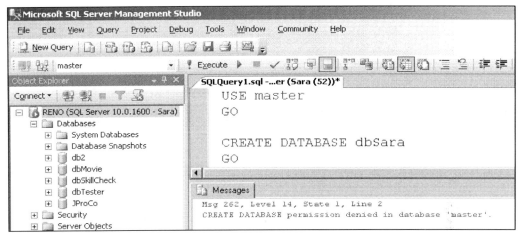

Figure 10.22 Sara does not have database-level DDL permissions.

To summarize what has been done to Murray and Sara, review Table 10.2. The change has been bolded to make it easy to find.

Table 10.2 A list of all permissions issued to Murray and Sara.

Principal	Permissions
Murray	Server Level : Control Server = Granted Server Level: Alter Any Database = Granted
Sara	Server Level : Control Server = Granted **Server Level: Alter Any Database = Denied**

Murray has control of the server. No permissions have been denied him. He has a second granting statement for altering databases that appears redundant. He would be unaffected if his "Alter Any Database" permission didn't exist.

We need to remove the "Alter Any Database" permission for Murray from the server's access list. You don't want to deny or grant this permission. You just want it to be unspecified or *revoked*. To turn off this permission, you would issue the following DCL statement:

```
REVOKE ALTER ANY DATABASE TO Murray
```

The REVOKE keyword simply removes an existing GRANT or DENY. After running the REVOKE, your permission structure is as seen in Table 10.3.

Table 10.3 After revoking the "Alter Any Database" server permission from Murray, he has one permission remaining.

Principal	Permissions
Murray	Server Level : Control Server = Granted
Sara	Server Level : Control Server = Granted Server Level: Alter Any Database = Denied

Log in as Murray and try to create the dbMurray database. Notice he has this level of permission (Figure 10.23).

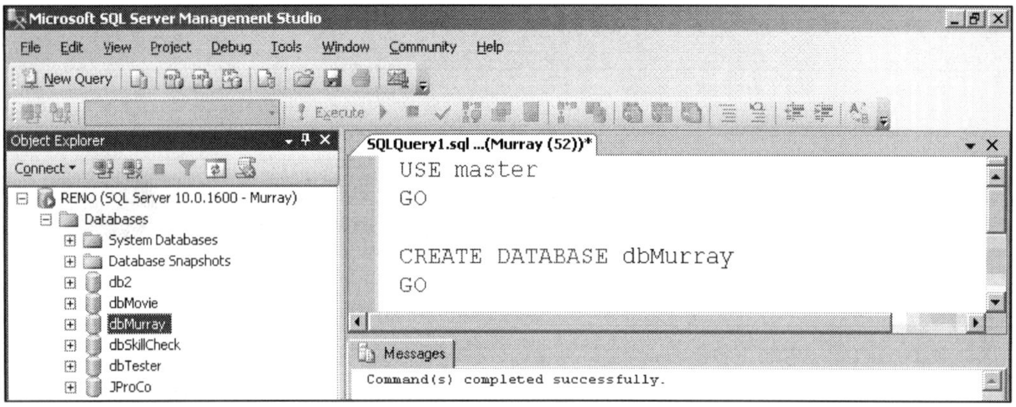

Figure 10.23 While logged in as Murray you can alter databases with control permission even after revoking the "Alter Any Databases" permission.

Revoke sounds like a penalty or a roadblock to someone's permissions. This indeed can be the case, as REVOKE takes away Grants. REVOKE also removes denied permissions. In reality, the REVOKE would free up Sara. The following code would again give Sara complete control over the server:

```
REVOKE ALTER ANY DATABASE TO Sara
GO
```

The end result is that Sara has server control and no more denied permissions. The Revoke freed her up to use more server resources. The server has the access list in Table 10.4.

Table 10.4 After revoking the "Alter Any Database" permission from both logins, only the Control Server permission remains.

Securable	Principal and Permission
Murray	Server Level : Control Server = Granted
Sara	Server Level : Control Server = Granted

There are many permissions at the server level. Table 10.5 lists the most common ones and a description of their uses.

Table 10.5 Common server-level permissions.

Permission Name	Description
ALTER ANY LOGIN	Allows the user to change a login name and password.
ALTER ANY DATABASE	Permission to run CREATE ALTER or DROP DDL statements against a database.
CONTROL SERVER	Permission to perform all operations.
SHUTDOWN	Permission allows you to shut down the SQL Server service.

A full detailing of all the possibilities with security would easily warrant an entire book. This chapter aims to familiarize you with the basic security concepts of SQL Server, along with the DCL statements. Any statement starting with keywords GRANT, REVOKE or DENY will set the level of control to principals and are therefore called Data Control Language statements.

Lab 10.3: Revoking and Denying Permissions

Lab Prep: Before you can begin the lab you must have SQL Server installed and run the Chapter10.3SetupAll.sql script.

Skill Check 1: Create a SQL login named Alan with the password of ABC$$123. Grant Alan a server-level permission that allows him full control of the server. Log in as Alan and create the dbAlan database. Upon completion, your screen should resemble Figure 10.24.

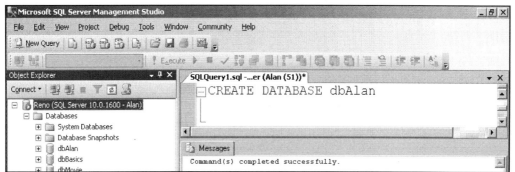

Figure 10.24 The new login "Alan" has control permissions and can create the dbAlan database.

Skill Check 2: Create a SQL login named Bruce with the password of ABC$$123. Grant Bruce a server-level permission that allows him full control to the server. Deny Bruce the ability to alter databases. Log in as Bruce and attempt to create the dbBruce database. Upon completion, your screen should resemble Figure 10.25.

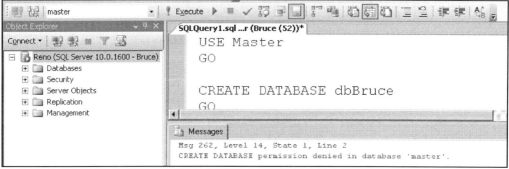

Figure 10.25 Bruce can do anything except alter databases.

Answer Code: The SQL code to this lab can be found from the downloadable files named Lab10.3_RevokingAndDenyingPermissions.sql.

Denying Permissions - Points to Ponder

1. Permissions can be manipulated with these DCL statements: GRANT, DENY and REVOKE.

2. DCL stands for Data Control Language.

3. To reduce a user's permission, use DENY and then list the permission.

4. If you DENY a permission, it trumps any other permissions to that object or scope. For example, if you grant control and deny control, the user would have no access to the securable.

5. To remove an existing granted or denied permission, use the REVOKE keyword.

6. Sometimes a REVOKE will not reduce the overall effective permission of a principal if that principal receives its permissions from other sources.

7. If you use REVOKE, you need to revoke all explicit and collection principal permissions to fully take away the permission.

Chapter Glossary

Authentication Mode: A security setting on SQL Server that specifies what types of logins are allowed access to the server.

Control: Permission that allows full control.

DCL: Data Control Language. A statement that affects the permissions a principal has to a securable.

Deny: A DCL statement that forbids a permission to a securable.

Grant: A DCL statement that allows a permission to a securable.

Login: A server-level principal in SQL.

Permission: A level of access to a securable given to a principal.

Principal: Any account or entity that is trying to access a resource.

Revoke: A DCL statement that undoes the last Grant or Deny for that permission.

Securable: A resource that you control access to by setting security limits. Databases and tables are examples of securables.

SQL Login: A SQL server level principal.

Windows Authentication: Authentication mode where all of your logins are part of a Windows domain.

Review Quiz

1.)The server-level principal account is called?

O a. A User
O b. A Login
O c. A Password

2.) How do you create a login named Dexter with the QAZ123ZZ password?

O a. CREATE LOGIN DEXTER WITH PASSWORD = 'QAZ123ZZ'
O b. CREATE USER DEXTER WITH PASSWORD = 'QAZ123ZZ'
O c. CREATE LOGIN DEXTER AS PASSWORD = 'QAZ123ZZ'
O d. CREATE USER DEXTER AS PASSWORD = 'QAZ123ZZ'
O e. CREATE LOGIN DEXTER FOR PASSWORD = 'QAZ123ZZ'
O f. CREATE USER DEXTER FOR PASSWORD = 'QAZ123ZZ'

3.) How do you grant full control of the server to Phil?

O a. GRANT CONTROL SERVER TO Phil
O b. GRANT SERVER CONTROL TO Phil
O c. REVOKE CONTROL SERVER TO Phil
O d. REVOKE SERVER CONTROL TO Phil

4.) If you granted Phil control to the server, but denied his ability to create databases, what would his effective permissions be?

O a. Phil can do everything.
O b. Phil can do nothing.
O c. Phil can do everything except create databases.

5.) If you granted Phil control to the server and revoked his ability to create databases, what would his effective permissions be?

O a. Phil can do everything.
O b. Phil can do nothing.
O c. Phil can do everything except create databases.

6.) Granting permissions is in what family of language statements?

O a. DML
O b. DDL
O c. DCL
O d. TCL

7.) You have a login named James who has Control Server permission. You want to elimintate his ability to Create databases without affecting any other permissions. What SQL statement would you use?

O a. ALTER LOGIN James DISABLE
O b. DROP LOGIN James
O c. DENY CREATE DATABASE To James
O d. REVOKE CREATE DATABASE To James
O e. GRANT CREATE DATABASE To James

Answer Key

1.) Because the server-level principal account is called a login, (a) and (c) cannot be the correct answer. The server-level principal is a login so (b) is the correct.

2.) Being that the correct syntax to create a login is CREATE LOGIN *LoginName* WITH PASSWORD = '*Password*' (b), (c), (d), (e) and (f) are all wrong answers Since (a) is the only one that has the correct syntax it is the correct answer.

3.) GRANT SERVER CONTROL will result in a syntax error because SERVER and CONTROL are reversed so (b) is incorrect. REVOKE undoes the last GRANT or DENY for a permission so (c) and (d) are also incorrect. The correct answer is (a) because it is the only one to use the correct syntax of GRANT CONTROL SERVER TO Phil.

4.) Phil cannot do everything because he was denied the ability to create databases so (a) is wrong. Phil can do some things because he was granted control of the server before being denied only the permission to create databases so (b) is also incorrect. Because Phil was granted control of the server and only denied the permission to create databases (c) is the correct answer.

5.) Because Phil is still allowed to create databases through the CONTROL SERVER permission (b) and (c) are incorrect. Phil can do everything because even though his permission to create databases was revoked, he still has the ability through the CONTROL SERVER permission so (a) is correct.

6.) Granting permissions does not manipulate or define data nor will it affect transaction control making (a), (b) and (d) all wrong answers. Because granting permissions affects the level of access or control a principal has over data it belongs to the DCL (Data Control Language) family of statements making (c) the correct answer.

7.) Disabling or dropping a login would affect all permissions that login had so (a) and (b) are both wrong. REVOKE only undoes the last DENY or GRANT on a permission and since CREATE DATABASE was never granted, revoking it will have no effect so (d) is also incorrect. GRANT CREATE DATABASE would give James the ability to create databases rather than eliminate the ability so (e) is incorrect too. To eliminate the ability to create databases you must use DENY CREATE DATABASE so (c) is the correct answer.

Bug Catcher Game

To play the Bug Catcher game run the BugCatcher_Chapter10.pps from the BugCatcher folder of the companion files. You can obtain these files from the www.Joes2Pros.com web site.

Chapter 11. SQL Summary

SQL Server works with more than just data. You need to protect data, structure data, and process data. A quick recap of what we covered and how it is used in the workplace wraps up this final chapter.

SQL Language Statement Types

The SQL language is comprised of four major parts. Data Manipulation Language (DML) statements affect the records in a table. Data Definition Language (DDL) statements handle the design of objects (e.g., databases, tables, and stored procedures). Data Control Language (DCL) allows you to control the level of access to securables. Transaction Control Language (TCL) allows you to manage transactions.

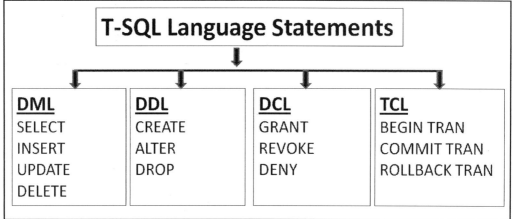

Figure 11.1 The breakdown of different language family statements which SQL supports.

Other SQL Language Statements

There are few SQL statements that support the four major types above. For example, setting the database context with a USE JProCo tells the next DDL statement into which database the object(s) will be created. Also, statements like IF and IF EXIST will conditionally run the next statement. For example, you might not want to create the Bruce login if it already exists. By putting an IF EXISTS above that DCL statement, it will support your code by running conditionally. This helps to avoid errors.

SQL has evolved and grown from just a data language to support more programming concepts. At its core are data, and how to use and protect it using DML, DDL, DCL and TCL. Remember that DML is about getting data in and out of your database. DDL is about the structure, and helps protect it by setting the fields and what data they can hold. DCL allows only the right logins to do certain actions. TCL protects your data by keeping transactions consistent.
When you see books on SQL queries or advanced query techniques, those typically are just a deep dive into the DML world. Getting data in and out of

databases is done more often than the other three areas combined. Most of your interview questions will be based on skills related to DML. Other examples outside of the scope of this book include structured error handling code.

What's Next

Having finished this book, you are ready to isolate and annihilate your next goal. In my experience, that often includes more advanced queries or administration involving DCL and TCL. Because of this next logical step, you can take this feather in your cap and build upon it. The next books in the *Joes2Pros* series are broken down according to Figure 11.2.

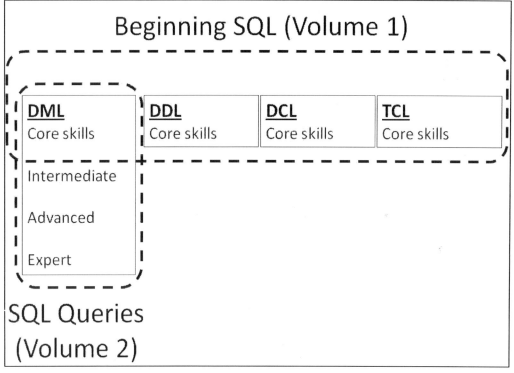

Figure 11.2 Book2 on SQL Queries are a deeper study of the DML section of the SQL language.

This SQL book covered the broad core of the language and how it works. If you finished this book and want to work towards your certification you can go directly to Volume 2 (SQL Queries Joes 2 Pros). With a solid understanding of the language you can delve deeper into the next discipline which is advanced DML statements. You can find more detail and keep in touch with the *Joes2Pros* community at *www.Joes2Pros.com*.

Please note that if you have finished this book there is really no need to buy or read the original (T-SQL 2008 Joes 2 Pros) book. Beginning SQL Joes 2 Pros and T-SQL Joes 2 Pros are essentially the same materials reprinted under a new title. This book you have read is the newest book with some minor improvements and a few extra labs. The next book on this progression series is the SQL Queries Joes 2 Pros book.

Beginning SQL Joes 2 Pros: The SQL Hands-On Guide for Beginners
ISBN 1-4392-5317-X

SQL Queries Joes 2 Pros: SQL Query Techniques for Microsoft SQL Server 2008
ISBN 1-4392-5318-8

SQL Architecture Basics Joes 2 Pros: Core Architecture Concepts
ISBN: 1-4515-7946-2

SQL Programming Development Joes 2 Pros: Programming & Development for Microsoft SQL Server 2008
ISBN: 1-4515-7948-9

SQL Interoperability Joes 2 Pros: SQL 2008 Techniques with XML, C#, and PowerShell
ISBN: 1-4515-7950-0

SQL Wait Stats Joes 2 Pros: SQL Performance Tuning Techniques Using Wait Statistics, Types & Queues
ISBN: 1-4662-3477-6

Index

G

GO, 26, 27, 47, 101, 102, 107, 108, 109, 111, 112, 113, 114, 115, 117, 120, 121, 124, 131, 145, 162, 198, 199, 206, 221, 233, 235, 240

GRANT, 30, 40, 42, 43, 44, 193, 233, 235, 236, 237, 240, 241, 243, 244, 245

I

Import, 168, 169, 171, 174, 175, 177, 178

In Operator, 33, 54

Information, 12, 17, 18, 20, 21, 23, 24, 25, 27, 31, 35, 45, 52, 54, 60, 61, 62, 63, 65, 87, 88, 92, 109, 114, 119, 122, 123, 133, 171, 186, 188, 230

Inner Join, 76

Inner join(s), 63, 64, 66, 69, 73, 74, 102, 103, 133

Inner Join(s), 63, 67, 69, 73

Insert, 116, 120, 121, 122, 123, 124, 125, 126, 128, 131, 138, 140, 142, 143, 144, 145, 155, 156, 157, 162, 163, 164, 176, 178, 206, 208

Intermediate state, 208, 210, 212, 213, 215, 216, 217

Intermediate State, 216

J

Join clause, 69, 78

K

Keyword, 24, 29, 54, 105, 119, 138, 143, 241

L

LIKE, 36, 37, 38, 39, 42, 43, 44, 45, 53, 54, 55, 57, 58, 59

locking, 211, 212, 215, 216

Login, 220, 221, 222, 224, 225, 226, 228, 229, 230, 233, 235, 236, 241, 242, 243, 244, 245, 248

M

Management Studio, 21, 23, 25, 106, 107, 108, 148, 149, 150, 152, 153, 154, 222, 227, 229, 237, 238

N

NOLOCK, 214, 215, 216, 217

Not Like, 45, 59

Null, 19, 23, 66, 71, 73, 75, 79, 96, 98, 99, 100, 119, 134, 163, 164, 166, 167, 176, 177, 178, 179, 208

O

Operator, 32, 33, 36, 38, 40, 41, 53, 54, 58, 79, 100

Outer Join, 76

P

Parameter(s), 195, 196, 197, 199, 200, 201, 202, 203

Permission, 241, 243

Permission(s), 29, 132, 170, 171, 219, 220, 222, 227, 230, 232, 233, 234, 235, 236, 237, 238, 239, 240, 241, 242, 243, 244, 245

Populate(d), 23, 155

Predicate, 32, 36, 41, 42, 43, 44, 53, 55, 56, 58, 74, 158

Primary Key, 115, 116, 117, 118, 120, 126, 131, 145, 162

Principal, 220, 231, 233, 237, 239, 240, 241, 243, 244, 245

Q

Query, 16, 18, 23, 24, 25, 26, 27, 28, 29, 31, 32, 33, 34, 35, 38, 39, 40, 42, 43, 44, 47, 48, 49, 50, 51, 52, 53, 54, 55, 58, 60, 61, 63, 64, 66, 67, 69, 70, 74, 75, 76, 77, 78, 79, 81, 82, 83, 84, 85, 88, 91, 92, 94, 95, 96, 97, 98, 99, 100, 101, 102, 103, 107, 109, 110, 116, 126, 132, 133, 134, 138, 141, 142, 143, 148, 149, 152, 156, 157, 160, 161, 163, 165, 166, 171, 180, 181, 186, 188, 189, 190, 191, 193, 196, 198, 208, 211, 212, 213, 214, 215, 216, 217, 222, 231, 238, 248

R

RDBMS, 20, 21, 23, 24, 129, 205

READUNCOMMITTED, 213, 214, 215, 216

Record, 23, 216

Record Set, 20, 23, 52, 53, 73, 92, 94, 196

Relational Database, 61

SQL Dev Volume 1

Beginning SQL Joes 2 Pros ®

The SQL Hands-On Guide for Beginners
(SQL Exam Prep Series 70-433 Volume 1 of 5)

Rick A. Morelan
Jessica Brown, Doug Fritz, Peter D. Kendall

SQL Dev Volume 2

SQL Queries Joes 2 Pros ®

SQL Query Techniques for Microsoft SQL Server 2008
(SQL Exam Prep Series 70-433 Volume 2 of 5)

Rick A. Morelan
Jessica Brown, Tom Ekberg, Irina Berger

SQL Dev Volume 3

SQL Architecture Basics Joes 2 Pros

Core Architecture Concepts
(SQL Exam Prep Series 70-433 Volume 3 of 5)

Rick A. Morelan
Jessica Brown, Tom Ekberg, Irina Berger, Joel Heidal

SQL Dev Volume 4

SQL Programming Joes 2 Pros ®

Programming and Development for Microsoft SQL Server 2008
(SQL Exam Prep Series 70-433 Volume 4 of 5)

Rick A. Morelan & Pinal Dave
Jessica Brown, Tom Ekberg, Joel Heidal, Simon Nicholson

SQL Dev Volume 4

SQL Interoperability Joes 2 Pros ®

A Guide to Integrating SQL Server with XML, C#, and PowerShell
(SQL Exam Prep Series 70-433 Volume 5 of 5)

Rick A. Morelan
Jessica Brown, Vinay Chopra, Joel Heidal, Simon Nicholson

Solution Series Book

SQL Wait Stats Joes 2 Pros ®

The Solutions Guide for Understanding SQL Wait Types & Queues

Pinal Dave, Rick A. Morelan
Jessica Brown, Joel Heidal, Simon Nicholson

Made in the USA
Lexington, KY
15 July 2012